D1435132

The new ave

 THE UNIV

012

Inside Popular Film

General editors Mark Jancovich and Eric Schaefer

Inside Popular Film is a forum for writers who are working to develop new ways of analysing popular film. Each book offers a critical introduction to existing debates while also exploring new approaches. In general, the books give historically informed accounts of popular film which present this area as altogether more complex than is commonly suggested by established film theories.

Developments over the past decade have led to a broader understanding of film which moves beyond the traditional oppositions between high and low culture, popular and avant-garde. The analysis of film has also moved beyond a concentration on the textual forms of films, to include an analysis of both the social situations within which films are consumed by audiences, and the relationship between film and other popular forms. The series therefore addresses issues such as the complex intertextual systems which link film, literature, art and music, as well as the production and consumption of film through a variety of hybrid media, including video, cable and satellite.

The authors take interdisciplinary approaches which bring together a variety of theoretical and critical debates that have developed in film, media and cultural studies. They neither embrace nor condemn popular film, but explore specific forms and genres within the contexts of their production and consumption.

Already published:

Harry M. Benshoff *Monsters in the closet: homosexuality and the horror film*
Julia Hallam and Margaret Marshment *Realism and popular cinema*
Joanne Hollows and Mark Jancovich (eds) *Approaches to popular film*

Forthcoming titles include:

Joanne Hollows *The state of the heart: re-mapping the field of women's genres*
Nicole Matthews *Comic politics: gender in Hollywood comedy after the new right*
Bennet Schaber *Everyday life and popular film*
Esther Sonnet *Sexuality and popular film*
Ben Taylor *Film comedy*

The new avengers

Feminism, femininity and the rape-revenge cycle

Jacinda Read

Manchester University Press
Manchester and New York

Distributed exclusively in the USA by St. Martin's Press

Published by Manchester University Press
Oxford Road, Manchester M13 9NR, UK
and Room 400, 175 Fifth Avenue, New York, NY10010, USA
http://www.man.ac.uk/mup

Distributed exclusively in the USA by
St. Martin's Press, Inc., 175 Fifth Avenue, New York,
NY 10010, USA

Distributed exclusively in Canda by
UBC Press, University of British Columbia, 2029 West Mall,
Vancouver, BC, Canada V6T 1Z2

British Library Cataloguing-in-Publication Data
A catalogue record for this book is available from the British Library

Library of Congress Cataloging-in-Publication Data applied for

ISBN 0 7190 5904 6 *hardback*
     0 7190 5905 4 *paperback*

First published 2000

07 06 05 04 03 02 01 00   10 9 8 7 6 5 4 3 2 1

Typeset in Sabon with Frutiger
by Northern Phototypesetting Co Ltd, Bolton

Printed in Great Britain
by Bell & Bain Ltd, Glasgow

Contents

Plates

Permission applied for.

Acknowledgements

I had rather looked forward to writing these acknowledgements, thinking they would be the easiest aspect of the whole process of producing a book. Now I come to write them, it seems finding the words to express my gratitude to the numerous people who have made this book possible is harder than finding the words to express the most difficult theoretical concept. I would like to start, however, by saying that I am enormously grateful to everyone who has helped me produce this book and I apologize to those I have not space to mention by name.

Among my colleagues, past and present, I would particularly like to thank Bob Ashley, Viv Chadder, Joanne Hollows, Tim O'Sullivan, Ben Taylor and Dave Woods. I am also grateful to Steve Chibnall who provided originals of some of the illustrative material used here. I would like to thank all the staff in the Department of Film and Television Studies at the University of Warwick. Very special thanks go, in particular, to my PhD supervisor, Charlotte Brunsdon, for making what I often thought was an impossible task possible.

This book would not have been produced without the love, help and encouragement of my friends and family. I would particularly like to thank Rachel Moseley whose friendship and support have been invaluable. I am extremely grateful to Lee Hughes, Sam Pickard and Julian Smith for providing the crucial technical support and advice that kept my computer up and running throughout this project. Love and gratitude go to my lifelong friend Richard Hall who not only supplied me with many of the film reviews referred to in this book but who wined and dined me in style during research trips to London. A close circle of friends helped prevent me from becoming a recluse during the writing of this book and, therefore, a very special thank you goes to Jools McCarthy, Sandy Villetet,

Mark Hutchinson, Alex Dean and Andrew Leam. The biggest thank you, however, goes to my family – my parents and step-parents, my sisters, Samantha McCann and Sarah Barrington, my brother, Tim Read, and last, but by no means least, my partner, Julian Smith, without whose love, patience and support this book would never have been written.

For my mother

Part I

Introductions

Introduction

Feminism and popular culture

The stories through which we make sense of ourselves are everywhere. In the media, they are not just in the articles and programmes labelled 'fiction' and 'drama', but in those on current affairs, sport, party politics, science, religion, the arts, and those specified as education and for children. They are in the advertisements. At work, the definition of tasks to be undertaken depend upon them, and the relations between the people involved – some face to face, some very distant. And in our intimate relations there are stories telling us who we are as individuals, who other individuals are and how to relate to them.[1]

As academics, it is tempting to believe that we can stand outside such 'stories', that in fact, we must, in order to gain the necessary critical distance to analyse them. However, we often fail to acknowledge not only the way in which, as individuals, we are shaped by such stories but also the way in which, as academics, our own critical positions are constructed by such stories. Most of all, we fail to recognize how, in attempting to make sense of such stories, we ourselves are telling stories.

The story I propose to tell is one that attempts to understand the relationship between two stories: the rape-revenge film and second-wave feminism. It is thus, in many ways, a response to the already existing account of this relationship given by Carol Clover in her book *Men, Women and Chainsaws*.[2] However, it is equally an attempt to make sense of my own relationship to feminism and of how this latter story informs the former. The latter story is one that is characterized by a feeling of 'inbetweeness' and contradiction. Too young to have experienced at first hand the feminist movement of the 1970s, feminism for me has existed largely through the theoretical abstractions of the academy. The decline of the feminist movement, however, has also meant that popular culture has become one of the primary realms in which feminism is now 'lived' and experienced by the majority of women including myself. As Jennifer Wicke has recently argued, 'the culture of celebrity is the material culture in which we have our being as feminists'.[3] Consequently, I have often been troubled by the gap between what I read and write as a feminist academic and my lived experience of feminism and social practice; between the story of feminism I am told as an academic and the story I experience everyday as a consumer of popular culture; between feminism's critique of popular culture as the site where normative femininities are constructed and the excited rush of recognition and identification a female avenger, such as Catwoman in the film *Batman Returns* (Tim Burton, 1992), inspires. My interest in the rape-revenge film thus lies in the way in which it (and indeed, critical work about it) dramatizes and articulates some of the gaps and contradictions that concern me, particularly those between the 'feminine' (victim) and the 'feminist' (avenger) and between the popular and the political. As I will show, in the distinction it draws between feminist and feminine stories, low and high rape-revenge films, Clover's analysis virtually reproduces these gaps. Yet, while the binary logic written into the very term 'rape-revenge' is itself suggestive of such contradictions and oppositions, the hyphen between the two words directs us towards the way in which these films can also be read as an attempt to bridge, and thus make sense of, these gaps.

During the course of this project I nevertheless spent much of my time leaping backwards and forwards across these gaps trying to 'find' feminism. But from wherever I stood it always seemed at one stage removed, was always just out of my grasp. It took me a while to realize that neither side of the divide represented the site of real, true, authentic feminism and that, in fact, in as far as *both* sides had produced my notion of what feminism was, 'feminism' was precisely in the very gap that troubled me. As Wicke points out: 'Feminism is not exempt from celebrity material, and more and more, feminism is produced (or feminisms are produced) and received in the material zone of celebrity.'[4] This project thus arises in part out of frustration at the failure of feminism to address or acknowledge the way in which it inhabits that gap. It is for this reason that I now leap into this abyss and begin a process of archaeology, of excavation, not in an attempt to find some authentic feminism but in order to unearth the way in which the meanings of feminism are produced through the cultural artefacts it has engendered. It is worth remembering, however, that like shattered pieces of pottery, these meanings are fragmented; some meanings will have been lost while those that remain will not always fit together to form a coherent whole. Moreover, some meanings will have migrated from the context in which they were originally produced, while others will be mixed together with fragments of meanings from different periods and discourses. I do not pretend to account for all the pieces or to fit them all together. Rather, I am looking for patterns among the fragments and the way in which, in attempting to make sense of feminism, they also produce understandings of feminism. In trying to understand those understandings and how they are produced, however, the act of critical analysis produces further understandings. 'Talking and writing about texts', as Jackie Byars has pointed out, 'actively involves critics in the production and circulation of meanings – that is, in the construction of culture.'[5]

Cultural texts tell many different stories and, in negotiating a route through the text, the critic can only pretend to tell one of those stories. Like an archaeologist who attempts to understand how a culture is lived by unearthing its cultural artefacts and monuments, I am interested in unearthing how feminism is lived and experienced through popular culture. As Sinfield argues: 'Stories are *lived*. They are not just outside ourselves, something we read or hear about. They make sense for us – of us – because we have been and are in them.'[6] In this respect, I will largely be concerned with how texts generate everyday, common-sense meanings and popular understandings of feminism and especially the current pervasiveness of such meanings. Writing at a moment when Britain is in the grip of 'Girl Power' and claims that 'the future is female', as espoused by the British pop group, the Spice Girls, I will be particularly concerned with exploring the way in which the story of second-wave feminism is being retold for the 1990s, with how the discourses of 1970s feminism are circulating and functioning in the popular texts of the 1990s, and with what this tells us about feminism past, present and future. Given the cultural pessimism that pervades many recent accounts of popular film as simply an articulation of a right-wing backlash against feminism, I will be giving specific consideration to the way in which contemporary Hollywood films might attempt to negotiate the competing and often contradictory demands of the discourses of feminism and the discourses of the New Right.

The coincidence between the rise of second-wave feminism and the emergence of specifically *female*-centred rape-revenge films, together with the latter's representation of 'angry women' and engagement with perhaps *the* quintessential feminist issue, suggests that female rape-revenge films might provide the ideal site through which to pursue such an analysis. While I recognize that these films are not necessarily the only, or indeed, the most obvious, way in which Hollywood can be seen to be making sense of feminism, their proliferation and increasing high-profile throughout this period means that they do represent a coherent, popular and ongoing site though which we can read the changing inscription of feminism in mainstream film and through which we can trace the significance of these changes. For example, in 1972 Helen Reddy's number one single 'I Am Woman (Hear Me Roar)' became one of anthems of the US Women's Liberation Movement. Twenty years later, in 1992, the song's title phrase reappeared in the film, *Batman Returns*, where Catwoman turns to the woman she has just saved from rape and pro-claims, 'I am Catwoman, hear me roar'. Similarly, in 1979, the Leeds Revolutionary Feminist Group pronounced that 'Men are the enemy. Heterosexual women are collaborators with the enemy'.[7] In 1991, these sentiments reappeared in the title of the film, *Sleeping with the Enemy* (Joseph Ruben, 1991). However, neither film's engagement with such discourses was straightforward or unmedi-ated. Rather, they represented a struggle between contradictory nar-rative and discursive levels, a struggle that, I will argue, can be read as an attempt to make sense of social and cultural change. *Batman Returns*, for example, presented us with the somewhat curious image of a pre-feminist incarnation articulating a feminist rallying cry in a supposedly post-feminist era, while *Sleeping with the Enemy* was structured so as to create a narrative lacuna around the very era its title evoked.

To the extent that cultural texts are founded on contradiction and struggle, they also speak to, and help to make sense of, the contra-dictions in our lives. As Ien Ang has argued, they function to con-struct 'imaginary solutions for real contradictions'.[8] The majority of women's relationship to feminism has always been characterized by a sense of contradiction, a feeling often summarized in the phrase 'I'm not a feminist, but …' My interest in the rape-revenge film, and especially with erotic female avengers, such as Catwoman, thus lies in the way in which they speak to that feeling of inbetweeness and contradiction, in the way in which, in particular, they live out the contradiction between discursively constructed ideas of the feminine and the feminist and, in so doing, produce popularly available and accessible versions of feminism. This process is perhaps nowhere more apparent than in Spice Girl Emma Bunton's articulation of this contradiction in her recent definition of girl power: 'I'm a feminist. But I could never burn my wonderbra.'[9] Of course, as Andrea Stuart points out, there is a disjunction between what this kind of popular feminism can supply and 'what women really need'.[10] However, as Christine Gledhill has argued:

> We need representations that take account of identities – representations that work with a degree of fluidity and contradiction – and we need to forge different identities – ones that help us make productive use of the contradictions in our lives. This means entering socio-economic, cultural and linguistic struggle to define and establish them in the media, which function as centres for the production and circulation of identity.[11]

Furthermore, we cannot afford to ignore the fact that we are living in a culture in which ideas about feminism and its history are as, if not more, likely to be gleaned from popular culture than from reading feminist theory. There is an increasingly urgent need for an analysis of this phenomenon and its implications for feminism.

Feminism's status as a story, the way in which it is imbricated in the forms and structures of popular culture is apparent in the way in which much recent feminist writing adopts the generic formulae of melodrama, with the writer often casting herself in the starring role. Margaret Walters, for example, has shown how the work of Catherine MacKinnon and Camille Paglia can be read as enacting a feminist melodrama with MacKinnon playing the role of the puritanical good girl to Paglia's villainous bad girl.[12] Similarly, Jennifer Wicke has demonstrated how, in her essay 'I'm for Tonya', the feminist writer and poet, Katha Pollitt, 'succumbs to the celebritizing of individual women as stock characters in a feminist melodrama'.[13] Suffice it to say, all three occupy the sphere of celebrity or popular feminism and trade in simplified, common-sense meanings of feminism. For all three, then, the forms and structures of popular culture help generate these meanings, help to make sense of feminism.

Of course, it may be that feminism is, by its very nature,

melodramatic. As Ien Ang has argued 'there is a fundamentally melodramatic edge to feminism':

> After all, are not the suffering and frustration so eminently materialised in melodramatic heroines the basis for the anger conveyed in feminism? And does not feminism stand for the overwhelming desire to transcend reality – which is bound to be a struggle, full of frustrations and moments of despair? While the melodramatic heroine is someone who is forced to give up, leaving a yawning gap between desire and reality, the feminist is someone who refuses to give up, no matter how hard the struggle to close that gap might be.[14]

The problem, however, with the melodramatic model of feminism is that in attempting to transcend the gap between desire and reality, feminism creates another gap between the feminine victim 'who is forced to give up' and the feminist heroine 'who refuses to'. This represents another of the gaps that concerns me, one that is, moreover, dramatized again and again in the rape-revenge film's emphasis on the transformation of the heroine from victim to avenger. Indeed, what I want to suggest is that the dramatization of this gap represents one of the primary ways in which the rape-revenge film can be seen to make sense of feminism.

As I have already suggested, however, the meanings of second-wave feminism are articulated not only through popular culture but in those critical texts that purport to analyse it (mine included). Furthermore, as Christine Gledhill has argued:

> The critical act is not finished with the 'reading' or 'evaluation' of a text. It generates new cycles of meaning production and negotiation – journalistic features, 'letters to the editor', classroom lectures, critical responses, changes in distribution or publication policy, more critical activity, and so on. In this way traditions are broken and remade. Thus critical activity itself participates in social negotiation of meaning, definition, identity.[15]

Thus my readings of rape-revenge films and the understandings of feminism they produce are, in many respects, constructed against, and in response to, those put forward by Carol Clover.[16] What I want to argue, in particular, is that the version of feminism Clover's analysis produces is one in which femininity and feminine competencies are repressed or disavowed. This is not to say, however, that femininity is repressed in the films themselves but rather that it is the 'repressed' *of* Clover's analysis. The most telling instance of this repression comes in Clover's discussion of *Ms. 45* (Abel Ferrara, 1981). Consider, for example, the following statement: 'The remainder of the film has Thana (*increasingly sexily dressed*) as a kind of *ultimate feminist vigilante* gunning down men who traffic in women'.[17] Why is the fact that Thana is 'increasingly sexily dressed' not only in parenthesis but unexplored in the rest of the analysis? I would suggest that the brackets operate as a form of disavowal. In other words, the sentence rests on the coexistence of two apparently incompatible terms – sexiness and feminism – and the parenthesis betrays Clover's belief that to claim Thana as 'a kind of ultimate feminist vigilante' necessitates a repression of her sexiness (indeed, the qualifying 'kind of' represents both an acknowledgement of, and an attempt to gloss over, the perceived contradiction). Similarly, in her introductory discussion of *Carrie* (Brian de Palma, 1976), Clover admits that 'with its prom queens, menstrual periods, tampons, worries about clothes and makeup, *Carrie* would seem on the face of it the most feminine of stories'.[18] She swiftly moves on, however, to Stephen King's claim that it is also a feminist one. For Clover, then, the repression of the feminine story, her insistence on the masculinization of the female victim-hero, is necessary in order for her to be able to tell her feminist story of the male spectator's cross-gender identification with the female victim-hero.

Clover's feminist analysis also depends on drawing a distinction between underground and mainstream rape-revenge films, a distinction that also translates into an opposition between feminist and feminine and that, therefore, again necessitates the exclusion of the latter. Thus, while the low-brow rape-revenge film is elevated to the status of a politicized avant-garde (consumed by male audiences), the mainstream version is implicitly analysed within a framework that condemns mass culture as a feminized and, therefore, depoliticized culture (consumed by 'normal', that is, mixed audiences). For example, the kind of adjectives Clover uses to denigrate and exclude mainstream examples of the rape-revenge film betrays a belief that they are too feminine to be feminist. In other words, they are variously described as 'civilized' (p. 147), 'pretty' (p. 150), 'safe' (p. 235), 'glossy' (p. 232), 'nice' (p. 20) and 'feel-good' (p. 147). The belief that feminism occludes femininity is not, however, peculiar to Clover or to academic analyses. For example, popular reviews of recent rape-revenge films often suggested that the feminist politics of such texts were compromised by their reliance on ideals of feminine beauty (*Bad Girls*, Jonathan Kaplan, 1994) or the presence of heterosexual romance (*Thelma and Louise*, Ridley Scott, 1991).[19] In this way, then, academic analyses and popular reviews alike can be seen as sites where the orthodox feminist position on femininity and popular culture is repeatedly inscribed.

In attempting to produce an alternative account of the relationship between feminism, femininity and popular film, I have thus been forced to look beyond the theoretical orthodoxies of traditional feminist film theory to cultural studies, and particularly to a model of cultural analysis underpinned by the concept of hegemony. In the hegemonic model of meaning production, as Christine Gledhill has observed, 'meaning is neither imposed, nor passively imbibed, but arises out of a struggle or negotiation between competing frames of reference, motivation and experience'.[20] Thus, as I argued earlier, cultural texts tell several different stories and, while the critic can only pretend to tell one of these stories, in so doing it is not sufficient (as Clover does) to simply repress or disavow the presence of apparently contradictory or mutually exclusive stories, since it is in the very struggle between such stories that meaning is produced. What this suggests, then, is that the understandings of feminism produced by the rape-revenge film are, in fact, crucially dependent on the way in which it negotiates the other stories present in the text, *particularly* the feminine stories. As the 'repressed' of Clover's analysis, therefore, my analysis depends on putting the feminine and the popular back into play, in order illuminate the processes of textual negotiation and struggle through which the rape-revenge film can be seen to be attempting to make sense of feminism. Contrary to Clover, then, I will argue that one of the primary ways in which it does this is precisely by addressing popular culture's repression of feminine stories or by retelling the stories popular culture has told about femininity. Within the sphere of popular culture, these stories are most clearly inscribed in genres or, as Charlotte Brunsdon has described them, 'mass cultural fictions of femininity'.[21] If we are to fully understand the significance of the feminist stories the rape-revenge film tells, we must also seek to understand the way in which the films engage with, negotiate and rework these 'mass cultural fictions of femininity'. Indeed, insofar as feminism can be defined as involving a struggle over the meanings of femininity, it is in its ongoing articulation of these struggles that the rape-revenge film can be seen to be attempting to make sense of feminism.

Because by their very nature these struggles are dynamic, competing and often contradictory, this attempt to make sense of feminism is, however, never complete, the understandings of feminism produced never secure or fixed. Such an analysis thus goes some way towards explaining the endurance and mutability of the rape-revenge story, its continual retelling across a variety of different genres throughout the post-1970 period. It suggests, moreover, that we might need to reappraise or question accepted understandings of the 1990s as a period of post-feminism or backlash – particularly the fixed and unitary meanings such concepts tend to ascribe to feminism. In other words, the endurance of the rape-revenge film suggests that the stories it attempts to make sense of must themselves be understood as complex, changeable, problematic and ongoing rather than as authentic singular or static moments. As Alan Sinfield observes: 'Notice how literary texts of any period return repeatedly to certain complex and demanding themes. This is because the stories that require most attention – most assiduous and continuous reworking – are the awkward, unresolved ones.'[22]

One of the main problems with Clover's generically specific model of the rape-revenge film is that, like much orthodox feminist film theory influenced by psychoanalysis, it is unable to adequately account for historical change, for either the endurance or the mutability of the rape-revenge story. In this model, the endurance of the story is understood simply in terms of the ahistorical and universal psychoanalytic concept of 'the repressed', while changes in the story are understood simply in terms of a decline from an original moment of authenticity.[23] Both explanations, therefore, tend to overlook the culturally and historically specific function of narratives and the way in which changes at their formal and thematic level are often indices of social change. Against Clover, then, I will be arguing that rape-revenge is not a sub-genre of horror, but a narrative structure which, on meeting second-wave feminism in the 1970s, has produced a historically specific but generically diverse cycle of films.[24] By showing how the meanings the rape-revenge film produces are generated from within an intricate matrix of shifting and contradictory discourses, the cyclic model will, I hope, help to produce a more subtle and sophisticated analysis of the changing inscription of feminism in popular film. Indeed, as Jackie Byars has argued: 'The general goal of feminist intervention is change, and theorizing change is crucial.'[25]

In endeavouring to trace the changing inscription of feminism in the rape-revenge cycle, then, I will be focusing in particular on the struggles and contradictions between these discourses or stories since, as Sinfield observes, it is in the competition between stories that social conflict and thus, by extension, social change manifests itself.[26] In order to isolate these conflicts and oppositions I will rely on a close textual analysis of narrative and genre. However, while I will be concerned to explore how these contradictions are resolved, I will be equally, if not more, concerned to identify and explore ideological gaps, moments of ambiguity, ambivalence and uncertainty, where negotiations around the meanings of feminism and femininity are at their most active. As I suggested earlier, one of the most obvious gaps the rape-revenge film opens up is that between the (feminine) victim and the (feminist) avenger and the way in which the films negotiate the transformation from one to the other, therefore, will be the focus of particular attention. Gaps are also apparent between the feminist stories the rape-revenge film can be seen to tell and the feminine stories inscribed in the genres it utilizes and these too will be the subject of specific analysis.[27] What I will argue is that these gaps represent what Christine Gledhill has called 'spaces of negotiation'. Following Gledhill, my analysis of these spaces will offer 'not so much resistant readings, made against the grain, as animations of possibilities arising from the negotiations into which the text enters'.[28] These readings, however, will arise not simply from these textual negotiations but from my own theoretical negotiations, my own attempts to build bridges, to traverse the gaps between film studies and cultural studies, the textual and the contextual, the academic and the public, the theoretical and the popular, the feminist and the feminine.

Neither Clover nor I doubt that the rape-revenge film tells a feminist story; what we offer, in negotiating different routes through the texts, is alternative versions of it. Moreover, the versions we offer can both be read as reactions to established aspects of the feminist story. Clover's version is a reaction to the story that feminist film theory has told about the male spectator, a reaction to its 'official denial' of cross-gender identification and a reaction to its assumption of woman's status as victim.[29] Her work exists at the end of a paradigm shift, at the end of a 'cycle of meaning' to use Gledhill's phrase, inaugurated by Laura Mulvey's 'Visual pleasure and narrative cinema' in 1975.[30] This cycle has been largely concerned with analysing the construction of femininity in popular texts. It is time, however, I think, that we applied the same kind of constructionist analysis to *feminism* itself. This would allow us to see that just as there is no innate, eternal essence to being a woman so too there is no innate, eternal essence to being a feminist. As Elizabeth Wilson has argued, feminists 'should not have to embody feminist virtues in the same way that western art for centuries has used the female form to represent uplifting abstract qualities'.[31] To paraphrase Simone de Beauvoir, then, 'One is not born, but rather becomes, a feminist.' From this perspective, it does not matter whether popular texts are truly feminist or not. Indeed, as Toril Moi argues: 'There is not, unfortunately, such a thing as an intrinsically feminist text: given the right historical and social context, all texts can be recuperated by the ruling powers – or appropriated by the feminist opposition.'[32] In other words, popular culture does not produce either purely dominant or purely oppositional meanings but is instead the site of contradiction where meanings are continuously contested and negotiated. Rather than futilely debating their relative feminist worth, as the delegates at a recent conference did with the Spice Girls, we need to concern ourselves with how these texts make such debates possible and with what they can consequently tell us, not only about what it means to be female, but about what it means to be feminist in the 1990s. Just as these texts construct certain versions of femininity, so too do they construct certain versions of feminism – and it is here, therefore, as much as in the ivory towers of academia, that we can find, alongside the inevitable reactionary deployments, tentative and evolving formulations of what the future of feminism might be. As Jennifer Wicke has argued: 'The celebrity zone is the public sphere where feminism is negotiated, where it is now in most active cultural play.'[33]

The structure of the book

In chapter 1, I will discuss at greater length my objections to existing analyses of the rape-revenge film, focusing specifically on the work of Carol Clover, and begin to flesh out in more detail an alternative approach. In particular, I will argue that the female avenger of the rape-revenge film has more in common with the violent woman of the erotic thrillers and neo-noirs of recent years than Clover's generically specific argument acknowledges. I will thus be situating Clover's work within the larger context of a burgeoning interest amongst feminist film theorists in these violent women. Against the tendency of both sets of analyses to distinguish the rape-revenge film from the erotic thriller or neo-noir, I will be developing an analysis that argues that both form part of an ongoing historically, rather than generically, specific cycle of films.

In line with my desire to give voice to the 'repressed' of Clover's work, the rest of the book will focus largely on those films Clover's analysis neglects – pre-1970 deployments of the rape-revenge structure and recent, mainstream articulations of the structure.[34] Chapter 2 will thus offer an analysis of *Sleeping with the Enemy*, one of the 'nice', 'glossy', 'safe' mainstream films Clover consigns to her 'Afterword'. Indeed, although *Sleeping with the Enemy* represents an example of a residual rather than a dominant deployment of the rape-revenge structure, this has the effect of foregrounding the feminine discourses of romance and fairy-tales over which that structure is mapped, discourses which Clover's analysis represses. Furthermore, I will show how this back-to-front rather than chronological approach (starting at the end of both the rape-revenge cycle and Clover's analysis, and with a residual rather than a dominant example of the structure) is also a structural feature of the film itself. My choice of *Enemy* also is informed by a desire to complicate linear models of cultural and social development and the moments of authenticity such models tend to assume. Thus, while this film is in many ways unique, it can also be read as paradigmatic of the rape-revenge cycle as a whole and particularly of the way in which the cycle can be read as an attempt to make sense of feminism. Consequently, it is through my analysis of *Enemy* that the import of my arguments as a whole can be gauged.

The rest of the book is organized in an attempt to facilitate an understanding of rape-revenge as a historically, rather than generically, specific cycle of films and to enable an analysis of the changing inscription of feminism in that cycle. In chapter 3, I examine the deployment of the rape-revenge structure over a range of genres from the silent period to 1970. In so doing, I hope to show how the structure functioned in relation to the discourses of gender and genre in the period prior to the rise of second-wave feminism. In particular, while I will be arguing that these pre-1970 rape-revenge narratives, like their post-1970s counterparts, emerged at key points in the history of twentieth-century gender relations, I will argue

that, in the absence of the discourses of rape, which emerged with
the rise of second-wave feminism in the 1970s, these early articulations of the structure did not attempt to tell feminist stories, or even
feminine stories, but instead largely functioned to endorse and
uphold the traditional conceptions of masculinity and femininity
inscribed in the genres over which it was mapped. For example, I
will show how in these films rape is often cast as a threat to the feminine career of heterosexual romance and family. In other words,
rape is frequently shown to result in the victim's rejection of this
career and the threat this represents is apparent in the way in which
these narratives work overtime to return the woman to her 'proper'
place within the confines of the family and heterosexual relations.
Even in those films in which rape can be seen to result *from* the heroine's rejection of her feminine vocation, the trajectory and ideological work of the narrative is the same – to reposition the heroine as
wife, fiancée or girlfriend. In this chapter, then, I will be examining
the various narrative and generic strategies employed to bring about
these 'narratives of transformation'.

In line with my claim that feminism is never available in a pure or
unmediated form, and with my interest in the popular and publicly
available meanings of feminism, chapter 4 will offer an analysis of
the way in which feminism was constructed in reviews of the rape-
revenge film. Focusing particularly on reviews of *The Accused*
(Jonathan Kaplan, 1988) and *Thelma and Louise*, I will argue that
extra-textual material such as reviews play an important part in the
construction of any particular text's meanings, particularly its dominant or preferred meanings. Traditionally, feminist analyses of
mainstream texts have read 'against the grain' of these dominant or
preferred meanings in order to produce resistant feminist readings.
Here, however, I will read '*with* the grain' of these dominant meanings as they are inscribed in reviews of *The Accused* and *Thelma and
Louise* in order to explore the ways in which they might produce
popular, common-sense understandings of feminism. Against
accepted understandings of the period in which these films were
produced – one in which feminism was the subject of a right-wing
backlash – I will argue that feminism instead underwent a process of
redefinition and negotiation. It will be my contention that this
process was, in fact, a *part of* the wider hegemonic project of the
New Right and that the meanings the reviews of *The Accused* and
Thelma and Louise constructed were particularly illustrative of these

processes. I will thus offer an analysis of these reviews as the discursive context for subsequent discussions.

Chapters 5 to 7, therefore, will analyse the changing inscription of feminism in the rape-revenge cycle itself. The organization of these chapters is thus diachronic and roughly chronological, with each chapter focusing on a different generic deployment of the rape-revenge structure. Given my interest in the way in which the discourses of 1970s feminism are circulating and functioning in the 1990s, the emphasis will be largely on recent films, although I will also be concerned to trace differences and similarities in the generic work of these films and those I discussed in chapter 3. Chapter 5 thus offers a broad sweep through the period with an analysis of the way in which the rape-revenge structure has been mapped over that of the western. Starting with Pam Cook's observation that 'the frontier has often been seen in symbolic terms as a boundary between opposing ideas', I will argue that the rise of second-wave feminism demanded a fundamental realignment of these oppositions and thus of the myths or stories the western articulates.[35] My analysis will thus offer a continuation of Will Wright's structural analysis of the western.[36] In the first section of this chapter, then, I will trace the differences and similarities between two female rape-revenge westerns – *Hannie Caulder* (Burt Kennedy, 1971) and *Handgun* (Tony Garnett, 1982) – and Wright's 'vengeance variation'. In so doing, I will explore the extent to which the introduction of new functions such as the rape-avenging woman brings about changes at the level of narrative structure, the oppositions it articulates and thus the meanings it generates. The second section of this chapter will look at a range of rape-revenge westerns from the 1990s and my analyses here will involve supplementing the preceding emphasis on the formal and thematic content of the texts themselves with an emphasis on the discourses surrounding them. In particular, I will argue that the rape-revenge film's move into the mainstream during this period has meant that the role played by stars such as Clint Eastwood and Sharon Stone has become increasingly significant to an analysis of the way in which these films articulate changing conceptions of masculinity and femininity and, by extension, to the way in which they produce a set of meanings around feminism. In so doing, I will begin to explore the extent to which popular understandings of the 1990s as a period of post-feminism and backlash are articulated in these films. Finally, I will also suggest that such an analysis must take account of the increasing influence of post-modern aesthetics on genre, gender and the deployment of the rape-revenge structure.

Picking up on some of the issues discussed at the end of chapter 5, chapters 6 and 7 will focus on two different and apparently contradictory directions the rape-revenge cycle has taken in the 1990s, and on the different versions of the feminist story they have produced. In chapter 6, I will explore the way in which the rape-revenge structure has been mapped over the codes and conventions of film noir in two neo-noirs of the period, *Batman Returns* and *The Last Seduction* (John Dahl, 1993). Against the tendency to argue that the neo-noir articulates a contemporary backlash against feminism similar to that articulated by the classic film noir against women's changing status following World War II, I will argue that such analyses fail to take into account those changes in the social, cultural and political context the pre-fix 'neo' should alert us to. Among these changes, I will suggest that the rise of second-wave feminism and of specifically female-centred deployments of the rape-revenge structure, the emergence and influence of the New Right, and the shift from a modernist to a post-modern aesthetic, are the most significant. Consequently, I will argue that the post-modern articulation of the codes and conventions of film noir found in the neo-noir is not nostalgic. Instead, I will suggest that the neo-noir reconfigures those codes and conventions in a way that can be seen as both specific to, and an attempt to make sense of, our own current experience in the late twentieth century. In particular, I will argue that within the context of the yuppie ethos of the 1980s, in which upward-mobility, consumerism and acquisitiveness were not only emphasized, but legitimated, both the femme fatale's transgressive greed and ambition and feminist desires to 'have it all' have been subject to reinterpretation. In my analysis of *The Last Seduction*, then, I will show how the negotiations that occur in the film between 1970s feminism and the 1980s culture of consumption, and between the codes and conventions of film noir and the rape-revenge structure, redefines feminism, particularly the archetypal feminist notion of 'having it all', according to the exigencies of the present moment. In the second half of the chapter, I will turn my attention to *Batman Returns* and explore how the film attempts to make sense of feminism within the context of increasing calls in the 1990s for a more morally restrained capitalism centred around family values. Anxieties about capitalism, I will suggest, are articulated in particular through the film's deployment of the codes and conventions of the vampire narrative. Although the construction of Catwoman would seem to owe more to the femme fatale of film noir and the erotic female avenger of rape-revenge than to the female vampire, I will argue that these figures have more in common than might at first appear and that it is in the combination and negotiation of these historically specific figurations of femininity that the film can be seen to be attempting to make sense of feminism past, present and future.

In chapter 7, I will analyse the erotic avenger's opposite number in the rape-revenge films of the 1990s – the maternal avenger. Given certain structural similarities between these maternal rape-revenge films and the 'vigilante-mom made-for-TV film' or 'trauma drama' analysed by Jane Feuer, I will start by exploring what happens to the feminist stories the rape-revenge structure articulates when it is juxtaposed with the vigilante and familial politics of the trauma drama in the maternal rape-revenge films of the 1990s.[37] In so doing, I will give particular consideration to Feuer's suggestion that 'when the trauma concerns women's issues' the politics of the trauma drama became less unambiguously right-wing.[38] In examining the extent to which the maternal rape-revenge film can be seen to conform to the structure and ideology of the trauma drama, I will also be concerned to evaluate Feuer's claim that it is the films that depart from the usual eight-step plot structure that can be 'read against the grain of the more hegemonic films that contain all eight steps'.[39] Against Feuer, I will argue that, in the maternal rape-revenge film at least, the omission of crucial functions has the effect of tipping the balance of the films away from the politicized public solutions of the trauma drama towards the depoliticized private solutions of the domestic melodrama. In the second part of the chapter, therefore, I will engage in a close textual analysis of the way in which the maternal rape-revenge film deploys the codes and conventions of classic melodrama. In particular, I will show how the deployment of these codes and conventions work to construct the mother as guilty and thus to legitimate a backlash politics, which demands women's return to the domestic sphere of home and family. Given the similarities between the ideological work of these films and those pre-second-wave feminist articulations of the structure discussed in chapter 3, I will suggest that, with the maternal rape-revenge film, the rape-revenge cycle has come full circle.

Following Gledhill's claim that 'the critical act is not finished with the "reading" or "evaluation" of a text', the conclusion will be concerned to assess not only my analysis of the rape-revenge cycle's textual negotiation of feminism, but the various theoretical negotiations with feminism that have underpinned this analysis.[40] In so doing, I will consider the implications of my research for the future of feminist film theory, pedagogy and politics.

Notes

1 Alan Sinfield, *Literature, Politics and Culture in Postwar Britain* (Oxford: Basil Blackwell, 1989), pp. 23–4.
2 Carol Clover, *Men, Women and Chainsaws: Gender in the Modern Horror Film* (London: BFI, 1992).
3 Jennifer Wicke, 'Celebrity Material: Materialist Feminism and the Culture of Celebrity', *South Atlantic Quarterly*, 93:4 (Fall 1994), 751–78 (p. 776).
4 Ibid., p. 754.
5 Jackie Byars, *All That Hollywood Allows: Re-reading Gender in 1950s Melodrama* (London: Routledge, 1991), pp. 2–3.
6 Sinfield, *Literature, Politics and Culture*, p. 24.
7 Leeds Revolutionary Feminist Group, 'Political Lesbianism: The Case Against Heterosexuality', in *The Woman Question: Readings on the Subordination of Women*, ed. by Mary Evans (London: Fontana, 1982), pp. 63–72 (p. 65).
8 Ien Ang, *Watching Dallas: Soap Opera and the Melodramatic Imagination* (London: Methuen, 1985), p. 135.
9 The Spice Girls, *Girl Power!* (London: Zone/Chameleon Books, 1997), p. 15.
10 Andrea Stuart, 'Feminism: Dead or Alive?', in *Identity*, ed. by Jonathan Rutherford (London: Lawrence and Wishart, 1990), pp. 28–42 (p. 40).
11 Christine Gledhill, 'Pleasurable Negotiations', in *Female Spectators: Looking at Film and Television*, ed. by E. Deidre Pribram (London: Verso, 1988), pp. 64–89 (p. 72).
12 Margaret Walters, 'American Gothic: Feminism, Melodrama and the Backlash', in *Who's Afraid of Feminism?: Seeing through the Backlash*, ed. by Ann Oakley and Juliet Mitchell (London: Penguin, 1997), pp. 56–76.
13 Wicke, 'Celebrity Material', p. 765.
14 Ien Ang, 'Melodramatic Identifications: Television Fiction and Women's Fantasy', in *Television and Women's Culture: The Politics of the Popular*, ed. by Mary Ellen Brown (London: Sage, 1990), pp. 75–88 (pp. 87–8).
15 Gledhill, 'Pleasurable Negotiations', p. 74.

16 Clover, *Men, Women and Chainsaws*.

17 Ibid., p. 141 (my emphasis).

18 Ibid., p. 3.

19 See for example: Leslie Felperin Sharman, '*Bad Girls*: Review', *Sight and Sound*, 4:7 (July 1994), 37–8; 'Daws', '*Thelma and Louise*: Review', *Variety*, 13 May 1991.

20 Gledhill, 'Pleasurable Negotiations', p. 68.

21 Charlotte Brunsdon, 'Pedagogies of the Feminine: Feminist Teaching and Women's Genres', *Screen*, 32:4 (1991), 364–81 (p. 365). It is worth noting that Brunsdon is referring specifically to 'women's genres' here, but I think the description can be usefully extended to cover genre in general.

22 Sinfield, *Literature, Politics and Culture*, p. 37.

23 Clover, *Men, Women and Chainsaws*, p. 11.

24 Clover's definition of the rape-revenge film as a sub-genre of horror also functions as one of the mechanisms through which she represses the feminine. In other words, existing theoretical paradigms demand that any attempt to tell a feminist story about the horror genre engage with the problem of the sadistic male gaze and thus with the masculine story of the male spectator. Clover's project is to square the feminist story that has enabled the representation of a female victim-hero with the masculine story of the male spectator.

25 Byars, *All That Hollywood Allows*, p. 24.

26 Sinfield, *Literature, Politics and Culture*, p. 26.

27 My use of the phrase 'feminist stories' here and elsewhere is not intended to imply that these films are actually '*feminist* texts' (although, as I argue below, there is, in fact, not such a thing 'as an intrinsically feminist text'). Rather, the phrase is intended as a shorthand for the 'stories *about* feminism' that these films can be seen to tell.

28 Gledhill, 'Pleasurable Negotiations', p. 87.

29 Clover, *Men, Women and Chainsaws*, p. 5.

30 Laura Mulvey, 'Visual Pleasure and Narrative Cinema', in *Feminism and Film Theory*, ed. by Constance Penley (London: BFI, 1988), pp. 57–68.

31 Elizabeth Wilson, 'Tell It Like It Is: Women and Confessional Writing', in *Sweet Dreams: Sexuality, Gender and Popular Fiction*, ed. by Susannah Radstone (London: Lawrence & Wishart, 1988), pp. 21–45 (p. 21).

32 Toril Moi, 'Feminist Literary Criticism', in *Modern Literary Theory: A Comparative Introduction*, ed. by Ann Jefferson and David Robey, 2nd edn (London: B. T. Batsford, 1986), pp. 204–21 (p. 220).

33 Wicke, 'Celebrity Material', p. 757.

34 It is perhaps worth conceding here that, beyond the implication that they are too feminine to be feminist, there are practical reasons for Clover's neglect of many of the recent, mainstream articulations of the

rape-revenge structure I will be discussing. In other words, most of them
had not been released at the time Clover was writing.

35 Pam Cook, 'Women', in *The BFI Companion to the Western*, ed. by
   Edward Buscombe (London: Museum of the Moving Image, 1991),
   pp. 240–3 (p. 241).

36 Will Wright, *Six Guns and Society: A Structural Study of the Western*
   (Berkeley: University of California Press, 1975).

37 Jane Feuer, *Seeing through the Eighties: Television and Reaganism*
   (London: BFI, 1995).

38 Ibid., p. 42n14.

39 Ibid., p. 37.

40 Gledhill, 'Pleasurable Negotiations', p. 74.

Chapter 1

Narratives of transformation: the rape-revenge cycle

From the final girls and monstrous women of the horror film, though the female avengers of rape-revenge, to the deadly dolls and fatal femmes of the erotic thriller or neo-noir, the 1990s have witnessed a burgeoning interest among feminist film theorists in representations of violent and vengeful women.[1] In their tendency to confine their analyses of these representations to specific genres, however, what these studies have failed to recognize are the continuities between these various representations and thus the way in which this apparent proliferation of deadly and dangerous women might be historically rather than generically specific. Moreover, the generic approach means that, even while they may question them, these studies tend to be constrained by the dominant theoretical approaches that have characterized the analysis of specific genres. Analyses of horror's violent woman tend to work within the psychoanalytical theoretical paradigms, which have dominated work on the genre. Carol Clover's work on the horror film, for example, is concerned to account for the pleasures such films afford their male viewers and, while this project involves challenging psychoanalytic film criticism's assumption of the sadism of the male spectorial position, Clover's alternative account of male spectatorial pleasure remains firmly rooted in psychoanalytic paradigms. Work on the deadly doll and fatal femme, on the other hand, has taken its cue from more historically contextualized studies of film noir, which have read the emergence of the femme fatale as an articulation of anxieties about the changing position of women following World War II. This emphasis on the way in which changes in the representation of women can be read as an attempt to make sense of feminism and women's new status closely parellels my own approach to the rape-revenge film. However, work on the deadly doll and femme fatale of the erotic thriller and neo-noir has tended to side-step discussion of the female avenger. Instead, rape-revenge receives its most extended discussion in Clover and Creed's studies of the horror genre. In what follows I want to counter this tendency to locate rape-revenge within the horror genre by developing an analysis, which argues that rape-revenge, together with the erotic thriller, form part of an ongoing historically, rather than generically, specific cycle. In so doing, I will attempt to displace the traditional emphasis on male spectatorial pleasure, which has characterized discussions of rape-revenge as horror, and begin to explore why these films and the representations of women they construct are of such interest to feminist critics.

The problems inherent in defining rape-revenge as a sub-genre of horror become particularly apparent in Clover's work. As Christine Gledhill has pointed out: 'While the existence of the major genres is in some ways a self-evident fact, the business of definition and demarcation is less clear-cut.'[2] Clover attempts to side-step such problems by claiming that:

> It has not been my concern to define horror or to adhere to the defin-
> itions of others ... I have been guided for the most part by video rental
> store categorizations, which ... seem to capture better than any defin-
> ition I know what the public senses to be 'horror'.[3]

Her categorization of US horror of the 1970s to mid-1980s is, there-fore, by her own admission, somewhat loosely defined. While I have no argument with Clover's definition of slasher and occult/posses-sion films as examples of horror, both she and I have more problems yoking rape-revenge films, such as *Deliverance* (John Boorman, 1972), to the genre and, as a result, she is constantly forced into making qualifications to her arguments:

> Although *Deliverance* is commonly taken less as horror than as a 'lit-
> erary' rumination on urban masculinity, its particular rendition of the
> country-city encounter has been obviously and enormously influential
> in horror – so much so that it is regularly included in cult horror lists.[4]

and:

> A number of the rape-revenge films I viewed in connection with this
> chapter are categorized in video rental stores under 'action' or 'sus-
> pense'. Production values, not just subject matter, play a role in the
> perception of genre. High-budget forms are likely to be categorized as

drama, suspense, or action and low-budget forms as horror or cult –
even when the plots are virtually identical.[5]

What these points belie is *precisely* a process of definition. In other
words, for a rape-revenge film to be 'horror' and, therefore, to fit
into Clover's thesis it must be both low-budget and represent a symbolic encounter between the city and the country (what Clover calls
the city-country axis). To my knowledge this rules out virtually every
female-centred rape-revenge film except *I Spit on Your Grave* (Meir
Zarchi, 1977), which, significantly, is the one to which Clover gives
the most detailed attention. Indeed, Clover's attempt to differentiate the horror film from the action film, and to explain the former's
preference for a *female* victim-hero over the latter's preference for
a *male* victim-hero on the basis of horror's greater emphasis on the
victim part of the story, forces her into another qualification (again
significantly tucked away in the footnotes): that 'the subgenre of
horror that most closely approximates the suffering-revenge pro-
portions of the male action film is the rape-revenge film'.[6] This,
along with her other qualifications, would seem to suggest that rape-
revenge is simply not assimilable to the horror genre. However,
instead, these qualifications are used as a defining principle by which
those films that might contradict Clover's thesis, while used to set
up the initial problematic, are successfully ruled out of the final
argument (single male-female axis rape-revenge films, high-brow
rape-revenge films, 'action' or 'suspense' rape-revenge films). Consequently, many significant features of the rape-revenge film go
unaddressed and unexplained, together with its predecessors and
successors in the filmic world.

Such an approach is, for example, simply unable to account for the
variations and developments that become apparent from even a cur-
sory glance at various rape-revenge films. Rape-revenge, for example, is not generically specific since, as a sequence of narrative events,
it quite clearly spans a whole range of genres from the western
(*Hannie Caulder*) to the erotic thriller or neo-noir (*The Last Seduction*), from melodrama (*In My Daughter's Name*, Jud Taylor, 1992)
to the detective genre (*Sudden Impact*, Clint Eastwood, 1983), and
from courtroom drama (*The Accused*) to, in rare cases, science fiction
(*The Handmaid's Tale*, Volker Schlöndorff, 1990). Some films, on
the other hand, appear to cover several genres at once. *Blue Steel*
(Kathryn Bigelow, 1990), for example, simultaneously draws on

melodrama, film noir and the detective genre. In addition, in some instances, rape-revenge forms the primary structure of the film (as in *I Spit on Your Grave*), while in others it is merely part of a larger narrative structure (as in *Showgirls*, Paul Verhoeven, 1995) or is given a self-conscious post-modern inflection (as in *The Last Seduction* or *Batman Returns*). What this suggests, I think, is that rape-revenge is best understood not as a genre, but as a narrative structure, which has been mapped on to and across not only a whole range of genres, but a whole range of historical and discursive contexts. Examples of the structure can be found in films from the silent period – *Broken Blossoms* (D. W. Griffith, 1919), *The Wind* (Victor Seastrom, 1928) and *Blackmail* (Alfred Hitchcock, 1929) – through to the present day – *Eye for an Eye* (John Schlesinger, 1995) and *A Time to Kill* (Joel Schumacher, 1996). The rape-revenge structure, however, has received perhaps its most widespread dissemination in the post-1970 period and I will thus be arguing that the confluence between the rape-revenge structure and the discourses of second-wave feminism that emerged during this period has produced a historically specific, but generically diverse, cycle of films.

Clover's impressive and persuasive discussion of horror's, or, more specifically, the city-country rape-revenge film's appropriation and transformation of elements from another genre, the western, would simply seem to support my contention that rape-revenge is not a genre but a narrative structure, which has been mapped over other genres. In addition, the parallel with the western not only illustrates how difficult it is to transfer Clover's persuasive arguments about the slasher film to rape-revenge, but supports the case for a historically rather than generically specific reading of rape-revenge. While I have no argument with the definition of slasher as an example of horror, rape-revenge is less easily assimilable to the genre. The parallels with the western, in some respects, only serve to point this up. The world of slasher lacks a social and historical context and, therefore, has little basis in reality. Both the western and the rape-revenge film, however, can be related to historical and social contexts and developments (US frontier history and the rise of second-wave feminism respectively) and have referents in the real world (for example, women's very real experience of rape). Of course, one may want to argue, as Clover does, that 'the notion of women going around ... putting bullets through male chauvinists has everything to do with fantasy and little to do with reality' and that it is, therefore, the revenge part of the drama that constitutes the horror.[7] However, one could also argue that these films actually represent an attempt to make sense of a reality in which radical feminists such as Valerie Solanis advocate the 'cutting up of men' and in which there are much publicized instances of women killing violent husbands (Sara Thornton) and castrating unfaithful ones (Lorena Bobbitt). In fact, as the legal consequences of Thornton's and Bobbitt's actions imply, Clover's charge of 'Pollyannaism' to *The Accused's* implication that 'the story is over when the men are sentenced' could equally be applied to the 'aftermathless' ending of *I Spit on Your Grave*.[8] Such issues underline my own argument that the theories that worked so well for the slasher film do not so easily apply to rape-revenge.

As Clover herself points out, in yet another qualification: 'Revenge dramas are by no means the sole property of horror; vengeance may very well be the mainspring of American popular culture.'[9] Yet, if this is the case, the question that surely needs to be asked is 'where is the horror in *rape-revenge*?' or 'what makes *rape-revenge* horror and other revenge dramas not horror?'. It is at this point that Clover's reliance on popular definitions becomes particularly problematic and at which *some* reference to the genre criticism and definitions she so studiously avoids clearly becomes necessary. While recognizing the problems associated with the definition of genres, I would agree with Robin Wood that one of the core characteristics of horror is that 'normality is threatened by the Monster'.[10] This also conforms with Stephen Neale's argument that genres do not consist of exclusive elements but of exclusive combinations of elements and of the weight given to those elements.[11] The presence of a monster – a threat to normality; an abnormal person – may be, but is rarely, an optional element in other genres, but in horror it plays a specific and distinctive role: its presence is essential. The question then arises 'where is the monster in rape-revenge?'. As Clover herself points out, the rapists in *I Spit on Your Grave* 'are not odd specimens but in the normal range of variation; their acts of brutal rape are not traced to dysfunctional upbringing', a point that actually contradicts her later assertion that such country people are indeed highly abnormal, a 'people not like us' but a 'threatening rural Other'.[12] In fact, the '"normalization" of the rapist' is later characterized as a feature of the films as a whole.[13] Are we then to assume that it is the female avenger's deviation from

standards of feminine behaviour through her adoption of violence
– what Clover calls the 'the "masculinization" of the rape victim' –
that is the threat to normality?[14] This would seem to be what Clover
is suggesting when she claims that in her definition of the female
victim-hero (of which the female avenger is an example) 'the hero
part [is] always understood as implying some degree of monstros-
ity'.[15] However, although her analysis of Stephen King's remark that
his novel, *Carrie*, represents 'an uneasy masculine shrinking from a
future of female equality' causes her to ask the question, 'If
"women's liberation" is the fear, is Carrie its representative monster?', it is one that is never satisfactorily addressed or answered.[16]
Instead, she prefers to argue that Carrie's status as a female victim-
hero has been enabled by women's liberation and that the cinematic
adaptation of *Carrie* (Brian De Palma, 1976) and subsequent films
articulate a feminist politics (although even here she tends to equiv-
ocate, her comments often qualified with the inclusion of an
ambivalent 'for better or worse').[17] Moreover, while Carrie's super-
natural powers place her firmly within the realm of horror and the
monstrous, the rape-avenging woman is less obviously assimilable
to the role of 'monster'.

If Clover's categorization of rape-revenge films as a sub-genre of
horror is problematic due to the absence of an adequately defined
monster, there is no such equivocation in Barbara Creed's work. My
disagreement with her classification of both rape-revenge films, such
as *I Spit on Your Grave*, and erotic thrillers, such as *Basic Instinct*, as
horror is consequently somewhat different. In other words, Creed's
genre argument rests precisely on an analysis of the female characters in her chosen films as representative of the *monstrous*-feminine,
not only, as has traditionally been argued, because man fears woman
because she is castrated, but, in Creed's reformulation, because she
is also castrator. Nevertheless, this formulation means that almost
any representation of woman as deadly or murderous can be classi-
fied as a horror film and, although this is, in fact, exactly what it
enables Creed to do, the category ultimately becomes so large and
all encompassing as to disintegrate into meaninglessness. Rather,
what I think Creed's discussion does, inadvertently, point up is a historically rather than generically specific proliferation of murderous
women. In other words, out of her corpus of 208 films spanning a
ninety-year period (1902 to 1992), well over half (124) were made
in the twenty-two years from 1970 to 1992. While I agree with

Creed, therefore, that there is a link between rape-revenge films and films such as *Basic Instinct*, I think this link is actually historically rather than generically specific and is thus better understood in terms of the rise of second-wave feminism and discourses of rape than in relation to ahistorical and universal psychoanalytic concepts such as castration anxiety.

Consequently, while the possibility, implicit in Clover's discussion of *Carrie*, that these films articulate anxieties about feminism is worth pursuing, it is one that is not exclusive to the horror genre. As Doane argues in relation to film noir, the femme fatale is 'not the subject of feminism but a symptom of male fears about feminism'.[18] What this points to is not horror and its monsters but a wider cultural process of demonization, which, like the revenge motif, is not 'the sole property of horror' but informs a wide cross-section of genres. In chapters 6 and 7, then, I will be exploring the extent to which specific generic deployments of the rape-revenge structure can be read as articulations of the backlash against feminism that occurred in the late 1980s and 1990s.

Some of the inconsistencies and ambivalence in Clover's arguments perhaps stem from this uneasy and never fully resolved alliance between psychoanalytical perspectives and socio-historical perspectives, from her desire to understand both the pleasures rape-revenge affords the male spectator and the way in which it articulates feminist discourses. In particular, Clover's reliance on an ahistorical, psychoanalytic analysis prevents her from seeing the discourses of genre and gender as anything other than fixed or static. Clover's analysis of the transformations that occur within and across the rape-revenge film thus does not allow for the complex temporality of the discursive formations in which the rape-revenge film has been produced and developed.[19] Rather, Clover offers a teleological account of the rape-revenge film's evolution. In other words, she argues that the rape-revenge film's move into the mainstream has been enabled by earlier, 'low' versions of such films and that this transformation has been accompanied by a concomitant erosion of their progressive politics. In its implication that there was a moment of authenticity that has now passed, Clover's argument installs the low-budget horror film as the site of the 'true' rape-revenge film from which mainstream or other generic examples are excluded and, in so doing, obviates any need to consider or account for changes in the cultural or political context.

This tendency becomes particularly apparent in Clover's decision to structure part of her discussion around a comparative analysis of a low-brow and a high-brow rape-revenge film (*I Spit on Your Grave* and *The Accused* respectively). Unsurprisingly, in comparison to the former, the latter is found wanting, with the analysis divided into 'virtues' and 'problems', but with the emphasis placed squarely on the problems. For example, Clover argues that *The Accused* is not as progressive in terms of its articulation of feminist discourses because, unlike *I Spit on Your Grave*, the legal system, rather than the rape victim, becomes the hero of the piece. However, in comparing *The Accused* with *I Spit on Your Grave*, Clover fails to take into account changes in the historical and political context in which the film was produced and consumed. For example, the shift from female revenge to legal revenge is perhaps best understood within the context of the right-wing populism of the Reagan era in which liberal institutions were increasingly subject both to critique and rejuvenation. Clover's evaluative analysis of the film's feminism thus overlooks the way in which the film might be read as an attempt to make sense of, or to construct a popular version of, feminism within a specific historical and political context.

In attempting to offer an alternative to Clover's teleological account of the rape-revenge cycle's politics and evolution, I will be focussing largely on the absences and gaps in Clover's analysis: the recent, mainstream, deployments of the rape-revenge structure and the cultural and political context in which they were produced and consumed. In so doing, I will be giving particular consideration to two key contextual developments: the emergence of the New Right during the 1980s and the increasing influence of post-modern aesthetics on Hollywood film. In exploring the impact of post-modernism on the evolution of the rape-revenge cycle and on the way in which specific generic deployments of the structure negotiate their social and political context, my arguments will be informed, in particular, by the work of Jim Collins on 'genericity in the nineties'.

Collins starts by pointing out that the traditional three-stage model of generic progression and decline – consolidation, variation and collapse into self-parody or reflexivity – is simply unable to account for recent developments in genre.[20] These developments, he argues, have been largely brought about by the advent of new technologies such as television and video and the subsequent growth in media literacy among consumers. However, the increasing availability of texts from the past brought about by these new technologies has, he claims, resulted neither in decline (generic exhaustion) or progression (a fourth stage) but a renaissance phase in which texts from the past are increasingly being recycled in the present. According to Collins this recycling manifests itself in two different ways. The first, 'eclectic irony', is 'founded on dissonance, on eclectic juxtaposition of elements that very obviously don't belong together' and 'involves an ironic hybridization of pure classical genres'.[21] Here, then, the features of conventional genre films are not simply recycled but rearticulated. They do not, in other words, represent 'the mere detritus of exhausted cultures past'. Rather

> those icons, scenarios, visual conventions continue to carry with them some sort of cultural 'charge' or resonance that must be reworked according to the exigencies of the present. The individual generic features then, are neither detritus nor reliquaries, but *artifacts* of another cultural moment that now circulate in different arenas, retaining vestiges of past significance reinscribed in the present.[22]

The second form of genericity, 'the new sincerity', on the other hand, is 'obsessed with recovering some sort of missing harmony, where everything works in unison' and consequently 'rejects any form of irony in its sanctimonious pursuit of a lost purity'.[23] Texts in this category tend use an originary genre text in order to facilitate and guarantee a 'move back in time ... toward a lost authenticity' in which the unresolvable problems of the present can be magically resolved in an imaginary and unrecoverable past.[24] Thus genre films of the late 1980s and 1990s either purposely confuse time and genre (eclectic irony) or attempt to construct 'an impossible temporality' (the new sincerity).[25] The way in which both these forms of genericity confuse linear notions of time by recycling traditional genre texts, therefore, not only militates against conventional accounts of generic development, but complicates conventional understandings of the way in which texts negotiate their cultural and social context:

> The fact that the old is not replaced by the new anymore does not just change the historical development of specific genres, it also changes the function of genre films, which, if they can still be said to be engaged in symbolically 'mapping' the cultural landscape, must do so now in reference to, and *through* the array that constitutes that landscape.[26]

This clearly has profound implications for the way in which we trace the transformations in the articulation of gender and genre both within and across the rape-revenge narrative. In other words, the complex temporalities of genre complicate linear notions of time and history, such that analysing the way in which the rape-revenge film attempts to make sense of feminism will involve rejecting any simple notions of a narrative of progression (or, indeed, decline). If the 1990s has witnessed an increasing cultural literacy concerning the discourses of genre, it has also witnessed an increasing circulation and popularization of specifically feminist-derived discourses of gender, as evidenced by the unprecedented book sales enjoyed by feminist authors, such as Susan Faludi, Naomi Wolf and Camille Paglia. However, as with the discourses of genre, we need to guard against reading these discourses either as a narrative of progression or as a narrative of decline.[27] With regard to the former, Imelda Whelehan has observed that 'the "new" feminism of the '90s, exemplified by writers such as Wolf, is ... not altogether "new" in its insights',[28] while Michele Barrett and Anne Phillips have warned against 'the simplistic teleology of assuming that later theory is therefore better theory'.[29] On the other hand, we need to be equally wary of the narrative of decline implied by 'post-feminism'. As Charlotte Brunsdon has pointed out, current usages of the term not only tend to install '1970s feminism as the site of "true" feminism, from which lipstick wearers and shoppers are excluded' but tend to reduce 'all feminisms, and their long histories, to that one 1970s movement'.[30] Thus, against Clover, I want to suggest that the rape-revenge structure, and the discourses of genre and gender over which it has been mapped, are best understood not as producing fixed meanings or authentic moments, but as narratives of transformation.

For example, Clover argues that in the rape-revenge film the sex of a character is 'performatively determined by the social gendering of the acts it undergoes or undertakes'.[31] Against this fixed binary logic, which sees the rape-revenge structure as always already gendered, and therefore as merely facilitating a movement from the 'feminine' (rape) to the 'masculine' (revenge), I will be arguing that the transformations that occur both within and across the rape-revenge film are not a product of the rape-revenge structure, but of the tensions and contradictions both within and between the discursive narratives of transformation over which that structure is deployed. In representing and articulating these tensions and

contradictions, the various deployments of the rape-revenge structure in turn produce negotiated versions of these narratives of transformation. Thus, the rape-revenge narrative is not a simple
reflection of its discursive context, but an active attempt to make
sense of it. Moreover, since this context is constantly shifting, so too
are the meanings the structure generates. The resulting narratives,
therefore, are not inert but themselves become the sites on, through
and against which the discursive formations that produced them are
subsequently constructed and transformed. Any attempt to understand the changing inscription of feminism in these narratives, the
way in which they articulate feminist narratives of transformation,
consequently must involve a close analysis of the diverse ways in
which the rape-revenge structure has engaged with and expressed
the often competing and opposing demands of the discourses of
gender and genre across which it has been mapped. In addition,
where the rape-revenge structure is mapped over more than one
genre consideration will also need to be given to the effects produced by the intersection of conflicting generic discourses.

If discussions of rape-revenge films are marked by their tendency to
situate them within the larger context of the horror genre, what is
also significant about these accounts is that all, at some point, critically engage with Roger Ebert's famous diatribe against *I Spit on
Your Grave*.[32] Indeed, a critique of Ebert's argument is commonly
taken as the starting point for analysis and I would suggest that such
an approach can largely be seen as accounting for the assumption of
a predominantly male audience and the concomitant emphasis on
explaining male spectatorial pleasure in discussions of such films.
Peter Lehman's analysis, for example, like Clover's, is predicated on
an initial disagreement with Ebert's presumption that 'the pleasure
of watching these films for men lies in identification with the rapists
and their assault on the woman'.[33] Instead, like Clover, Lehman
argues that 'male spectators are positioned to be disgusted by the
rape and to identify with the avenging woman'.[34] What I want to
suggest, however, is that both Clover's and Lehman's critiques are
based on a superficial reading of Ebert's arguments and that these
actually have little to do with cinematic point of view.
    Ebert's intentions are, on the surface, ostensibly noble. He criti-
cizes what he refers to as 'the woman-in-danger' film (a categorization that covers both rape-revenge and slasher films) on the basis of

their 'sick attitude toward women' and their 'antifemale theme' and even concurs with fellow critic Siskel's claim that:

> this has something to do with the growth of the women's movement in America in the last decade. These films are some sort of primordial response by *very sick people* saying, 'Get back in your place, women!' The women in these films are typically portrayed as independent, as sexual, as enjoying life. And the killer, typically – not all the time but most often – is a man who is sexually frustrated with these new aggressive women, and so he strikes back at them.[35]

Clearly this ignores what these films, with their rape-avenging women and final girls, are actually about – women's refusal to get back in their place, their refusal to be killed off, their refusal to live in fear and danger. Indeed, Ebert's characterization of such films as about women in danger ignores the way they are equally about men in danger. Yet, ironically, reading between the lines reveals that it is, in fact, the latter rather than the former that concerns Ebert – not in any simple way as the victims of female violence, but as victims of a representational seachange in the depiction of male rapists and murderers. As my emphasis on the 'very sick people' in the above quote is intended to highlight, what concerns Ebert in the second half of this article is not cinematic devices or point of view but the representation of male villains as either normal or abnormal. In other words, Ebert admits that he has nothing against horror films *per se*, that he in fact quite enjoys them and is not 'automatically turned off, let's say, just because a film is about *a berserk raving homicidal madman*'.[36] To this end he praises John Carpenter's *Halloween* (1978) and claims that *The Texas Chainsaw Massacre* (Tobe Hooper, 1974) has redeeming features because the latter features '*heinous villains*' and in the former a psychiatrist testifies to the fact that the killer is 'the embodiment of *evil*'.[37] In other words, such films are acceptable not because they do not encourage audience identification with the killer through the use of cinematic point of view (the opening sequence of *Halloween* is perhaps the most famous and influential example of such techniques), but because they distinguish the 'normal' male audience from the 'abnormal' male killer and the male spectator is consequently not implicated in the male violence against women depicted on the screen.[38] Films such as *Prom Night* (Paul Lynch, 1980) or *Terror Train* (Roger Spottiswoode, 1979), however, come under attack from Ebert because 'the killer is never

clearly seen nor understood once the killings begin'.[39] The implication here, then, is that since the killer is 'never clearly seen' he could
be any man, and that, as he is never 'understood', that is, as he is
never given an adequate (psychopathic) motive, he could be any
normal man – as Ebert himself points out the killer becomes 'a *non-
specific* male killing force'.[40]

It is not, therefore, the use of shots from the killer's point of view
to establish audience identification with the killer that differentiates
these two sets of films – since both use these techniques – but the fact
that, in those Ebert endorses, the male viewer is able to get pleasure
from such identification, while the abnormality of the killer enables
him to disavow his complicity in the violence depicted and to find
the destruction of the abnormal Other enjoyable. In those, such as *I
Spit on Your Grave*, which Ebert criticizes, on the other hand, the
nonspecificity of the killer and the 'normalization' of the rapist
means that the pleasure of identification is undercut not only by
implication but by violent female retribution.[41] That it is not actually
'the terrible things [that] are happening to women' in such films
which concerns Ebert, but the way in which normal men are implicated in (and punished for) male violence against women, is
betrayed in his final sentence: 'Now the "victim" is the poor, put
upon, traumatized male in the audience. And the demons are the
women on the screen.'[42] Clearly, this suggests that it is not so much
male spectatorial pleasure that concerns Ebert but rather issues surrounding the representation of, and motivation for, male violence.

In predicating their analyses on a disagreement with what is essentially a misconception of Ebert's argument, both Clover and Lehman
are forced into finding alternative ways to account for the pleasures
these films afford male viewers. While the pleasures male viewers
obtain from images of rape have already been well documented by
feminist theorists, the question as to why they might enjoy the spectacle of a woman violently attacking her male rapists is less well
understood and, therefore, more interesting. Clover's answer rests
on challenging the widely held view that spectators, irrespective of
gender, identify with the male heroes on the screen. Within the
terms of this argument, female spectators are believed to get
masochistic pleasure from seeing women victimized by men in
horror films, and male spectators sadistic pleasure. Yet, as Clover
points out, this fails to explain the appeal to a largely male audience
of films, such as rape-revenge, which feature a *female* hero who,

after an initial period of victimization, turns the tables on her male attackers. Instead, she argues that 'these films are predicated on cross-gender identification' not of the female spectator with the male hero, but of the male spectator with the female hero.[43] In other words, she suggests that during the rape part of these films, shots from the victim's point of view solicit identification with, rather than objectification of, the rape victim on the part of the male spectator. This, along with the increasing masculinization of the rape victim, functions to secure the male spectator's identification with the female avenger in the revenge part of the story. For the male spectator, then, 'the revenge fantasy derives its force from *some* degree of imaginary participation in [the rape] itself, in the victim position'.[44]

What this argument fails to take into account, however, and what Clover's observations about many of her films gloss over, is that the avenging woman is frequently eroticized rather than masculinized. For example, as I pointed out in the introduction, Clover's observation that, in the revenge part of *Ms.45*, Thana is 'increasingly sexily dressed' is not only unexplored in the rest of the analysis, it is considered so insignificant that it is put in parenthesis.[45] Similarly unexplored (and also in parenthesis) is the observation that, in her final rampage, Thana is 'dressed as a nun'.[46] Indeed, one of the most memorable moments in *Ms.45* is a below-the-waist shot of Thana, nun's habit pulled up to reveal a stockinged leg into which is inserted her gun, and this highly erotic image surely plays on a whole range of male sexual fantasies. Thus the idea that male spectorial pleasure lies in identification is too often unproblematically assumed in Clover's analysis:

> The success among young male audiences of single-axis films like *Ms. 45* makes it clear that narrative and cinematic positioning can in themselves go a long way in insuring sympathy with the humiliation and rage of a raped person.[47]

Clearly, the process of eroticization radically compromises this reading of the rape-revenge film as telling a story of cross-gender identification, and it is perhaps for this reason that it is repressed in Clover's analysis. As I argued in the introduction, however, Clover's disavowal of eroticization can also be seen as arising from a more deep-seated conviction that sexiness is inimical to the feminist story she is seeking to tell about the rape-revenge film. In so doing,

Clover's analysis betrays a belief that in order to claim a text as feminist it must reflect such feminist orthodoxies. Yet as Pam Cook has argued: 'The quest for feminism in popular texts is ... self-defeating, in the sense that these texts produce popular versions of feminism, rather than reproduce an "authentic" feminist politics.'[48] In reinscribing the erotic female avenger as a central figure within the rape-revenge cycle, I will thus be particularly concerned to trace the way in which she functions in the construction of these popular versions of feminism.

In fact, the issue of eroticization seems to me one of the central ways in which the slasher film and the rape-revenge film differ. It represents another of the reasons why Clover's arguments about slasher are not transferable to rape-revenge. In other words, with regards to slasher, Clover's argument for the male spectator's cross-gender identification with a masculinized female victim-hero finds credence in the fact that the final girl of slasher is not only dowdy and virginal but frequently known by a boy's name (Stevie, Terry, Will, Joey, Max). Rape-revenge, on the other hand, is frequently either peopled with beautiful actresses – Raquel Welch in *Hannie Caulder*, Margaux Hemingway in *Lipstick* (Lamont Johnson, 1976), Sondra Locke in *Sudden Impact*, Farah Fawcett in *Extremities* (Robert M. Young, 1986) – or involves a transformation in which the initially rather plain rape-victim is transformed into a deadly but irresistible femme fatale – Thana (Zoë Tamerlis) in *Ms. 45* and Bella (Lia Williams) in *Dirty Weekend* (Michael Winner, 1992). Indeed, if Clover's initial selection procedure was guided by video 'box covers (screaming women, poised knives, terrified eyeballs)', then the erotic depiction of the female avenger on the video box covers and publicity material for many rape-revenge films (including *I Spit on Your Grave*) should have alerted her to these differences (see plates 1–3).[49]

The similarities between the erotic female avenger and the femme fatale suggest, moreover, that, while the origins of the rape-revenge structure *do* lie in the horror genre, they go back much further than the relatively recent slasher sub-genre. As I will argue in chapter 6, the femme fatale emerged as a key representational figure in the nineteenth century and the inspiration for these representations can be traced largely to the vampire narratives that had circulated widely since the publication of John Polidori's *The Vampyre* in 1819. Indeed, as I will go on to demonstrate in chapter 6, the similarities

1 Publicity poster for *I Spit on Your Grave*. The female avenger is clearly eroticized rather than masculinized.

2 Publicity poster for *Dirty Weekend*. Erotic codes (high heels, short skirts, parted legs) are deployed to construct an image of an erotic female avenger.

3 Publicity stills for *Dirty Weekend*. The initially rather plain rape victim, Bella (Lia Williams), is transformed into a deadly but irresistible femme fatale.

between the rape-revenge film and the vampire story extend beyond the level of representation to the level of narrative structure and ideology. In particular, I will show how vampirism, like rape, represents a violent sexual act which has similar effects on the subsequent representation and narrative trajectory of its female victim. Finally, I will argue that the female vampire (particularly as she is figured in the ultimate vampire narrative – Bram Stoker's 1897 novel, *Dracula* – and in the 1970s cycle of lesbian vampire films) emerges at key points in the history of feminism (the 1890s and the 1970s) and thus, like the female avenger, can be read as an attempt to make sense of the spectre of the 'New Woman' and a gathering women's movement.

If the vampire narratives of the nineteenth century can be seen as enacting symbolic forms of rape, by the mid-1980s, according to Clover 'rape moved virtually offscreen'.[50] However, not only does she fail to interrogate why this might be so, she fails to recognize the way in which this observation actually compromises many of her existing and subsequent arguments. For example, the disappearance of rape and the frequent eroticization of the vengeful woman suggest that the rape-revenge film has more in common with the erotic thrillers and neo-noirs of recent years than Clover's generically specific argument acknowledges. In addition, the disappearance of rape, along with the 'very brief and very unerotic' rapes of *Ms. 45* and *Lipstick*,[51] radically undermine her argument that for the male spectator 'the revenge fantasy derives its force from *some* degree of imaginary participation in [the rape] itself, in the victim position', and consequently her claim that 'these films are predicated on cross-gender identification of the most extreme, corporeal sort'.[52] Indeed, what Clover fails to recognize in her celebration of the move away from a representation of rape that 'exudes a kind of lascivious sadism with which the viewer is directly invited to collude', is that the 'very brief and very unerotic' nature of rape-revenge's representation of rape is often more than made up for in the concomitant 'eroticization' of the female-avenger.[53]

In attempting to account for the pleasures rape-revenge films afford male viewers, Peter Lehman fills a significant gap in Clover's analysis by pointing out that, while the rapist is nearly always repulsive, the women are nearly always beautiful. This allows him to argue that although both the rapist and the spectator have a similar desire for the erotic woman, the spectator cannot acknowledge this similarity with the rapist. Consequently, the spectator projects his repressed desires onto the rapist and this is why the rapist is always characterized as so repulsive. In this way, according to Lehman, 'The male spectator can hate rather than simply identify with these men who embody desires similar to their own.'[54] However, the fact that the female character is frequently not eroticized until *after* the rape and that the rape, in fact, is a process through which she is transformed, I think problematizes this argument for the spectators' and rapists' objects of desire being one and the same. Furthermore, despite the fact that this analysis is constructed against Ebert's, in effect, it merely reverses its polarity, defending *I Spit on Your Grave* for the same ideologically suspect reasons that Ebert defended *Halloween* and criticized *I Spit on Your Grave*. In other words, defending either film on the basis that men do not identify with the killer/rapist because they are abnormal/repulsive fails to criticize the way in which this facilitates a collective male disavowal of their complicity in violence against women.

The emphasis on male spectatorial pleasure is consequently not only misguided and limiting, but the psychoanalytical theoretical parameters in which such analyses tend to be set provide few openings for critical engagement and debate and are consequently tenuous and unconvincing. Nevertheless, Lehman does identify an important and consistent feature in the films themselves, which I think not only offers a simpler and more plausible explanation for the pleasures these films afford the male viewer, but which also serves to undermine the generic specificity usually attributed to the rape-revenge film. This is what Lehman calls the films' 'structures of erotic anticipation'.[55] In other words, although men are violently punished in these films, it is more often than not in a context that is overtly erotic and punishment is frequently preceded by the promise of sexual pleasure. That is, the avenging woman leads her victim (and the male spectator) to believe she is about to make love to him but instead hangs, castrates or shoots him. This structure features in what can perhaps be identified as one of the first rape-revenge films of the period, Wes Craven's *Last House on the Left* (1972). While this differs from the later films in terms of the fact that it is the woman's parents who exact revenge for her rape and murder, and while the structure of erotic anticipation is only used in one out of four deaths (the mother seduces one of the rapists, fellates him, then bites his penis off), it can be seen as a feature which is both consistent with, and influential on, the later films. By 1977 and the release of *I Spit On Your Grave*, then, not only were all the deaths marked by this structure but its deployment had also become more complex and sophisticated. Here, the first murder establishes the structure, with Jennifer first seducing Matthew and then, as they begin to have intercourse, slipping a noose over his head and hanging him. The second murder, however, initially reverses this structure. In other words, when Jennifer first confronts Johnny, it is the threat of violence rather than the promise of sexual pleasure that is anticipated as she forces him to remove his trousers at gun point, clearly intending to shoot him in the genitals. Nevertheless, in response to Johnny's pleas, Jennifer appears to yield and they return to her house where they take a bath together. Consequently, with the threat of violence apparently overcome, erotic anticipation would appear to be uncompromised for both Johnny and the male spectator. Yet, the film quickly effects a double reversal, re-establishing the traditional structure as Jennifer castrates her unsuspecting victim.

What I want to argue, moreover, is that the influence of these structures of erotic anticipation extend far beyond the rape-revenge film and that they find expression in the very term used to describe a recent cycle of films. I am thinking, of course, of the erotic thriller, which similarly features violent women whose attacks on men are frequently preceded by erotic overtures. Consider, for instance, the opening sequence of *Basic Instinct* (Paul Verhoeven, 1992), which has all the markings of pure erotic spectacle but which suddenly and without warning degenerates into frenzied and bloody violence. More explicit an example still is *Body of Evidence* (Uli Edel, 1992) in which sex is itself the murder weapon as an aged millionaire anticipates a night of sexual pleasure with dominatrix Rebecca Carlson (Madonna) only for the exertion and the kinkiness of the sex to give him heart failure. Furthermore, whereas, unlike the rape-revenge film, there is no apparent motivation for such attacks, this coupling of sex and violence suggests a similar reversal of, and therefore revenge for, the sexual violence men commit against women. While these structures of erotic anticipation may explain the male viewer's pleasure in such films, I take exception to Lehman's assertion that 'such eroticized deaths are male fantasies which are unlikely to be of "interest" to women'.[56] Although I do not wish to make similar, unsupported, claims for a female audience for such films, the literature on both the rape-revenge film and the erotic thriller demonstrates that, within the academy at least, these films have proved to be of remarkable interest to women, with Clover even situating herself as 'something of a fan'.[57] My discussion of this literature will attempt, therefore, to displace the traditional emphasis on male spectatorial pleasure through an exploration of why these films, like film noir, are of such interest to feminist critics. Moreover, within the context of the enduring and increased popularity of these films in the last twenty years, and against the tendency of these analyses to distinguish the rape-revenge film from the erotic thriller, I will also be developing an analysis that argues that both form part of an ongoing historically, rather than generically, specific cycle.

While Barbara Creed's discussion of the *femme castratice* embraces both sets of films they are differentiated on the basis of whether the castrating woman is justified or unjustified, motivated or motiveless. In other words, she argues that in film, the *femme castratice* assumes two forms, 'the castrating female psychotic (*Sisters*, *Play Misty for Me*, *Repulsion*, *Basic Instinct*) and the woman who seeks revenge on men who have raped or abused her in some way'.[58] According to Creed, then, these two groups of films are unified by the motif of the *femme castratice* and the genre of horror and where they differ is in their representation of rape. In other words, when the rape is simply 'not there', as for example in *Sisters* (Brian De

Palma, 1973), the castrating woman is depicted 'as psychotic, a mad-woman who wishes to avenge herself against the whole male sex'.[59] While this formulation of the motif of the *femme castratice* allows Creed to embrace films beyond those typically regarded as rape-revenge films, both groups of films are still categorized as falling within the genre of horror and are thus understood in those terms. In other words, by interpreting the link between rape-revenge and films like *Basic Instinct* in terms of the universal and ahistorical psychoanalytical concepts that have characterized the study of the horror genre (specifically, castration anxiety), Creed overlooks the way in which this link might be historically rather than generically specific.

Unlike Creed's analysis of the *femme castratice*, Julianne Pidduck's discussion of the 'fatal femme' cycle of the 1990s is concerned to account for a historically specific proliferation of violent women. Like Creed, Pidduck also distinguishes rape-revenge films from fatal femme films on the basis of the presence or absence of a motive such as rape. In other words, she distinguishes the justified revenge fantasy of, for example, *Thelma and Louise* from the violence of the fatal femme who, she claims, 'rarely lines up in any straightforward way with the forces of righteousness, feminist or otherwise'.[60] However, in claiming that the fatal femme film 'specializes in *turning the tables* on what is perhaps *the* quintessential (and most high profile) male crime against women: sexual assault coupled with violent attack', Pidduck inadvertently points out that rape-revenge is precisely what the fatal femme cycle is often all about.[61] The motivating rape is no longer there partly because since it has now become '*the* quintessential (and most high profile) male crime against women' it no longer needs to be depicted and is frequently only alluded to.

Creed and Pidduck suggest that what differentiates erotic thrillers, such as *Basic Instinct*, from rape-revenge films, such as *I Spit On Your Grave* and *Thelma and Louise*, is the absence in the former of a motive such as rape, and, therefore, the representation of characters, such as Catherine Trammell (Sharon Stone) in *Basic Instinct*, as psychotic rather justified in their deadliness. Against them, I would suggest that rape may have moved offscreen but it has not disappeared altogether. In fact, it is surprising how often rape does still figure in the erotic thrillers and neo-noirs of the 1980s and 1990s. Christine Holmlund's discussion of 1980s 'deadly doll' films, for example, despite similarly attempting to distinguish the rape-revenge film from the deadly doll film on the basis of motive, actually points up the continuing presence of rape as a motive in the latter, and thus their similarities with the rape-revenge film: 'Regardless of genre, several films still promote female violence as self-defence or revenge for rape and/or abuse'.[62] Of the six deadly doll films Holmlund analyses – *Black Widow* (Bob Rafelson, 1987), *Aliens* (James Cameron, 1986), *Fatal Attraction* (Adrian Lyne, 1987), *Blue Steel*, *Mortal Thoughts* (Alan Rudolph, 1991) and *Thelma and Louise* – half feature rape and violence against women as a motivation (*Blue Steel*, *Mortal Thoughts* and *Thelma and Louise*).

In *Blue Steel*, something of a generic hybrid, both sexual and domestic violence against women pervades the film. It opens with a mock scene of domestic violence during a police training exercise. The heroine, Megan (Jamie Lee Curtis), is later raped by the psychopathic Eugene (Ron Silver). There is also a suggestion that the domestic violence suffered by Megan's mother is behind her choice of career in the police force. As Harriet E. Margolis points out, the film works on a double structure of investigation.[63] In other words, while Megan investigates male violence against women, the men in the film investigate her motives for becoming a cop (she is asked why no less than three times during the film). Whereas Megan's answer to this question is initially flippant – 'I like to slam people's heads against walls', 'I want to shoot people' – the answer eventually becomes simply 'Him'. Although this is clearly intended to refer to Eugene, the fact that she uses a generalized third person pronoun rather than a specific name, suggests that it is a more generalized and pervasive male violence she wishes to investigate and avenge; desires which materialise in both her arrest of her father and her killing of Eugene. Similarly complex is the Hitchcockian *Final Analysis* (Phil Joanou, 1992) in which incestual rape is first given as the explanation for the disturbed younger sister, Diana's (Uma Thurman), psychosis but actually finally emerges as the reason for the apparently normal older sister, Heather's (Kim Basinger), murder of father and husband. Finally, given that all the female characters in *Basic Instinct* could be characterized as deadly, one of them, Beth (Jeanne Tripplehorn), is at least given some sort of motive – date rape at the hands of the hero, Nick (Michael Douglas).

The more traditional rape-revenge structure has also recently reappeared in the British erotic thriller, *Dirty Weekend* and in the female road/buddy movie, *Thelma and Louise*. As the example of *Thelma and Louise* illustrates, the deployment of the rape-revenge structure is not confined to the erotic thriller or neo-noir. Rather the structure has been mapped across a whole range of genres, including the western and the domestic/maternal melodrama. The erotic thriller, the neo-noir and the domestic/maternal melodrama, however, represent the two key directions the rape-revenge cycle has taken in the 1990s and these will be explored in chapters 6 and 7, respectively. A particularly interesting example of the latter direction, often cited in academic analyses of the violent woman film, is *The Hand That Rocks the Cradle* (Curtis Hanson, 1992).[64] Here the revenge drama is motivated not by the rape of the violent and vengeful female protagonist, Peyton (Rebecca de Mornay), but by the charge of sexual assault brought against Peyton's gynaecologist husband by the good wife and mother of the film, Claire Bartel (Annabella Sciorra). The charge results in the husband's suicide and Peyton's miscarriage and sexual violation can consequently be seen as directly responsible for the violent retribution that ensues. In chapter 7, however, I will focus on the more conventional deployments of the rape-revenge structure found in the maternal rape-revenge melodramas *In My Daughter's Name* and *Eye for an Eye* (John Schlesinger, 1995).

Given these examples, I find it remarkable that, despite the huge critical interest in what is seen as a *recent* proliferation of deadly and murderous women in the films of the 1980s and 1990s, so few critics have been willing to acknowledge the connection between these representations and the rape-revenge film. While Creed makes this connection, it is one that I have argued is problematized by its reliance on an unconvincing genre argument and a universal and ahistorical notion of the castrating woman. She consequently ignores the specificity of both the historical context and the issues of rape and revenge since these latter defining principles are what are seen as distinguishing the one set of films from the other. Yet, despite the fact that work on the violent women in the films of recent years shows a greater willingness to recognize the historical specificity of such representations and to acknowledge the generic hybridity of Hollywood film in the post-modern age, such distinctions continue to be either implicitly or explicitly made and the desire to locate (and contain) cinema's violent women within a traditional generic home still informs some work.

Both Christine Holmlund and Julianne Pidduck, for example, trace the origins of the violent women of contemporary cinema to the femme fatale of film noir. This tendency is particularly apparent in Pidduck's article on what she terms the 'fatal femme'.[65] While she refers throughout to films featuring such women as part of the 'fatal femme cycle' this *cycle* is seen as belonging to the larger and more specific *genre* of the thriller or neo-noir. Thus, as this rearticulation of terms suggest, for Pidduck, such killer women are seen as the off-spring of the femme fatale of film noir. Where Creed's location of the monstrous-feminine within the horror genre relied on re-conceptualized psychoanalytical approaches to the genre, Pidduck's situation of the fatal femme within neo-noir depends on re-articulated feminist readings of the femme fatale of film noir. Pidduck consequently argues that:

> if the *femme fatale* in wartime and post-war cinema is often connected to a deep-seated unease in the shifting gender roles in that society, the fatal femme … marks the ongoing troubled status of issues of gender, violence, and power within North American society.[66]

Like Doane, then, who suggested that the femme fatale was 'a symptom of male fears about feminism', Pidduck argues that the 1990s fatal femme can be seen as a manifestation of the contemporary backlash against feminism documented by Susan Faludi.[67] To this end, Pidduck identifies a number of similarities between the film noirs of the 1940s and 1950s and the neo-noirs of the 1990s. Both are marked by the absence of family; in both, males are put at risk by the femme fatale/fatal femme and their authority is undermined; and, finally, both often 'contain' or punish the aberrant woman for the attack she has made on patriarchal society through strategies such as insanity and death. However, implicitly following Doane's argument that the representation of the femme fatale is 'not totally under the control of its producers and, once disseminated comes to take on a life of its own', Pidduck points out that the fatal femme often eludes complete containment and that there is frequently a certain ambivalence about her defeat.[68] Such ambivalence, she argues, can be read as supporting the fatal femme's attack on the family (often already dysfunctional) and male authority (often already undermined). She claims that 'the generic proliferation of the fatal femme can never perform a *merely* repressive, "containing" gesture' and that, despite the films' mysogynistic aspects, their irony, self-referentiality, ambiguity and intertextuality open up alternate readings, which 'identify moments of struggle (for example, over representation and closure) and even moments of rupture which allow for pleasurable feminist readings'.[69]

Pidduck's reference here to 'generic proliferation' suggests that although her argument is fairly firmly situated within, and dependent on, existing work around film noir, she has a more flexible approach to genre than either Creed or Clover. Consequently, despite her initial claim that the fatal femme cycle is 'an extensive 1990s cycle of *thrillers* featuring women who kill', she later concedes that the cycle blends the genres of 'suspense, melodrama/ romance, and horror'.[70] Similarly Christine Holmlund's work on the deadly doll film suggests that while the innocent killers of the rape-revenge films of the 1970s 'were confined to a single genre: the thriller', the deadly doll films of the 1980s 'widen the range of possible genres'.[71] Both Pidduck's and Holmlund's emphasis on the generic hybridity and historical specificity of the fatal femme and deadly doll cycles thus clearly point to a number of similarities with my own approach to the rape-revenge cycle. I find it remarkable, therefore, given these similarities in emphasis and the fact that Pidduck's final section is entitled 'Violence against Women and the "Violent Femme"', that virtually no reference is made in either analyses to the rape-revenge film or to its possible influence on the fatal femme/deadly doll cycles.

While I not wish to deny the obvious influence of film noir and the femme fatale on the fatal femme/deadly doll films of recent years, I want to suggest that these films owe an equal debt to the rape-revenge film and the female avenger and that this is evidenced by a number of similarities and continuities between the two sets of films. For example, although Pidduck initially argues that both femme fatales and fatal femmes come out of a similar historical context of backlash against feminism, she ultimately ends up arguing against this thesis in relation to fatal femmes. The rape-revenge and fatal femme cycles, which both emerged during the period of second-wave feminism, can perhaps be seen as sharing more in terms of historical context. In particular, while both cycles can be partially understood in terms of backlash politics, it can also be argued that it is precisely second-wave feminism that has enabled such representations. Clover articulates this ambiguity when she states that 'the figure of the self-saving Final Girl and the self-avenging rape victim may, *for better or worse*, be the main contribution to popular culture of the women's movement and the "new family"'.[72] Furthermore, while for both Holmlund and Pidduck, the deadly doll or fatal femme 'ups the ante of earlier, more muted cinematic codes of sexuality and graphic violence', the deadly doll/fatal femme cycle and the rape-revenge cycle are roughly equivalent in this respect, particularly since, as I have been suggesting, the rape-revenge film was perhaps the first to present overt displays of female violence as specifically eroticized. In addition, Pidduck, although noting that the containment of the fatal femme, unlike that of the femme fatale, is often ambivalent or bypassed altogether, fails to recognize that the fatal femme has more in common with the vengeful rape victim, who is also rarely shown to be punished for her violent attacks on men. Finally, as I have pointed out, rape does feature, albeit more subtly, as a motive in the fatal femme cycle. Linda Williams picks up on some of these similarities when she argues that:

> erotic thrillers may almost have done away with the *femme fatale*, but this doesn't stop their women from being unsettlingly exciting. However audacious they are, they don't get punished for it, and having enjoyed the sex they can then switch roles as the films slip genres and the women take their revenge.[73]

Sexual Intent (Kurt MacCarley, 1992), for example, 'turns from erotic thriller to rape-revenge narrative, when three of the women overcome their sexual rivalry to round up the villain and shoot him, only so a fourth can run him over'.[74] Nevertheless, although Williams notes the continuity between the two sets of films her analysis is mainly predicated on distinguishing and contrasting straight to video erotic thrillers such as *Sexual Intent* and high budget blockbusters such as *Basic Instinct*, arguing, like Clover, that the lower forms of the genre are more progressive in terms of feminism than the higher versions. Against this tendency to make various distinctions between the fatal femme and the female avenger, neo-noir and rape-revenge, I want to argue that the fatal femme, or what I would call the erotic female avenger, is a product of the negotiations that occur when the rape-revenge structure is mapped over the genre of film noir. In other words, the erotic female avenger is a product of the negotiations between the noir story and the rape-revenge story, the femme fatale and the female avenger, the backlash politics of noir and contemporary feminism. As such, the politics of the erotic thriller and the neo-noir are best understood not as relatively progressive or reactionary but as an attempt to make sense of feminism, not as reflecting or deflecting authentic feminist politics but as constructing popular versions of feminism.

The tendency of Pidduck and others to look straight to film noir for the fatal femme/deadly doll's most famous and well-defined antecedents is perhaps partly to blame for this failure to make connections between the female avenger and fatal femme/deadly doll.[75] However, this tendency is perhaps itself symptomatic of what is at stake in feminist appropriations of the violent woman film. In other words, I would tentatively suggest that feminists, myself included, are drawn to film noirs, erotic thrillers and neo-noirs because they represent a fantasy of being conventionally feminine but strong. Rape-revenge, on the other hand, thanks largely to the widespread success and circulation of Clover's work, would seem to offer the rather less appealing prospect of a masculinized female victim-hero constructed for the pleasure of the male spectator. In summary, the pleasures the femme fatale, fatal femme and female avenger offer feminist critics would appear to lie in the way in which they imaginarily resolve the opposition between feminine and feminist identities on which feminism has for so long depended.

Pidduck's characterization of the rape-revenge film also points towards another of the reasons why feminists interested in the violent woman film have tended to circumvent the rape-revenge film. In other words, Pidduck's references to rape-revenge films emphasize their depiction of violence against women rather than of violent women. Thus she argues that although

> aspects of violence *against* women have been explored through a handful of films like *Loyalties*, *Living with Billy*, *The Accused*, *The Burning Bed*, *Extremities*, or *Thelma and Louise* ... with the exception of the latter, these dramas have largely been eclipsed in profits and notoriety by the likes of *Fatal Attraction* or *Basic Instinct*.[76]

However, this clearly ignores the fact that several of the former films not only explore violence against women but violent women (*The Accused*, *The Burning Bed*, *Extremities*, *Thelma and Louise*). Thus, while I agree with Pidduck that one of the pleasures of the fatal femme cycle lies in the way in which its 'consistent turning of the tables allows (female) spectators to explore a shift at the level of fantasy and representation, as Lenz suggests, "from being the object of violence (victimization) to being its subject (aggression)"', what she fails to recognize is that this shift and the 'venting of rage and revenge fantasies' it facilitates is not specific or new to the fatal femme cycle but has its roots quite firmly in the rape-revenge structure.[77]

In Clover's reading of the rape-revenge film, however, this shift from being the object of violence to being its subject involves a con-comitant transformation of the feminized victim into a masculinized avenger, a shift which, according to Clover, facilitates cross-gender identification and thus *male* spectatorial pleasure. Yet as Christine Holmlund points out, the deadly doll film, like the rape-revenge film, eroticizes female violence and 'the murderesses in these films are, to a woman, white, lithe and lovely'.[78] To this end Holmlund contends that of the six films she analyses all

> are really more obsessed with the changing shape and status of het-
> erosexual femininity than with homicide. Most translate this obsession
> visually, paying hyper-attention to costume and make-up and offering
> lingering and/or shock close-ups of soft and hard bodies.[79]

I will be arguing that the rape-revenge cycle is similarly preoccu-pied with articulating and making sense of the transformations that have occurred in and around heterosexual femininity in the post-1970 period. In so doing, I will argue that the rape-revenge struc-ture is best understood as articulating a movement not from the feminine (rape) to the masculine (revenge) – since, as I have pointed out, the process of eroticization complicates such an analysis – but from private to public femininities. Clearly, the private/public binary, like the rape/revenge binary, traditionally has been under-stood as being gendered feminine and masculine respectively. How-ever, as Hilary Radner has observed, in the twentieth century this gendered distinction came increasingly under historical pressure. In other words, she argues that:

> As women came to work outside the home, and acquired economic
> independence from the family (as they came to make their own deci-
> sions rather than following the wishes of the father, head of that
> family) new categories and structures of femininity and its attendant
> virtues emerged and new stories ... came to be told in which the het-
> erosexual contract was of necessity figured differently.[80]

These 'new categories and structures of femininity', of which the working girl is the archetype, Radner terms 'public' femininities. As Radner's use of the term 'working girl' (rather than the more neutral 'career woman') suggests, these femininities were explicitly sexual-ized and were thus distinct from the desexualized private femininity of the mother. According to Radner, the work of Helen Gurley Brown has played a key role in the construction and development of these femininities. In particular, her work 'emphasized reproducing femininity through consumer practices' such as the buying and wear-ing of clothes.[81] As I hope to show, in the female rape-revenge film, femininity is similarly transformed and reproduced through changes in clothing and appearance. In particular, the female avenger, like the working girl, frequently becomes a specifically eroticized figure whose sexuality represents her 'capital' (for the female avenger read 'weapon') within the public domain. In this way, then, the female avenger can be seen as representing one articulation of the new public femininities Radner describes. Eroticization thus not only problematizes the gendered binary implicit in the movement from rape to revenge, it destabilizes the distinction between the masculine public sphere and the feminine private sphere.

Although discussions of both the rape-revenge film and the fatal/deadly woman film are concerned with their feminist credentials, the latter tend to be more interested in exploring and accounting for the male spectator's stake in such representations, while critical debates around deadly doll films, as Holmlund points out, tend to centre on 'perceived changes in femininity'.[82] Nevertheless, as I have been arguing, this emphasis on the transformation of feminine iden-tity is a feature of both sets of films and not only suggests a way in which we can argue for their similarities and approach their feminist politics, but also perhaps offers a way in which we can redress the emphasis on the male spectator and begin to account for femin-ist/female interest and pleasure in such films. Academic analyses of *Thelma and Louise* are perhaps worth exploring here since the film is cited in accounts of both the rape-revenge film and the violent woman film and, out of the six analyses I surveyed, all cite the trans-formation of the heroines as a trangressively pleasurable aspect of the text. Cathy Griggers, for example, argues that this transforma-tion results in Thelma and Louise becoming hybrids 'not restricted to strict codes of femininity or masculinity'.[83] More explicit still and significant for the way in which it identifies the reconstruction of femininity as a current trend in cinema, is Sharon Willis' assertion that:

one of the more compelling pleasures of this film, for me, is the radical change in women's body language – posture, gait, and gesture –, a
change that went along with the shift from dressy clothes to tee-shirts
and jeans ... the prominence of this bodily transformation sets the film
in an associative chain of recent images of women clearly 'recon-
structed' on screen, like Sigourney Weaver's Ripley in *Aliens* [1986],
and most recently and spectacularly, Linda Hamilton's Sarah Connor
in *Terminator 2* [1991]. These revised embodiments of femininity
stress the body's constructed character as costume, a costume that asks
us to read it both as machine and as masculinity.[84]

While these analyses account for female pleasure through their
celebration of the move away from traditional stereotypes of femininity, they fail to explain the pleasures to be found in the transformation of female characters into violent but hyper-feminine and
eroticized woman. However, against the tendency to assume that
such representations are spectacles designed purely for male enjoy-
ment, it is worth noting, as Jane Gaines has, that although early
second-wave feminists saw glamorous and erotic women as antithetical to feminism, more recently it has become possible for feminists 'to declare an interest in and even to confess a serious passion
for clothes'.[85] As Linda Williams maintains, 'sexiness is not an index
of sexism'.[86] Indeed, in line with my suggestion that eroticization
might function to destabilize the distinction between the masculine
public sphere and the feminine private sphere, Gaines, following
Carol Ascher, has argued that we need to be aware that self-decora-
tion may give 'women a sense of potency to act in the world'.[87] Such
representations and the current surge of feminist interest in them
can, perhaps, only be fully understood in terms of the fact that, as
Janey Place argues in relation to film noir, they are among the few
in which 'women are active, not static symbols, are intelligent and
powerful, if destructively so, and derive power, not weakness, from
their sexuality'.[88] What this suggests is that the distinction between
feminism and femininity on which second-wave feminism depended
is currently undergoing a process of negotiation and transformation.
The rape-revenge cycle and the narratives of transformation it articulates represents, I would suggest, one of the privileged sites
through which we can analyse this process and assess its political and
theoretical implications for contemporary feminism.

Moreover, against Lehman's claim that these films 'do not even
masquerade as seriously concerned with women and rape', I would

argue that the rape-revenge film can be seen as both enabled by, and a response to, the feminist discourses that emerged at virtually the same historical moment (the 1970s).[89] More specifically, I will argue that the transformations that occur in the representation of gender when the rape-revenge structure is mapped over existing genres can be read as an attempt to make sense of, and to produce popular understandings of, these discourses. As I have suggested, insofar as feminism can be defined as involving a struggle over the meanings of femininity, it is in its ongoing articulation of these struggles that the rape-revenge film can be seen to be attempting to make sense of feminism.

While Clover makes some attempt to analyse the rape-revenge film in relation to modern, and particularly feminist, debates about sexual violence, her claim that these films 'repeatedly and explicitly articulate feminist politics' tends to be too generalized and simplistic.[90] In particular, 'feminist politics' are taken as a homogenous and static thing rather than as an ongoing and changing debate, while the relationship between feminism and film, text and context, culture and social change, is undertheorized. Furthermore, such historical contextualization is never adequately married with Clover's psychoanalytically based arguments around gender identity and identification. Yet, the fact that an emphasis on challenging established concepts of femininity and gender identity has informed second-wave feminist politics and theory from its inception in the early 1970s, suggests that the proliferation of violent women in film during this period cannot be seen simply in terms of ahistorical psychoanalytical concepts (Creed) or 1980s-based backlash politics (Siskel and Ebert). Instead, I would argue that the ambivalence towards these representations, articulated by both Clover and Pidduck and echoed in Holmlund's claim that 'although they are in part a response to feminist gains, these deadly dolls are not necessarily a cause for feminist jubilation', is symptomatic of the negotiated, popular versions of feminism they articulate.[91]

Notes

1 See Carol Clover, *Men, Women and Chainsaws: Gender in the Modern Horror Film* (London: BFI, 1992); Barbara Creed, *The Monstrous-Feminine: Film, Feminism, Psychoanalysis* (London: Routledge, 1993); Christine Holmlund, 'A Decade of Deadly Dolls: Hollywood and the

Woman Killer', in *Moving Targets: Women, Murder and Representation*, ed. by Helen Birch (London: Virago, 1993), pp. 127–51; Julianne Pidduck, 'The 1990s Hollywood Fatal Femme: (Dis)Figuring Feminism, Family, Irony, Violence', *Cineaction*, 38 (1995), 65–72.

2 Christine Gledhill, 'Genre', in *The Cinema Book*, ed. by Pam Cook (London: BFI, 1985), pp. 58–64 (p. 59).

3 Clover, *Men, Women and Chainsaws*, p. 5n5.

4 Ibid., p. 126.

5 Ibid., p. 153n39.

6 Ibid., p. 18n34.

7 Ibid., p. 142.

8 Ibid., p. 149 and p. 118.

9 Ibid., p. 115.

10 Robin Wood, 'An Introduction to the American Horror Film', in *Movies and Methods, Volume II: An Anthology*, ed. by Bill Nichols (Berkeley: University of California Press, 1985), pp. 195–220 (p. 203).

11 Stephen Neale, *Genre* (London: BFI, 1980).

12 Clover, *Men, Women and Chainsaws*, p. 119 and p. 124.

13 Ibid., p. 144.

14 Ibid., pp. 143–44.

15 Ibid., p. 4.

16 Ibid., pp. 3–4.

17 Ibid., p. 64 and p. 162.

18 Mary Ann Doane, *Femmes Fatales: Feminism, Film Theory, Psychoanalysis* (London: Routledge, 1991), pp. 2–3.

19 Carol Clover, 'High and Low: The Transformation of the Rape-Revenge Movie', in *Women and Film: A Sight and Sound Reader*, ed. by Pam Cook and Philip Dodd (London: Scarlet Press, 1993), pp. 76–85.

20 Jim Collins, 'Genericity in the Nineties: Eclectic Irony and the New Sincerity', in *Film Theory Goes to the Movies*, ed. by Jim Collins, Hilary Radner and Ava Preacher Collins (London: Routledge, 1993), pp. 242–63.

21 Ibid., pp. 242–3.

22 Ibid., p. 256.

23 Ibid., pp. 242–3.

24 Ibid., p. 259.

25 Ibid., p. 262.

26 Ibid., p. 247.

27 As Denise Riley has observed: 'Equality; difference; "different but equal" – the history of feminism since the 1790s has zigzagged and curved through these incomplete oppositions upon which it is itself precariously erected. This swaying motion need not be a wonder, nor a cause for despair. If feminism is the voicing of "women" from the side

of "women", then it cannot but act out the full ambiguities of that category.' 'Am I That Name?': Feminism and the Category of 'Women' in History (Basingstoke: Macmillan, 1988), p. 112.

28 Imelda Whelehan, Modern Feminist Thought: From the Second Wave to 'Post-Feminism' (Edinburgh: Edinburgh University Press, 1995), p. 220.

29 Michele Barrett and Anne Phillips, 'Introduction', in Destabilizing Theory: Contemporary Feminist Debates, ed. by Michele Barrett and Anne Phillips (Cambridge: Polity Press, 1992), pp. 1–9 (p. 7).

30 Charlotte Brunsdon, Screen Tastes: Soap Opera to Satellite Dishes (London: Routledge, 1997), p. 102.

31 Clover, Men, Women and Chainsaws, p. 159.

32 Roger Ebert, 'Why Movie Audiences Aren't Safe Anymore', American Film, 6:5 (March 1981), 54–56.

33 Peter Lehman, '"Don't Blame this on a Girl": Female Rape-revenge Films', in Screening the Male: Exploring Masculinities in Hollywood Cinema, ed. by Steven Cohan and Ina Rae Hark (London: Routledge, 1993), pp. 103–117 (p. 104).

34 Ibid., p. 104.

35 Ebert, 'Why Movie Audiences Aren't Safe Anymore', p. 55 (my emphasis).

36 Ibid., p. 56 (my emphasis).

37 Ibid., p. 56 (my emphasis).

38 Ibid., p. 56.

39 Ibid., p. 56.

40 Ibid., p. 56 (my emphasis).

41 Clover, Men, Women and Chainsaws, p. 144.

42 Ebert, 'Why Movie Audiences Aren't Safe Anymore', p. 56.

43 Clover, Men, Women and Chainsaws, p. 154.

44 Ibid., p. 154.

45 Ibid., p. 141.

46 Ibid., p. 141.

47 Ibid., pp. 163–4.

48 Pam Cook, 'Outrage', in Queen of the 'B's: Ida Lupino Behind the Camera, ed. by Annette Kuhn (Trowbridge: Flicks Books, 1995), pp. 57–72 (p. 70).

49 Clover, Men, Women and Chainsaws, p. 19.

50 Ibid., p. 140.

51 Ibid., pp. 139–40.

52 Ibid., p. 154. See also p. 152, 'the slasher genre is predicated on spectatorial identification with females in fear and pain'.

53 Ibid., p. 139.

54 Lehman, '"Don't Blame this on a Girl"', p. 112.

55   Ibid., p. 106.
56   Ibid., p. 111.
57   Clover, *Men, Women and Chainsaws,* p. 20.
58   Creed, *The Monstrous-Feminine*, p. 123.
59   Ibid., p. 128.
60   Pidduck, 'The 1990s Hollywood Fatal Femme', p. 72.
61   Ibid., p. 72 (my emphasis).
62   Holmlund, 'A Decade of Deadly Dolls', p. 127.
63   Harriet E. Margolis, '*Blue Steel*: Progressive Feminism in the '90s?', *Postscript*, 13:1 (1993), 67–76.
64   See also: Deborah Jermyn, 'Rereading the Bitches from Hell: A Feminist Appropriation of the Female Psychopath', *Screen*, 37:3 (Autumn 1996), 251–67.
65   Pidduck, 'The 1990s Hollywood Fatal Femme'.
66   Ibid., p. 65.
67   Doane, *Femmes Fatales*, pp. 2–3.
68   Ibid., p. 3.
69   Pidduck, 'The 1990s Hollywood Fatal Femme', p. 71 and p. 70.
70   Ibid., p. 65 (my emphasis) and p. 67.
71   Holmlund, 'A Decade of Deadly Dolls', p. 127.
72   Clover, *Men, Women and Chainsaws,* p. 162 (my emphasis).
73   Linda Ruth Williams, 'Sisters Under the Skin: Video and Blockbuster Erotic Thrillers', in *Women and Film: A Sight and Sound Reader*, ed. by Pam Cook and Philip Dodd (London: Scarlet Press, 1993), pp. 105–14 (p. 112).
74   Ibid., p. 109.
75   See for example: Yvonne Tasker, *Spectacular Bodies: Gender, Genre and the Action Cinema* (London: Routledge, 1993); Robert E. Wood, 'Somebody Has To Die: *Basic Instinct* as White Noir', *Postscript*, 12:3 (1993), 44–51.
76   Pidduck, 'The 1990s Hollywood Fatal Femme', p. 71 (my emphasis).
77   Ibid., p. 72.
78   Holmlund, 'A Decade of Deadly Dolls', p. 128.
79   Ibid., p. 135.
80   Hilary Radner, 'Pretty Is as Pretty Does: Free Enterprise and the Marriage Plot', in *Film Theory Goes to the Movies*, ed. by Jim Collins, Hilary Radner and Ava Preacher Collins (London: Routledge, 1993), pp. 56–76 (p. 57).
81   Ibid., p. 58.
82   Holmlund, 'A Decade of Deadly Dolls', p. 145.
83   Cathy Griggers, '*Thelma and Louise* and the Cultural Generation of the New Butch-Femme', in *Film Theory Goes to the Movies*, ed. by Jim Collins, Hilary Radner and Ava Preacher Collins (London: Routledge,

1993), pp. 129–41 (p. 139).

84 Sharon Willis, 'Hardware and Hardbodies, What Do Women Want?: A Reading of *Thelma and Louise*', in *Film Theory Goes to the Movies*, ed. by Jim Collins, Hilary Radner and Ava Preacher Collins (London: Routledge, 1993), pp. 120–28 (p. 127).

See also Manohla Dargis, '*Thelma and Louise* and the Tradition of the Male Road Movie', in *Women and Film: A Sight and Sound Reader*, ed. by Pam Cook and Philip Dodd (London: Scarlet Press, 1993), pp. 86–92; Lynda Hart, *Fatal Women: Lesbian Sexuality and the Mark of Aggression* (London: Routledge, 1994); Kathleen Murphy, 'Only Angels Have Wings', *Film Comment*, 27:4 (1991), 26–9; Tasker, *Spectacular Bodies*, pp. 132–41.

85 Jane Gaines, 'Introduction: Fabricating the Female Body', in *Fabrications: Costume and the Female Body*, ed. by Jane Gaines and Charlotte Herzog (London: Routledge, 1990), pp. 1–27 (p. 6).

86 Linda Ruth Williams, 'Sisters Under the Skin', p. 107.

87 Jane Gaines, 'Fabricating the Female Body', p. 6.

88 Janey Place, 'Women in Film Noir', in *Women in Film Noir*, ed. by E. Ann Kaplan (London: BFI, 1978), pp. 35–67 (p. 35).

89 Lehman, '"Don't Blame this on a Girl"', p. 107.

90 Clover, *Men, Women and Chainsaws*, p. 151.

91 Holmlund, 'A Decade of Deadly Dolls', p. 128.

Chapter 2

From romance to revenge: *Sleeping with the Enemy*

While *Sleeping with the Enemy* substitutes domestic violence and marital rape for the more sensational 'stranger rape' of other films in the cycle, its narrative can, nevertheless, be seen to represent a clear rendition of the rape-revenge structure. Indeed, its title's almost verbatim use of radical feminist injunctions against heterosexuality would appear to explicitly invite readings in terms of the film's engagement with feminism. In her discussion of Julia Roberts' previous film, *Pretty Woman* (Garry Marshall, 1990), and of *Working Girl* (Mike Nichols, 1988), Charlotte Brunsdon produces such a reading, arguing that: 'However problematic, some form of feminist discourse is occurring within these women's films for the 1990s.'[1] A similar point could be made about *Sleeping with the Enemy* and, in fact, a number of similarities between *Pretty Woman* and *Enemy* imply an attempt to capitalize on the success of the former film and indicate that *Enemy*'s deployment of the rape-revenge structure can perhaps only be fully understood within the context of the discourses both implicit in and surrounding *Pretty Woman*. That these discourses are largely those of femininity and heterosexual romance suggests, moreover, that *Enemy*'s specific articulation of the rape-revenge structure might represent a particularly privileged example of the negotiations that occur between feminism and femininity within the rape-revenge cycle as a whole.

The most obvious similarity between the two films is, of course, *Sleeping with the Enemy*'s trying-on-hats sequence, which is clearly based on *Pretty Woman*'s famous and exceptionally popular shopping sequence. While both sequences suggest an engagement with the construction of feminine identity, the use of pieces of nineteenth-century romantic classical music signal an equivalent concern with heterosexual romance. However, although there are clear confluences between the narratives of these pieces of music and those of the films in which they appear, both films ultimately offer revised versions of these classical narratives. For example, unlike Violetta in *La Traviata*, who 'sends her lover away so that his sister may marry, knowing that as a fallen woman she herself will never become a bride', Vivian (Julia Roberts) in *Pretty Woman* is saved from a life of prostitution precisely *through* marriage.[2] *Sleeping with the Enemy*, on the other hand, features Berlioz's *Symphonie Fantastique*, which tells the story of 'the artist's obsession with the woman he adores' and culminates in 'an opium dream in which he dreams he has murdered his beloved'.[3] While *Enemy* similarly features an obsessive and violent man, it concludes with *his* murder at the hands of his 'beloved' rather than vice-versa.

By far the most thoroughgoing similarity between the two films is, however, their reliance on a frame of reference located within the world of fairy-tales.[4] Several critics have commented on the similarities between the narrative of *Pretty Woman* and the Cinderella story and the connection is perhaps so explicit that there is no need to rehearse such arguments here. Despite being rather more subtle and complex, *Sleeping with the Enemy's* fairy-tale references can be seen to support my argument for reading the film as a kind of sequel to *Pretty Woman*. Moreover, they represent a continuation of the process of narrative and generic revision identified above in both films' deployment of classical music. In other words, if *Pretty Woman* represents a popular feminist rewriting of the Cinderella story for the 1990s, then *Sleeping with the Enemy* continues this act of revision by picking up where *Pretty Woman*/Cinderella concluded, with the union of Cinderella/Vivian and Prince Charming/Edward. In *Sleeping with the Enemy*, we are reminded both of this conclusion and of one of the Cinderella narrative's central tropes (the ball) through early references to Martin and Laura's honeymoon and 'the night [he] taught [her] to dance', while Laura's role as 'Mrs Prince Charming' is assured by Martin's continual reference to her as 'princess'. In this sequel to the Cinderella tale, however, Prince Charming turns out to be no better than the Ugly Sisters and he is, in fact, shown to be even more tyrannical and exacting. Far from being rescued from a life of drudgery in the domestic realm, Laura/Cinderella (Julia Roberts) remains firmly located within this realm: she digs for clams, cooks and tidies. Furthermore, if the Ugly Sisters set Cinderella impossible and pointless tasks such as picking

dishes of lentils from the ashes, so too does Martin/Prince Charming (Patrick Bergin): the towels in the bathroom must be perfectly
straightened and the canned goods lined up on the shelves with mil-
itary precision. By substituting Martin/Prince Charming for the Ugly
Sisters, *Sleeping with the Enemy* replaces the Cinderella story's
attack on the notion of sisterhood with an attack on patriarchal
oppression and thereby exposes the reality behind the fairy-tale.

The early part of the film also contains a feminist rewriting of the
Rapunzel tale – one in which a witch imprisons a young woman with
preternaturally long hair in a tower where she is visited by a prince
who reaches her by climbing her hair. The film references the tale
not only by giving Julia Roberts longer hair than we know her naturally to have, but also by verbally evoking the image of the woman
imprisoned in the tower in the doctor's comment to Martin: 'So that
must be your wife I keep seeing staring down from the window.' The
film partially rewrites the story as one of domestic violence in which
the role of the malevolent woman is again taken by Martin who
believes that Laura, like Rapunzel, has allowed the doctor/prince
into her 'tower'. 'When was he in here?' he asks before striking her
so hard that she flies across the room. Of course, in *Rapunzel*, the
witch's punishment takes the form of cutting off Rapunzel's hair,
thereby denying the prince access to her. In a further twist on the
tale, therefore, Laura cuts off her own hair as part of her plan to
escape from Martin. In other words, if, in *Rapunzel*, Rapunzel's hair
was, quite literally, the route to heterosexual romance, then, to cut
off one's hair, as Laura does in *Sleeping with the Enemy*, implies a
rejection of heterosexual romance. In this way, the film clearly follows the first two stages of the rape-revenge structure: rape (or, in
this case, domestic violence) followed by physical transformation.[5]
Furthermore, as I hope to have shown, the deployment of this structure involves a concomitant transformation of the generic discourses
over which it is mapped.

Thus Laura frees herself from myths of femininity and heterosexual romance by transforming the agents of those myths (long hair
and fairy-tales). Moreover, by changing the fairy-tale's narrative,
Laura takes control of her own story. This is clearly illustrated in the
final fairy-tale reference in this section of the film. Escaping from
Cape Cod on a bus, Laura, disguised in a black wig, is offered an
apple by an older woman.[6] The reference to *Snow White*, particularly
Disney's version in which Snow White has black hair, is obvious.

However, in line with the film's eradication of evil women from its fairy-tales, here the older woman is benevolent rather than malevolent and encourages Laura to tell her about herself. Laura obliges but constructs her story as a fairy-tale, telling it in the third person and using the kind of terms and phrases usually found in such narratives: 'he was a horrible man', 'at first he was charming', 'she escaped, started a new life'. This story thus represents the third and final instalment of the film's retelling of the fairy-tale as a narrative of domestic violence.

The prominence of elemental imagery, particularly fire and water, in *Sleeping with the Enemy* not only adds credence to my arguments about the influence and importance of fairy-tales in the film, but works to highlight the film's theme of gender antagonism. As Ruth B. Bottigheimer observes in her study of *Grimms' Tales*: 'In this dualistic world ... water (or at least certain kinds of water), appertains exclusively to women. Wells, springs, brooks, and streams seem peculiarly under feminine sway' while its opposite, fire, 'belongs peculiarly to male figures and is closely associated with gender antagonism'.[7] Opening with a shot of Laura gathering clams at the sea's edge, water imagery permeates *Sleeping with the Enemy*. Indeed, the film's most widely circulated publicity still featured a shot from the end of the film of Roberts in the bath. With one exception, then, this imagery is always associated with Laura. The introduction of the character of Ben (Kevin Anderson) proves to be the exception, since we first see him *watering* the garden. The symbolism of the scene (the hose pipe, the spurting water), however, suggests that we read it as symbolic of ejaculative male sexuality rather than of femininity, particularly given that it introduces the film's romantic/sexual interest and that Ben is singing a song celebrating masculine identity ('The Jet Song' from *West Side Story*). At the very least, the association functions not so much to code Ben as 'feminine' as to suggest that he is not typically 'masculine'. It also marks him as different to Martin for whom water brings nothing but misfortune. Indeed, while in a later scene Ben is also associated with the more masculine fire, it is shown to be an element not totally under his control (he inadvertently sets fire to the pot roast he has cooked for Laura). Elsewhere, then, elemental imagery functions to reaffirm gender duality. For example, when Laura goes to visit her mother in the nursing home disguised as a young man she is shown drinking from a water fountain. Immediately afterwards Martin is shown attempting to drink from the same fountain, which promptly spurts a jet of water into his eye. By showing the water fountain performing in gender specific ways, this incident serves to alleviate any potential anxiety or confusion about gender identity brought about through Laura's use of sexual disguise. In other words, the fountain (the modern equivalent of a spring) is shown to be 'peculiarly under feminine sway' while being 'dangerous for boys'.[8] This gender duality is further reinforced by the elementally derived names of the characters: Martin's surname is *Burn*ey (and at key moments his face is suffused with a burning red light) while Laura chooses to change her name to Sara *Waters*. At the end of the film, then, the final, fatal confrontation between Laura and Martin is signalled initially through their totemic elements which, like Martin and Laura's relationship, are shown to be dangerously out of control. Thus, as Laura's bath water overflows, the toast burns in the toaster (which almost electrocutes Laura when she unplugs it).

This discussion has, of course, so far failed to address the film's most obvious and important piece of water imagery: Laura's 'death' by drowning and her 'rebirth' as Sara Waters. Laura narrates the flashback to this accident:

> That was the night I died and someone else was saved. Someone who was afraid of water but learnt to swim. Someone who knew that there'd be one moment when he wouldn't be watching. Someone who knew that the darkness from the broken lights would show the way.

The broken lights referred to here are clearly a motif borrowed from the world of fairy-tales where, as they venture into unknown realms, the hero or heroine leave a trail of stones or grain in order to mark the way back to safety. What is most striking about this narration, however, is the disjunction it sets up between identities, between old and new selves, crucially suggesting that what is at stake here is a process of transformation. Again, the influence of fairy-tales is apparent, as Bottigheimer points out in her analysis of the archetypal Grimms' tale 'The Three Little Men in the Wood':

> Rinsing yarn through a hole in the ice on the river results, however, not in [the good girl's] death, but in her meeting and marrying the king. Water thus functions as a locus of reversal and transformation: the poor harried stepdaughter becomes queen of the realm.[9]

Despite being similarly mediated through water, *Sleeping with the*

Enemy's transformations, nevertheless, would appear to depart from the archetypal fairy-tale transformations apparent both here and in *Pretty Woman*. In other words, while the latter examples rely largely on a rags-to-riches Cinderella transformation, *Enemy* seems to offer a feminist-inspired transformation of consciousness. Whether or not the film follows through on the logic of this transformation, however, remains to be seen.

In reference to *Pretty Woman*, Charlotte Brunsdon has observed that: 'The explicitness of the reference to Cinderella in this very successful romance has tempted some critics to see this film as a reversion to a pre-feminist narrative.'[10] She goes on to argue, however, that 'just as the reference to Cinderella is contemporary and self-conscious, so is the invocation of the romance genre and the construction of the heroine'.[11] Thus far, *Sleeping with the Enemy* would seem to concur with Brunsdon's arguments. I have already shown in some detail how the film's deployment of the initial stages of the rape-revenge structure updates various fairy-tales by retelling them in terms of contemporary feminist discourses about domestic violence. Moreover, the world into which these discourses are inserted is clearly constructed as contemporary. The house in which Martin and Laura live is exceptionally modern and minimalist and the food they eat – lamb with rosemary and peach chutney, new potatoes, baby peas and herb bread – is contemporary in its sophistication and continentalism. In addition, with the exception of Berlioz, the only pieces of music used within the diegesis during this section of the film are contemporary pop songs: Maxi Priest's 'Close to You' (1990) and Oleta Adams' 'Circle of One' (1991).

In contrast, the world into which Laura escapes is the magical and idyllic world of childhood innocence and fairy-tales. The small midwest town into which she arrives is sunny, leafy and clean. Children paddle in the fountain (girls, naturally) and skip in the square. Old-fashioned values of community and nationalism are reinforced as an old man helps a US marshall raise the Stars and Stripes flag, which, reflected in the window of the coach, flickers across Laura's smiling face. Here, Laura rents a neglected old-fashioned, wooden fronted house with veranda and swing, which she transforms, with loving care, to its former glory. In many respects, this is the film's key transformation sequence, functioning as a metaphor for Laura's transformation. As Laura pulls off the dust sheets, the house's old-fashioned natural charm and beauty is revealed and the pretension and sophistication of Cape Cod rejected. Simultaneously Laura makes the transition from modern, sophisticated woman to old-fashioned, pretty girl-next-door (quite literally as far as Ben is concerned since the pair live next door to each other). Furthermore, that this transformation functions as a revelation of the natural self rather than of the constructedness of identity is assured both by the film's use of natural, elemental imagery to define the sexes and in a brief exchange between Martin and Laura at the beginning of the film. Laura is preparing for a party when Martin comes up and comments that the dress she is wearing is 'pretty'. Sensing his displeasure, she asks if he was thinking of 'the red', to which he replies that he was thinking of 'the black'. The latter, the archetypal sexy little black dress, is the one Laura ends up wearing. Thus, although Laura's reversion to 'pretty' dresses in the second half of the film could be interpreted as an attempt at self-determination, I think this transformation must be understood not only within the context of *Pretty Woman* and Roberts' star persona, which both rely on what Brunsdon describes as 'a natural model of femininity', but also in terms of the apparent retreat from feminism that occurs in the second half of the film.[12]

If the contemporary setting and feminist inflection given to the various fairy-tale references prevents the first part of *Sleeping with the Enemy* from being seen as 'a reversion to a pre-feminist narrative', the same cannot be said for the second part of the film. Here, various factors combine to conjure up the pre-feminist era of the late 1950s and early 1960s. What is more, these are clearly intended to contrast with the contemporary world of Cape Cod. Indeed, as Colin McArthur has observed, 'the small town here operates as the binary antinomy not, strictly speaking, of the city itself but of [the] "city values"' embodied by Cape Cod.[13] Thus, like many of the rape-revenge films Clover discusses, *Enemy* can be seen as working primarily on a city–country axis. Against Clover, however, I will argue that the sub-antinomies that proceed from the master antinomy of city/Cape Cod versus midwest town are not understandable in terms of class or gender but are instead largely temporal. For example, whereas in the early part of the film the diegetic music consisted of contemporary pop, here it consists of a number of well-known and extremely successful songs from the late 1950s and 1960s: 'The Jet Song' (1957) from *West Side Story*, 'My Girl' (1965) by The Temptations, 'Brown-eyed Girl' (1967) by Van Morrison and 'Runaround

Sue' (1961) by Dion. In addition, in contrast to the sophisticated, continental food eaten by Martin and Laura in Cape Cod, Ben and Laura eat plain, old-fashioned American food, such as pot roast and apple pie. Finally, Laura exchanges her modern, designer clothes for the long, full skirts and dresses, jeans and fitted tops and cardigans, usually in pastel colours, which were popular with young women in the early 1960s. The film, therefore, also positions Ben and Laura within the newly defined category of the teenager, showing them playing at dressing up, dancing to pop music and going to the fair in an era, it is implied, before feminism caused the relationship between the sexes to turn sour. Indeed, given the marked changes in the colour scheme and lighting of the *mise-en-scène* in this part of the film, we might be forgiven for believing we had suddenly donned a pair of rose-tinted spectacles. In other words, in the Cape Cod sequences high-key lighting and a *mise-en-scène* dominated by whites, silvers and blues combine to give a cold, contemporary feel while, in the later sequences, low-key lighting and a *mise-en-scène* dominated by oranges, browns and pinks combine to produce a nostalgic, rosy glow.

Significantly, many of these features are concurrent with those Steve Neale identifies as elements of a cycle of films he terms the 'new romance', in which, incidentally, he includes *Pretty Woman*.[14] This cycle, Neale argues, involves 'a persistent evocation and endorsement of the signs and values of "old-fashioned" romance' and these include a number of the components outlined above.[15] The most notable of these are the influence of fairy-tales and, in particular, 'the knight-in-shining-armour figure' and the 'use of "standard" songs' and 'nineteenth-century romantic' music.[16] However, Neale also cites signs such as the vintage car and the presence of poetry or poetic speech as signifiers of old-fashioned romance. Both are evident in *Sleeping with the Enemy* and are associated with the character of Ben who not only drives a vintage car but, in a long, and otherwise unmotivated sequence, recites a lengthy romantic speech from a play to his students. Furthermore, Neale identifies the old-fashioned values of the new romance as marking a reaction to the nervous romance of the late 1970s and early 1980s in which the 'breakdown of monogamy' was largely blamed on the '"post-feminist" woman', thus supporting my contention that *Enemy's* deployment of the old-fashioned motifs of the new romance constitutes an attempt to return to a pre-feminist era.[17]

This, then, is also an era when the issue of domestic and sexual violence against women was, quite literally, unspeakable and the film's evocation of this era through the motifs of the new romance consequently functions to legitimate and account for its suppression of a feminist inspired discourse against domestic violence. In particular, as Neale argues, the elements of infantilism, regression and having fun fundamental to the new romance, and apparent in Ben and Laura's relationship, 'help to repress or disavow those aspects of "adult" difficulty or "adult" responsibility characteristic of real ("adult") relationships'.[18] However, this repression does not amount to a wholesale disavowal of the domestic violence depicted in the first half of the film. Rather, the film creates a number of opportunities for such a discourse that are simply not taken up. For example, when Ben starts asking Laura awkward questions on their first date, she retorts, 'Look I really don't want to talk about this OK', and brushes him off when he notices the cut on her head. Similarly, after returning from the theatre, Ben and Laura start kissing passionately on the stairs. Suddenly Laura gets very upset and tells Ben to stop, but when Ben asks, 'God, what did he do to you?', Laura merely replies, 'Please go'. Nevertheless, the next day the following exchange takes place:

> LAURA What you said is right. I had a husband. He hurt me. I guess I'm just really afraid.
> BEN Of what?
> LAURA Of never getting my life back together.
> BEN It just feels like that. Some day you might surprise yourself.
> LAURA I'm glad you're here.
> BEN Me too.

This discussion, however, is not informed by a feminist critique of Martin's behaviour but by Laura's desire to explain her own behaviour and, while it may initially be about domestic violence, it is ultimately about a developing heterosexual romance. Furthermore, lest we be tempted to interpret Laura's reticence on the subject of Martin's violent behaviour towards her as simply a matter of her inability to trust another man, her conversation with her mother is similarly evasive. 'God, what did he do?', asks Chloe (Elizabeth Lawrence). 'Doesn't matter now', Laura replies. Laura's conversation with the woman on the bus as she travels towards this pre-feminist world thus represents one of the few instances where female experience of male violence is articulated and the legal and social system which implicitly supports such behaviour criticized. Along with the swimming lessons Laura takes at the YWCA, this is also the closest the film comes to depicting female bonding or sisterhood. Indeed, that Laura is shown to join the YWCA rather than a support group specifically aimed at addressing domestic violence merely serves to reinforce the film's apparently regressive tendencies.

Insofar as it too articulates a nostalgia for an idealized, pre-feminist past, the second part of *Enemy* can thus, in many ways, be read as an articulation of the backlash against feminism that occurred in the late 1980s under the influence of the New Right. However, because this past must, by necessity, always be represented from a contemporary perspective, the attempt to disavow the feminist politics of the intervening period is never entirely successful. There is in the film a kind of reinscription and rearticulation of the 'sixties-in-the-eighties' (or early 1990s in this instance). According to David Glover and Cora Kaplan, this was a key aspect of the New Right's hegemonic project. I will argue, however, that this involved not so much a rejection of 1960s and 1970s radicalism as a negotiation of it; not so much the disavowal of feminism as the production of popular, hegemonic, common-sense versions of it.[19] The film's title is, for example, clearly informed by the kind of radical feminist rhetoric espoused by the Leeds Revolutionary Feminist Group in 1979:

> Men are the enemy. Heterosexual women are collaborators with the enemy ... Every woman who lives with or fucks a man helps to maintain the oppression of her sisters and hinders our struggle.[20]

While the second part of the film ostensibly fails to follow through on the logic of its title, the first part of the film is fairly self-conscious about its deployment of the discourses of both feminism and femininity. Charlotte Brunsdon argues an equivalent point in relation to *Pretty Woman*:

> *Pretty Woman* is very knowing about its retrenchments, simultaneously informed by feminism and disavowing this formation. Thus the narrative scenario, although deeply indebted to the screen history of the whore with the heart of gold, would be unimaginable without second-wave feminist perspectives on sex-work.[21]

Similarly, while the later sections of *Sleeping with the Enemy* may attempt to render as unspeakable the feminist discourses that made

the early sections of the film representable, they are not entirely successful. Thus, although this part of the film may be interpretable as
pre-feminist on the basis of its disavowal of domestic violence, it
nevertheless depicts a woman taking her first, tentative steps
towards social and financial independence (even if that independence is somewhat compromised by the presence of a man). Indeed,
the film's evocation of a pre-feminist era suggests a simultaneous disavowal and acknowledgement of feminism. In other words, by relocating itself 'before' feminism, it simultaneously acknowledges the
very existence of an 'after' that *is* feminism. Indicative of this
ambivalence is the fact that the film specifically chooses to relocate
itself in the 1960s, an era which, although pre-feminist, both her-
alded profound social upheaval and change and saw proto-feminists,
such as Betty Friedan, struggling to give voice to the 'problem that
has no name', to speak the, as yet, unspeakable.[22]

It should perhaps come as no surprise, then, that the film's ending
attempts to articulate this emerging feminism. Consequently, while
the final sequence contains several allusions to the conclusion of the
Cinderella story these are subject to revision and transformation.
For example, we are reminded again of the tale's central narrative
trope (the ball) not only through Martin's reference to the night he
taught Laura to dance, but by the fact that he comes bearing a 'glass
slipper' in the form of Laura's wedding ring. Here, however, the
slipper/ring no longer fits and this rejection of the fairy-tale's conventional narrative resolution is perhaps nowhere more apparent
than in the film's final frame – a shot of Laura's discarded wedding
ring.[23] If Vivian in *Pretty Woman* is '"saved" through marriage',
then, Laura is 'saved' through her rejection of marriage.[24] Yet, in
fairy-tales rings are typically invested with magic properties, and this
one is no exception. As it lies discarded in the foreground of the
frame – while in the background Laura embraces the injured Ben –
it twinkles in the light and a single 'ping' is heard above the soundtrack suggesting that its power and, by extension, the power of
romance, has not been entirely vanquished by feminism.

Unlike Vivian, however, Laura does not need a man to save her.
While Vivian rewrites the fairy-tale narrative by claiming that she'll
rescue Edward 'right back', Laura rewrites it by rescuing *herself*.
Thus, while *Sleeping with the Enemy* maps the rape-revenge structure across traditionally feminine genres such as romance and fairy-
tales, it also clearly utilizes those films that have been seen as both

enabled by, and a response to, feminism, particularly the slasher or stalker genre. For example, while much of the second half of the film is constructed around the developing romance between Ben and Laura, it is also organized around Martin's pursuit of Laura and thus comes complete with the slasher film's trademark point-of-view shots. Indeed, Martin's steadfast refusal to die at the end (despite being shot at close range several times) and almost super-human ability to tidy the cupboards *and* stalk his victim suggest clear similarities with the monster of the slasher genre. Although this construction of the violent husband as psychopathic monster is, in many ways, problematic (for reasons I have outlined in chapter 1), with Ben swiftly dispatched, Laura is able to take her place as the 'final girl' or, more specifically, as the vengeful woman of rape-revenge. Thus, Laura's attack on Martin is not only inspired by feminist discourses of self-defence (she incapacitates him by kneeing him in the groin) but is clearly cast as revenge. Training the gun on Martin with one hand and holding the phone in the other, Laura is given the opportunity to take the legitimate, legal solution to the problem of domestic violence. However, as Martin taunts her with the ineffectualness of such a response, she calls the police to tell them she has killed an intruder. In line with the film's earlier feminist critique of legal solutions, therefore, and despite crying and shaking almost uncontrollably, Laura shoots Martin in a deliberate and calculated act of anger and revenge.

The rape–transformation–revenge structure is clearly discernible within the narrative of *Sleeping with the Enemy*. While rape is replaced by a more generalized domestic violence, as feminist work in this area has highlighted, domestic violence frequently involves marital rape and there is, in fact, a scene early in the film that suggests that Laura is, indeed, an unwilling participant in her husband's lovemaking. The transformations that subsequently occur are, as I argued in chapter 1, largely a product of the contradictions within and between the discourses of gender and genre across which this structure is deployed. These discourses come into particular conflict and contest in the film's final sequence, which, despite having all the markings of a slasher film, continues to make allusions to the romance genre, for example, through Martin's reference to his and Laura's fairy-tale honeymoon. While Laura's violent revenge against Martin apparently signifies a rejection of this fairy-tale, the film's final shot would seem to suggest the possibility of the coexistence of romance and revenge: in the foreground lies Laura's discarded wedding ring, in the middleground, the body of the man she has killed, and in the background, Laura and Ben embracing. Thus, while *Enemy* maps the rape-revenge structure over both the new romance and the slasher/stalker genres, the transformation Laura undergoes is neither the Cinderella transformation associated with the new romance, and *Pretty Woman* in particular, nor the process of masculinization associated with the heroines of the slasher genre. Rather, as the film's emphasis on disguise and dressing up and on the disjunction between different identities suggests, what is at stake here is the movement through, and negotiation of, a range of public femininities. Indeed, Laura's trajectory through the narrative can be seen as indicative of the various transformations in the popular representations of heterosexual femininity that, Charlotte Brunsdon has argued, have occurred over the past three decades in response to feminism.[25] In other words, Laura moves from the 'independent woman' of the 1970s cycle of films, through the 'girly heroine' of films such as *Pretty Woman*, to the 'final girl' of slasher. In the final sequence, however, Laura ultimately emerges as a composite and contradictory figure, combining the resourcefulness, resilience and independence of the 'final girl' with the hyper-femininity of the 'girly heroine' (she wears, for example, a pale pink dress and her long, curly hair loose). Laura's transformation into a female avenger thus involves not so much a movement through these various femininities as a negotiation of them and the understandings of feminism they articulate.

It is, therefore, only within the context of these transformations that we can fully understand *Enemy's* division of its narrative into two distinct and clearly identifiable post- and pre-feminist eras since, in so doing, the film foregrounds the historically specific processes of transformation that, I have argued the rape-revenge cycle can be seen to articulate. Yet, to all intents and purposes, this is a post-feminist narrative, which, by reverting to a pre-feminist era, ostensibly disavows the transformations brought about both by, and within, feminism in the intervening period. What, I want to argue, however, is that precisely the reverse is true and that the film is a particularly good example not only of current popular articulations of feminism but of the meaning of post-feminism itself. Indeed, the film is careful to remind us, through brief incursions of the contemporary world, that its pre-feminist narrative is told very much from a post-feminist perspective. Here, Charlotte Brunsdon's understanding of the term post-feminism proves to be especially illuminating. Brunsdon argues that while the term can be seen to imply a disavowal or rejection of feminism, it only does so if we insist on seeing '1970s feminism as the site of "true" feminism, from which lipstick wearers and shoppers are excluded' but that when used in 'an historically specific sense to mark changes in popularly available understandings of femininity and a woman's place' the term is quite useful.[26] Thus *Enemy's* evocation of both post- and pre-feminist eras must be understood not as a rejection of feminism *per se* but as a rejection of certain elements of the 1970s radical feminism invoked in its title. In other words, the articulation of both a post- and pre-1970s narrative allows the film to embrace the discourses of heterosexual romance and femininity traditionally rejected by radical feminism, while simultaneously demonstrating a certain knowingness and self-consciousness in its deployment of such discourses. Similarly, while the film disavows (or maybe simply takes for granted) feminist discourses of domestic violence, it simultaneously embraces the popular representation of the violent and angry woman, which those discourses have enabled.

In her analysis of the rape-revenge film and transformation, Carol Clover argues that the rape-revenge film's move into the mainstream has been enabled by earlier, low versions of such films and that this transformation has been accompanied by a concomitant erosion of their progressive politics.[27] In its implication that there was a moment of authenticity that has now passed, Clover's argument is informed by the same kind of binary logic that has tended to mark understandings of post-feminism. Against both these perspectives, I have suggested that the rape-revenge film *and* feminism itself are perhaps better understood not in terms of authentic moments but as narratives of transformation. The various transformations the rape-revenge film has undergone do not, therefore, represent celebrations or rejections of feminism according to their status as low or high respectively, but are rather attempts to negotiate and make sense of the various transformations within feminist thinking during the post-1970 period. Nicci Gerrard provides a succinct summary of these transformations when she observes that: 'We used to say, gladly: I am a feminist. Then: I am a feminist, but…Then: it depends what you mean by feminism. Then: what is feminism, anyway?'[28] While 'some people label this gradual crumbling of certainties the backlash', the meaning of feminism has, in fact, always been a site of struggle and therefore contradiction.[29] Moreover, as I have been arguing, the rape-revenge cycle can be seen as one of the privileged sites on, through and against which these struggles and contradictions are played out and the meanings of feminism produced *and* transformed. The answer to Gerrard's final question can thus be found in popular texts such as *Sleeping with the Enemy*, which, through an attempt to reconcile the contradictions between the discourses of feminism and the discourses of femininity, construct a popular version of feminism for the 1990s and, in the process, provide Gerrard with a fifth feminist phase/phrase: 'I may be feminine, but...'.

Notes

1 Charlotte Brunsdon, *Screen Tastes: Soap Opera to Satellite Dishes* (London: Routledge, 1997), p. 101.
2 Hilary Radner, 'Pretty Is as Pretty Does: Free Enterprise and the Marriage Plot', in *Film Theory Goes to the Movies*, ed. by Jim Collins, Hilary Radner and Ava Preacher Collins (London: Routledge, 1993), pp. 56–76 (p. 65).
3 Stanley Sadie, ed., *The New Grove Dictionary of Music and Musicians*, 20 vols (London: Macmillan, 1980), Volume II, p. 594.
4 Julia Roberts' association with fairy-tales culminated in her being cast in the role of Tinkerbell in *Hook* (Steven Spielberg, 1991).
5 Indeed, the motif of hair-cuting can be found in two other articulations of the rape-revenge structure: *Handgun* (Tony Garnett, 1982) and *The Accused* (Jonathan Kaplan, 1988).
6 The wig can be seen as a further reference to *Pretty Woman*, at the beginning of which Roberts is shown wearing a similar blonde wig.
7 Ruth B. Bottigheimer, *Grimms' Bad Girls and Bold Boys: The Moral and Social Vision of the Tales* (New Haven: Yale University Press, 1987), p. 29 and p. 25.
8 Ibid., p. 33.
9 Ibid., p. 31.
10 Brunsdon, *Screen Tastes*, p. 94.
11 Ibid., p. 94.
12 Ibid., p. 100.
13 Colin McArthur, 'Chinese Boxes and Russian Dolls: Tracking the Elusive Cinematic City', in *The Cinematic City*, ed. by David B. Clarke (London: Routledge, 1997), pp. 19–45 (p. 24).
14 Steve Neale, 'The Big Romance or Something Wild?: Romantic Comedy

Today', *Screen*, 33:3 (Autumn 1992), 284–99.

15 Ibid., p. 295.

16 Ibid., pp. 295–6.

17 Steve Neale and Frank Krutnik, *Popular Film and Television Comedy* (London: Routledge, 1990), p. 172.

18 Steve Neale, 'The Big Romance', p. 299.

19 David Glover and Cora Kaplan, 'Guns in the House of Culture?: Crime Fiction and the Politics of the Popular', in *Cultural Studies*, ed. by Lawrence Grossberg, Cary Nelson and Paula A. Treichler (London: Routledge, 1992), pp. 213–26 (p. 222).

20 Leeds Revolutionary Feminist Group, 'Political Lesbianism: The Case Against Heterosexuality', in *The Woman Question: Readings on the Subordination of Women*, ed. by Mary Evans (London: Fontana, 1982), pp. 63–72 (p. 65).

21 Brunsdon, *Screen Tastes*, p. 95.

22 Betty Friedan, *The Feminine Mystique* (Harmondsworth: Penguin, 1965).

23 The motif of the discarded wedding ring occurs in other films in the cycle. See, for example, *The Last Seduction* and *Thelma and Louise*.

24 Radner, 'Pretty Is as Pretty Does', p. 61.

25 Brunsdon, *Screen Tastes*, p. 101.

26 Ibid., p. 102 and 101.

27 Carol Clover, 'High and Low: The Transformation of the Rape-Revenge Movie', in *Women and Film: A Sight and Sound Reader*, ed. by Pam Cook and Philip Dodd (London: Scarlet Press, 1993), pp. 76–85.

28 Nicci Gerrard, 'The New Feminism: Hello, boys…', *Observer* (Review), 27 April 1997, p. 5.

29 Ibid.

Part II

Pre-feminism

Rape-revenge and mass cultural fictions of femininity: from the silent era to 1970

While the rape-revenge structure has received its most wide-spread deployment and dissemination in the post-1970 period, several examples of the structure can be found in the films of the pre-1970 period. Rape and revenge, for example, formed an integral part of one of the earliest and most famous feature films, D. W. Griffith's *The Birth of a Nation* (1915). Indeed, the themes of defilement and retribution are particularly evident in Griffith's work in the 1910s as witness, *Broken Blossoms* (1919) and *The Greatest Question* (1919). Such issues also appear in other films of the period, including *The Wind* (Victor Seastrom, 1928) and *Blackmail* (Alfred Hitchcock, 1929). In order to begin to identify precisely what is specific and significant about the representation of feminism and femininity in articulations of the rape-revenge structure in the post-1970 period, I want to start by looking at some of these earlier examples of the structure. In particular, while I will be arguing that these pre-1970 rape-revenge narratives, like their post-1970s counterparts, emerged at key points in the history of twentieth-century gender relations (the late 1910s/1920s and the late 1940s/1950s), I will argue that, in the absence of the discourses of rape, which emerged with the rise of second-wave feminism in the 1970s, these early articulations of the structure did not attempt to tell feminist stories or even, feminine stories, but instead largely functioned to endorse and uphold the traditional conceptions of masculinity and femininity inscribed in the genres over which it was mapped.

Rape

The silent era, 1915–29
Given that early film technology lent itself to expressive forms of

representation it is perhaps not surprising that melodrama, along
with comedy, formed the mainstay of film production in the early
silent era. Both were flourishing forms of popular theatre in the late
nineteenth century, and it was from here that the nascent cinema
drew both its inspiration and its actors. As Sandy Flitterman-Lewis
points out:

> A specifically generic definition of melodrama ... would involve the-
> atrical conventions – for example, domestic location, familial conflict,
> the stock types of brave hero, evil villain, and suffering heroine, the
> struggle of good and evil, and plot motifs such as kidnap or seduction.[1]

It is in this context that we need to understand the early representation of rape and revenge. In other words, the themes of rape and
revenge were particularly suited to the silent melodrama's emphasis
on emotional heightening and the battle between good and evil.
This is especially evident in *Broken Blossoms* where the fight
between good and evil is embodied in the figure of the Yellow Man
(Richard Barthelmess) and Battling Burrows (Donald Crisp). Burrows is an archetypal 'baddie', complete with thick, black, angular
eyebrows; he is a prize-fighter who eventually beats his daughter,
Lucy (Lillian Gish), to death. The Yellow Man, on the other hand, is
a gentle and peaceful man, a Buddhist eventually driven to violence
in order to avenge Lucy's death. While many may want to argue that
it is Lucy's death that the Yellow Man avenges, rather than her rape,
Julia Lesage has made a convincing case for reading the film's
famous closet scene as a symbolic rape.[2] There is much evidence to
support such a reading, not least that Burrows's fatal beating of Lucy
arises out of his belief that she is having a sexual relationship with
the Yellow Man and, therefore, revolves around issues of ownership
and possession. Furthermore, the scene is predicated on Burrow's
penetration of the closet that Lucy has locked herself in and in which
she writhes around in a futile attempt to escape this penetration.
Lastly, and perhaps most significantly, the sexual connotations of the
final beating and Lucy's death are cemented not only by the fact that
they occur on the *bed*, but by the fact that the beating is carried out
with a whip handle which, in appearance and positioning, has obvious phallic connotations. Clearly such a symbolic representation of
rape allowed Griffith to show much more than he would have been
able to do had he depicted an actual rape since, while silent film and
the codes of melodrama clearly lent themselves to such depictions,

standards of decency limited the extent to which rape could be fully represented.[3] Thus other silent films dealing with the issue of rape, such as *The Birth of a Nation*, *The Greatest Question*, *The Wind* and *Blackmail*, tend to feature only an *attempted* rape.[4]

Griffith, however, was master of even the attempted rape scene and his *The Birth of a Nation* contains no less than two such scenes. While there are clearly some racial tensions at work in Battling Burrows and the Yellow Man's fight for ownership of the white woman in *Broken Blossoms*, *Birth*'s rape sequences are far more heavily marked by the relationship between rape and race since one of the potential rapists is a black man (Gus) while the other is a mulatto (Lynch). Griffith thus draws heavily on the myth of the black male rapist and this is particularly evident in Gus' pursuit of Flora (Mae Marsh) in the film's first rape sequence. In other words, that the chase takes place in the forest, with Gus (Walter Long) bent double and thus almost on all fours, virtually foaming at the mouth, suggests a man reduced to his base and animalistic instincts. Flora, on the other hand, while also connected to the natural world through both her name and her fascinated observation of the forest's small animals, is linked to the purity and innocence of that world.

Again then, there is a reliance here on the melodramatic exaggeration of the battle between good and evil, purity and bestiality. Yet, while evil and bestiality were signalled in these early films in a variety of ways, though most clearly through the figure of the black (Gus), mulatto (Lynch) or working-class (Burrows) rapist, it was in the star persona of Lillian Gish that the motif of the pure rape victim found its most cogent expression. Gish starred in four out of the five films under discussion here – *The Birth of a Nation*, *The Greatest Question*, *Broken Blossoms* and *The Wind* – and Richard Dyer's analysis of Gish's star persona is suggestive of the ideology behind these early representations of rape. Dyer argues that it is the 'concatenation of gender, race and light that is a key part of [Gish's] stardom', in other words, the way in which she embodies an ideal of white womanhood.[5] While this is most apparent in *The Birth of a Nation*, all Gish's performances, particularly in *Broken Blossoms* and *The Wind*, carry overtones of nineteenth-century conceptions of women as bastions of morality and virtue, as redemptive 'Angels in the House'. Such rape narratives, therefore, function to underline this ideal and to uphold it. Although in both *Birth* and *The Greatest Question*, Gish is saved from rape, generally the message

is that it is better to die than to be despoiled; that rape is tantamount to death. Thus, in *Birth*, Flora leaps to her death rather than
succumb to Gus' lustful intentions and at the end of the film, where
the Cameron family are trapped in a cabin besieged by black soldiers, the men prepare to kill the women rather than allow them to
fall into the hands of the black soldiers. In *Broken Blossoms*, the
outcome of the 'rape' is Gish's death. In the original ending of *The
Wind*, Gish runs out into the desert to die after having killed the
man who attempted to rape her.[6] It is perhaps within this context,
then, that we can also understand the fact that these films depict
only *attempted* rapes. In other words, in depicting attempted rapes,
the films not only maintain standards of decency, they maintain the
purity and innocence of white womanhood.

In this respect, then, Hitchcock's *Blackmail* is something of an
anomaly. To start with it is a British film but I include it here not only
because of Hitchcock's massive influence on filmmaking worldwide,
but because his thematic concerns with both violence against women
(*Psycho*, 1960; *The Birds*, 1963; *Frenzy*, 1972) and violent women
(*Under Capricorn*, 1949; *Marnie*, 1964) make some reference to his
work essential.[7] Secondly, unlike the films discussed above, in *Blackmail* the woman neither dies nor is saved, but kills the man who
attempts to rape her and escapes. Nor do the victim or the rapist fit
the established stereotypes. Despite the fact that Alice White's surname *suggests* purity and innocence, she is actually flirtatious and
coquettish, a woman who willingly goes out with another man,
Crewe (Cyril Ritchard), behind her boyfriend's back. The man turns
out to be her rapist and while, as an upper-class, white artist, he does
not obviously fit the stereotypes of the black or working-class rapist,
his profession and lifestyle do carry connotations of decadence and
licentiousness. In many respects, the differences between Griffith's
and Hitchcock's articulation of the rape motif has much to do with
their own particular obsessions. As Schickel observes: 'One is
reminded of how often, before and after *Birth*, Griffith arranged
confrontations between the beautiful and the bestial, how obsessive
was his belief that innocence must, almost inevitably, be brutally
despoiled.'[8] Hitchcock's work, on the other hand, is peopled not
with beautiful and innocent heroines, but with beautiful and aberrant ones of which Alice (Anny Ondra) is perhaps the earliest example. Furthermore, while both *Broken Blossoms* and *The Birth of a
Nation*, despite the latter's added dimension of historical epic, fit

almost exactly the definition of melodrama cited above, Hitchcock worked largely in the thriller genre and, according to Pam Cook, 'objected to the fact that Hollywood produced so many "women's pictures"'.[9]

As with many representations of rape in this period, Hitchcock manages the delicate nature of his subject matter through the use of a distanced, non-subjective camera and shadows. In other words, it is the shadows that the bodies of the protagonists cast on the wall behind them rather than the characters themselves that we see as the victim and rapist struggle. However, Hitchcock then cuts to a shot of a bed that is hidden from our view by the surrounding curtains and out of which pokes Alice's struggling forearm. That this later shot is not entirely motivated by decorum or convention is suggested by the fact that Hitchcock was to repeat this representation of rape, in which the woman's body is fragmented, in the later *Frenzy*, where there are repeated shots of Brenda Blaney's ankles and breasts as she is raped by Rusk. What this suggests is that, for Hitchcock, woman is little more than the sum of her (sexual) body parts. Furthermore, that this fragmented female sexuality is possessed not by the woman herself but by men is made clear through the motif of Alice's lost gloves, which she leaves in Crewe's apartment. According to Selim Eyüboglu, the gloves connote Alice's sexuality: 'Gloves here work as a signifier of a lost object that positions the desire of the "guilty" subject in relation to the desire(s) of the other.'[10] Thus when one of the gloves is taken by her boyfriend, Frank (John Longden), and the other by the blackmailer, Tracey (Donald Calthrop), her body is not only further fragmented, it is further possessed. Indeed, the fact that immediately prior to finding one of the gloves, Frank is shown looking at the female nude Crewe helped Alice paint the previous night further confirms the link between the gloves and female sexuality. The gloves, however, are also the signifier of Alice's guilt, which, because of their sexual connotations, function to signify not only that she is guilty of the murder but that she is guilty of precipitating the rape in the first place. Thus, contrary to Griffith's melodramatic representation of rape, which functions to construct and uphold the nineteenth-century ideal of white womanhood, Hitchcock's representation of rape functions to construct the woman as both a sexual and a guilty subject.

This construction of Alice as a desiring '"guilty" subject' causes Eyüboglu to argue that the film constructs Alice as a prospective femme fatale.[11] Early silent cinema did indeed tend to represent women as either virgins (as embodied by actresses such as Lillian Gish) or vamps (as embodied by actresses such as Theda Bara) and I will have more to say about the influence of the femme fatale or vamp on subsequent deployments of the rape-revenge structure in chapter 6. In particular, I will argue that the vamp can be seen as an articulation of the anxieties that accompanied the emergence of first-wave feminism in the 1890s. It is perhaps worth noting, however, that the ideal of woman as 'Angel in the House' was actually used to support US suffrage leaders' arguments for the female vote. As Nancy McGlen and Karen O'Connor have observed, suffrage leaders 'claimed that the ballot would enable women to reform society, a task that they were particularly suited to *as women*' on the basis of 'the inherent incorruptibility of women and their acknowledged superior moral character'.[12]

With the winning of the vote in 1920, however, a new female stereotype emerged, one with which Alice is much more closely associated – that of the emancipated new woman. While, as Molly Haskell has pointed out, the new woman was 'either a suffragette or a flapper, depending on what she wanted and how she chose to get it', it was the image of the flapper that most frequently found its way into the films of the period.[13] According to Haskell, the flapper 'wanted social and sexual, rather than political and intellectual, power'.[14] In dress and manner, Alice is clearly constructed in this image: she wears the cloche hat popular with women in the 1920s, a fur-trimmed coat and behaves flirtatiously with the men she meets. Likewise, Alice is clearly attracted to Crewe's upper-class, decadent life-style and to the apparent sexual power she wields over him. These associations are cemented in the song Crewe sings as Alice undresses in readiness to have her portrait painted – 'Miss Up-to-Date' – at the conclusion of which Crewe comments 'that's a song about you my dear'.[15] Indeed, the song's lyrics are indicative of the ideology behind the representation of Alice as new woman. In other words, while ostensibly constructed as a defence of 'Miss Up-to-Date', the song simultaneously chronicles the backlash against the emancipated woman, significantly constructing her against the 'woman of the past age'. For example:

> They praise the woman of the past age,
> And loath her daughter of this last age,

They sing a hymn of hate about Miss Up-to-Date,
And spend their spite from morn to night.

Continuing with the lines 'They say you're wild, a naughty child
Miss Up-to-Date/A goofy few predict for you an awful fate', this
'hymn of hate' is clearly endorsed by the events that follow (Crewe's
attempted rape of Alice). Moreover, later, as Alice roams the streets
having killed Crewe by stabbing him with a carving knife, the film
specifically links her crime with her role as a new woman. Miss Up-
to-Date, as the song has pointedly reminded us, is partial to 'a cocktail or two', and thus in this sequence there is a point-of-view shot
of Alice staring absently at a neon advertisement for Gordon's Gin.
Surrounded by the words, 'The Heart of a Good Cocktail', is a
moving cocktail shaker, which gradually turns into an image of a
hand holding a knife which moves in stabbing motions, the implication being that the transition from new woman to murderess is but
a small one. To the left of this central image is the slogan 'Gordon's,
White for Purity'. The connection made here between Alice's surname and the accoutrements of the new woman not only further
serves to confirm her role as Miss Up-to-Date, but functions as an
ironic comment on the inappropriateness of her surname (Alice is
clearly neither sexually or morally pure). Finally, that the film represents an articulation of the backlash against Miss Up-to-Date evident in the song is apparent not only in the way in which the film
subsequently effects a transformation of Alice into the asexual
'woman of the past age' (on returning home she changes into a floral
dress and a shapeless cardigan), but in the 'awful fate' awaiting Alice
in Hitchcock's intended ending. In this ending, Alice does not escape
but is pursued, caught and locked up in a cell.[16]

Despite their differences, the question that remains, however, is to
what extent these early films are actually *about* rape and its effects;
to what extent can they be described as rape *narratives*? I have
already explored the way in which Lillian Gish's role in several of
these films functions to uphold an ideal of white womanhood and
thus, in *The Birth of a Nation* in particular, rape appears simply as a
narrative motif in the film's larger ideological project of defining
white male supremacy. In *Broken Blossoms* and *The Wind*, while the
narrative appears to centre more on the woman's story, the positioning of the rape at the end of the narrative leaves little room for
the exploration of its consequences beyond the message that rape

itself is a resolution, an end point tantamount to death. Finally, in
Blackmail, although the rape occurs near the beginning of the film,
the subsequent emphasis is not on Alice's rape but on the consequences of her murder of the rapist. Thus, it is the murder rather
than the rape that is replayed throughout the film in the repeated
stress, both symbolically and aurally, on knives, an emphasis which,
moreover, serves to position Alice as guilty party rather than victim.
Indeed, as the title of the film and its narrative trajectory suggests, if
Alice is a victim at all, she is the victim of blackmail rather than rape.
Within the wider ideological project of the film as a whole, however,
Alice is the victim of the backlash against the emancipated new
woman that occurred in the 1920s.

The sound era, 1930–70

While this section spans the period from 1930 to 1970, the earliest
example of the rape-revenge structure I was able to find was *Johnny
Belinda* (Jean Negulesco, 1948). Like the previous examples, then,
the articulations of the rape-revenge structure I will be discussing in
this section span a period of profound upheaval in gender relations.
While the feminist movement largely lay dormant during this time,
World War II brought about its own form of female emancipation.
During the war, as men went off to fight, leaving factories and offices
quite literally 'unmanned', women entered the workforce in unprecedented numbers. The post-war backlash against the working
woman, the drive to push her back into the home, cannot, however,
be understood simply in economic terms (that is, in terms of the fact
that, with war production over and a returned male workforce,
there simply were not enough jobs to go around). Rather, as Jackie
Byars has observed: 'A family-centred culture became America's bul-
wark … against the insecurity caused by the discovery of atomic
energy, and against communism.'[17] Thus the family came to stand for
the unity and moral integrity of the nation as a whole. The desire to
return women to their roles as wives and mothers consequently also
arose from the belief that the working woman compromised the
moral integrity of the family/nation, from the fear, in other words,
that the working woman was not only financially independent but
sexually independent and available as well. As a narrative motif, rape
would appear to be ideally suited to conveying the dangers of
(sexual) independence and encouraging a return to the family. Thus,
whether she is a working woman or not, in the articulations of the

rape-revenge structure in this period, rape functions in various and complex ways to position the heroine within the traditional feminine career of wife and/or mother. Given that the late 1940s and 1950s are seen by many to be the golden age of melodrama (or the 'woman's film'), it should perhaps come as no surprise that, during this period, female-centred deployments of the rape-revenge structure such as *Johnny Belinda* and *Outrage* (Ida Lupino, 1950) appeared solely in this genre. Indeed, as I hope to show, the combination of the rape-revenge structure and the codes and conventions of melodrama worked to forcefully reinscribe women's role within the family.[18]

In *Johnny Belinda*, Belinda (Jane Wyman) is rejected by her family, partly because her birth caused her mother's death and partly because she is deaf and mute. In her discussion of the woman's film, Mary Ann Doane argues that: 'This muteness is in some ways paradigmatic for the genre. For it is ultimately the symptoms of the female body which "speak" while the woman as subject of discourse is inevitably absent.'[19] Thus, when we first meet Belinda, it is her body, her dirty and dishevelled appearance, that signifies her position outside of the feminine sphere of the family. As Doane points out, in the woman's film:

> The female body is located not so much as a spectacle but as an element in the discourse of medicine, a manuscript to be read for the symptoms of her story, her identity. Hence the need, in these films, for the figure of the doctor as reader or interpreter, as the site of knowledge which dominates and controls female subjectivity.[20]

Accordingly, in *Johnny Belinda*, Belinda is befriended by the hero, Doctor Robert Richardson (Lew Ayres), who teaches her sign language and who, thus, quite literally, becomes the interpreter of the signs she subsequently makes with her body. Moreover, in line with Doane's suggestion that what the doctor's active reading of the female body constructs is an identity, under Richardson's tutelage Belinda is transformed from a neglected child known only as 'The Dummy' into a beautiful young woman; she is made 'feminine'.[21] For Belinda, however, the consequence of this transformation is her rape at the hands of one of the locals who visits her father's farm, an event that leads her to again reject the accoutrements of heterosexual femininity. While Richardson at first misdiagnoses Belinda's physical neglect (interpreting it as the symptom of loneliness), another doctor's examination of Belinda's body reveals that she is pregnant and this diagnosis then becomes subsumed into Richardson's initial misdiagnosis (he tells Belinda that, as a mother, she will never be lonely again). Thus, despite the fact that Belinda's body attempts to speak 'the symptoms of her story', the symptoms of rape are repeatedly reinterpreted as the symptoms of motherhood. Here, then, rape reinterpreted as motherhood not only brings the dysfunctional family together, but results in Belinda's further 'feminization' as a mother. This privileging of the maternal and the familial over women's experience of, and responses to, rape is perhaps nowhere more apparent than in the film's title, which, in defining its heroine in terms of her feminine role as mother to Johnny, suggests that it is the definition and control of female subjectivity, rather than Belinda and her experiences which are the subject of this woman's film.

In contrast, *Outrage's* title clearly announces the film's attitude towards rape. Like *Johnny Belinda*, the film also maps the rape-revenge structure over the codes and conventions of melodrama. Pam Cook has observed:

> Feminist study of the genre has emphasized its creation of a 'feminine', domesticated world in which women's experience and point of view are privileged, not least by the employment of *mise en scène* and sound to convey heightened affect.[22]

She goes on to argue that:

> In *Outrage* the moralistic, punitive trajectory of the narrative is undercut and commented on by the visual and auditory codes, which are used expressionistically to convey Ann's state of mind and existential predicament.[23]

Cook's analysis, however, provides little evidence to support such claims, and in fact, most of her observations about the film would actually seem to support a reading of its narrative as 'moralistic' and 'punitive'. Cook's discussion of *Outrage* is interesting, nevertheless, for the way in which she analyses the film both in terms of melodrama and in terms of the rape-revenge genre as it has been defined by Carol Clover. This allows her not only to map historical changes between the two genres but also to explore some of the limitations of Clover's approach. According to Cook:

> The rape-revenge reading produces a view of *Outrage* diametrically opposed to that produced by the melodrama reading. The first sees the film as endorsing the female victim position, while the second sees it as putting the drama of female subjectivity centre-stage.[24]

In other words, by comparing *Outrage* with the post-1970s rape-revenge films discussed by Clover, Cook's analysis, not unexpectedly, reveals that the film 'falls far short of the ideological disturbances detected by Clover in her 1970s and 1980s feminist-influenced examples'.[25] My project here, while similarly concerned to explore the way in which the rape-revenge structure functioned in the pre-1970 period, is informed by a somewhat different approach. Rather than producing a comparative reading of *Outrage* across different generic and historical contexts, my purpose is to explore the effects of the *intersection* between the rape-revenge structure and the codes and conventions of melodrama within the specific historical and ideological context of post-war USA I outlined at the beginning of this section.

What I want to argue, in particular, is that, in *Outrage*, rape is cast as a threat to the feminine career of heterosexual romance and family. Thus, the beginning of the film is centred around the heroine, Ann's, embarkation on this career, with her boyfriend's proposal of marriage and her parent's blessing on their subsequent engagement. However, on an evening on which Ann (Mala Powers) has worked late and must walk home alone in the dark, she is raped. The film consequently sets up an opposition between the two careers open to women in the post-war period – marriage or work – an opposition underlined by Ann's colleague, who comments to her during a coffee break that she has to return to work: 'You're the one that's getting married, I need my job'. Yet, while in line with the post-war drive to get women back into the home, the rape is clearly shown to be a consequence of the latter rather than the former career, after the rape Ann rejects fiancé and family and flees the city for the country, where she is taken in by a preacher named Doc (Tod Andrews). The preacher's name, however, is, of course, significant, since like Doctor Richardson in *Johnny Belinda*, it is his role to 'cure' Ann of her rejection of the feminine career and return her to fiancé and family.[26] As I argued earlier, this emphasis on the need for the standard family can be seen as a response to the crisis of national identity that occurred after the war. Indeed, if, as Cook suggests, the rape can be read as symptomatic of the USA's own lost innocence, then Ann's trajectory through the narrative can be seen as an attempt to recover that innocence through a return to family values.[27] Consequently, the rape is also shown as arising from the disturbances to family life, and the traditional gender relations inscribed therein, brought about by the war. In other words, not only is the rape constructed as a consequence of women's work outside the home, the rapist is constructed as a victim of the trauma inflicted by war and of what Cook describes as 'postwar impaired masculinity'.[28] Hence, as Cook observes: 'The rapist is absolved of guilt ... with the consequence that the specificity of Ann's experience of rape is subsumed into the rapist's experience of war, and both are perceived as neurotics who need to be cured.'[29] This 'cure', as I have suggested, involves reasserting traditional gender roles through a return to family values.

While *Outrage* is ostensibly framed as Ann's story, the second half of the film tends to shift the focus from Ann to Doc, with Ann merely playing the passive role to Doc's active role of 'healer'. Like *Johnny Belinda*, then, *Outrage's* deployment of the rape-revenge structure across the women's film would appear to similarly deny Ann the opportunity to articulate her experience of rape and to become the subject of her own story. Thus, despite the fact that the women's film purports to articulate a female point of view, the women in both these films are never allowed to speak for themselves. Rather, as is indicated most forcefully in the trial scenes at the end of each film, it is the role of the doctor to speak for the woman and thus to define and control her. What I want to suggest is that the deployment of the rape-revenge structure colludes in the ideological project of these women's films. In other words, by including as a central narrative motif an event that, at the time, was not only unrepresentable but quite literally unspeakable, the films are able to legitimate the erosion of the woman's story from their narratives.

The remaining articulations of the rape-revenge structure in this period demonstrate an even more pervasive emphasis on the male protagonist and thus a concomitant disavowal of women's experiences of, and responses to, rape, not least because in two of them (*Rancho Notorious*, Fritz Lang, 1952; *The Virgin Spring*, Ingmar Bergman, 1959) the victim dies and the subsequent emphasis, therefore, is on the hero's revenge.[30] This increasing repression of a female perspective is marked, in particular, by a shift from the codes and conventions of melodrama to those of the western (*Rancho*

Notorious) and the medieval fable (*The Virgin Spring*). I will consequently discuss these films at greater length in the section on
revenge. For now I want to turn to Otto Preminger's *Anatomy of a
Murder* (1959), which, despite the shift from melodrama to courtroom drama, would seem to offer the woman the opportunity to tell
her story.

Like Hitchcock's *Blackmail*, which appeared at the tail end of the
silent era, *Anatomy of a Murder* appeared towards the end of the era
of the production code, and there is a sense in which as a result both
are watershed films quite different from anything that has gone
before them. As such, both depart from the conventional representation of the raped woman in both the silent and the production
code eras as innocent victim. Preminger's work, like Hitchcock's,
also shows a preoccupation with the representation of 'woman as
enigma'.[31] While *Anatomy's* narrative is ostensibly centred around
establishing the guilt or innocence of Lieutenant Manion (Ben Gazzara), on trial for the murder of a bartender who allegedly raped his
wife, Laura (Lee Remick), it is ultimately the question of whether or
not Laura was raped and her guilt or innocence in this matter that
becomes central to the narrative. Consequently, unlike the films discussed previously in which rape, if not directly represented, was
always *visually* signalled within the diegesis, in *Anatomy* the alleged
rape not only occurs outside of the narrative framework but it is
never visually represented or signalled within that framework. As
with *The Accused* (1988), attention is drawn to the victim's physical
injuries as evidence of rape, but such evidence is undermined
through the construction of the victim as a woman who is sexually
inviting in both appearance and behaviour and who also frequents
bars alone. Nevertheless, whereas *The Accused* resolved the issue of
the victim's guilt or innocence by representing the rape in flashback
through the eyes of a male witness at the end of the film, in *Anatomy*
we have only the oral testimony of two women, Laura herself and
the rapist's stepdaughter, Mary Pilant (Kathryn Grant), as proof of
Laura's innocence. The jury accepts these testimonies and Lieutenant Manion is acquitted. The final scene of the film, however, in
which lawyer Paul Biegler (James Stewart) goes to the Manion's
mobile home to collect his fee only to find that Manion has left a
note citing the legal precedent of irresistible impulse used to help
acquit him as an excuse to leave without paying, throws the court's
verdict into question.[32] Thus, despite the opportunity given to Laura

to articulate her experience of rape, this is not a woman's story but one in which, as Richard Lippe has observed, 'the primary issue at stake is male identity and power and the ability of the male to manipulate a situation to his advantage'.[33]

Despite the way in which *Anatomy's* narrative structure tends to deny or question the existence of rape, perhaps more than any other film of the pre-1970 period, it contributed to making rape 'speakable'. In other words, while earlier films always visually *implied* the threat or occurrence of rape, rape was simultaneously shown to be visually *unrepresentable*. For example, in *Johnny Belinda*, Belinda's fate is visually implied by a shadow falling over her as she cowers back but the actual rape is visually absent as the screen fades to black. In *Johnny Belinda* this absence functions to render rape as both unrepresentable and, despite Belinda's new found communication skills, unspeakable. In *Anatomy*, on the other hand, the visual absence of rape functions to create a narrative lacuna as a result of which rape must and does become speakable. Nevertheless, although *Anatomy* can be seen as indicative of the increasing openness towards sex and sexuality that occurred in the 1950s and that would lead, in the late 1960s, to women beginning to speak out about sexual violence, as yet there was still no way of thinking about rape from a female perspective.[34] Like the films previously discussed, therefore, *Anatomy* is not *about* rape or women's experience of rape. Rather, rape here functions largely to endorse and uphold traditional conceptions of masculinity and femininity.

Rapists and their victims

I have already demonstrated how, in early silent films, the rape victim is largely represented as innocent and, with the exception of *Blackmail* and *Anatomy of a Murder*, this is also true of the rest of the films I have discussed. These exceptions are to some extent suggestive of the motivation behind the representation of the innocent rape victim, at least in those films which represent male revenge. In other words, if, in *Anatomy*, Laura's appearance and behaviour threw the existence of the rape and thus the legitimacy of her husband's revenge into question, in films such as *Rancho Notorious* and *The Virgin Spring*, the victim's innocence would appear to function to help legitimate male revenge. The purity of the woman is largely assured by making her either a child (Flora in *Birth*, Lucy in *Broken Blossoms*, Belinda in *Johnny Belinda* and Karin in *The Virgin Spring*)

or by defining her in relation to marriage as either a fiancée (Elsie in
Birth, Ann in *Outrage* and Beth in *Rancho Notorious*) or a wife
(Letty in *The Wind*). Even the less than innocent heroines of *Black-mail* and *Anatomy* are respectively girlfriend and wife. Moreover,
while the roles of fiancée and wife clearly define these women in
relation to men rather than as individuals, even the children are
male-identified since, apart from Karin (Brigitta Pettersson) in *The
Virgin Spring*, their fathers are present while their mothers are dead
or absent.

With the exception of *Broken Blossoms*, in which father and rapist
are one and the same, these fathers, husbands and fiancés in part
function as signifiers of a good and honourable white masculinity
against which the rapists' difference and deviance can be defined.[35]
Thus, the rapist is represented variously as black (Gus in *Birth*),
mulatto (Lynch in *Birth*), a potential bigamist (Roddy Wirt in *The
Wind*), an upper-class artist (Crewe in *Blackmail*), a violent woman-izer (Locky McCormick in *Johnny Belinda*), a convicted criminal (in
Outrage), an outlaw (Kinch in *Rancho Notorious*), and goatherds (in
The Virgin Spring).[36] Even in *Anatomy of a Murder*, where the rapist
is characterized simply as a bartender, the husband still holds the
superior moral ground as a lieutenant in the US army. In this way,
then, rape is constructed not as a product of heterosexual power
relations but as the deed of a minority of abnormal men who are rep-resented as distinct from the majority who make up normal, patri-archal society. Some of the later films also construct similar
oppositions between their female characters, using deviations from
the established standards of feminine behaviour in order to under-line the rape victim's goodness and purity. For example, in *Johnny
Belinda*, Belinda is contrasted with the vain and worldly Stella
McGuire (Jan Sterling). In *Rancho Notorious*, the hero's raped and
murdered fiancée, Beth (Gloria Henry), is contrasted with the
femme fatale, Altar Keane (Marlene Dietrich). Finally, and perhaps
most clearly, in *The Virgin Spring*, the blonde and virginal Karin is
opposed to her pregnant and unmarried dark-haired foster sister,
Ingeri (Gunnel Lindblom).

In the films of the pre-1970 period, rape would appear to function
to endorse and uphold traditional conceptions of masculinity and
femininity. These films often allow little room for the change or
transformation of such categories. Indeed, in many of these films no
discernible change or transformation takes place. This may be largely

due to the limited passage of time between the occurrence of the rape and either the exacting of revenge or the victim's death. Even when transformation does hold a central position in the narrative, however, it remains to be seen whether it is the raped or avenging person who is transformed, given that they are not always the same person, and what the ideological implications of such transformation may be. It is, therefore, the way in which the films of the pre-1970 period articulate this central structuring convention of the rape-revenge narrative that I will be exploring in the next section.

Transformation

I have already pointed out how rape often *results in* the rejection of the feminine career and how the transformation that subsequently takes place functions to restore the heroine to her proper feminine vocation within the confines of heterosexual romance and family. However, rape can also be seen to *result from* such a rejection of the feminine career. Here it is rape itself that is transformative, functioning to reposition the heroine as wife, fiancée or girlfriend. For example, in *The Birth of a Nation*, Elsie (Lillian Gish) breaks off her engagement with Ben Cameron (Henry B. Walthall) because of his involvement with the Ku Klux Klan and it is only after her near rape at the hands of Lynch (George Siegmann) that they are reunited. Similarly in *The Wind*, Letty (Lillian Gish) rejects her husband, Lige (Lars Hanson), until she is nearly raped by Roddy Wirt (Montagu Love) whereupon she declares her true love for him. Finally, in *Blackmail* Alice stands her boyfriend, Frank, up to go out with another man who attempts to rape her but becomes dependent on Frank when she is subsequently threatened by a blackmailer. That the narrative resolutions and the final shots of all three films centre around the reunited couple further serves to underline the message that a woman's proper place is within a heterosexual relationship. Thus, as I suggested in my discussion of both *Blackmail* and *Outrage*, these films can, in many ways, be seen as a response to historical contexts in which women were increasingly rejecting traditional feminine images and roles. In other words, in these films, rape can be seen as functioning both as a warning and a corrective to women who step outside of their designated position within society.

Those films that do not rely on restoring the heroine's femininity or teaching her her proper place through rape or its consequences

tend, nevertheless, to effect a concomitant transformation or punishment of the heroine's other or double. Thus, in *Johnny Belinda*,
Stella must undergo the humiliation of admitting publicly not only
that she married a rapist, but that she was willing to violate the sanctity of the mother–child relation. In *The Virgin Spring*, Ingeri's
remorse for her part in Karin's rape and murder and renunciation of
evil are apparent in her confession to Karin's father and in her purifi-
cation at the virgin spring. Finally, in *Rancho Notorious*, Altar must
pay with her life for her involvement with the masculine world of
crime and for harbouring outlaws (including Beth's rapist), although
not before the hero, Vern (Arthur Kennedy), has made her change
from her usual masculine attire into her finest and most feminine
clothes.

As this latter example suggests, the transformation of the female
character is frequently a process effected by the male character.
Moreover, such transformations do not always occur as a result of
rape but, in fact, can contribute to its occurrence. Thus, for example, in *Broken Blossoms* it is the Yellow Man's feminization of Lucy
– he bathes her, changes her rags for a robe and gives her a doll – and
his sexualization of her – his attempt to kiss her – that makes her
'rapable'. Likewise, in *Johnny Belinda*, Doctor Richardson effects an
analogous feminization of Belinda with similar consequences. Nevertheless, while the heroine's responses to rape in *Johnny Belinda*
and *Outrage* suggest a recognition that it is femininity that engenders rape, their subsequent rejection of femininity and its accoutrements is not represented as the central narrative transformation,
which, instead, again charts their feminization by male agents.
Indeed, even this narrative division of labour, in which women are
defined merely as passive victims while men are given the active role
of bringing about change and transformation, serves to endorse and
restore traditional conceptions of masculinity and femininity. Yet, it
is not always the lack or rejection of femininity that is represented
as a problem to be solved by the male character in these films, as evidenced by the fact that in *Anatomy of a Murder* it is the *excess* of
femininity that is shown to be problematic. Moreover, *Anatomy*
illustrates that if it is femininity that makes women 'rapable', then it
is also femininity that makes them 'not rapable'. In other words,
Laura's excessive femininity and sexuality calls into question
whether she was raped or whether she consented to intercourse and
thus threatens not only her husband's trial, but the career of his

lawyer, Paul Biegler. Biegler, therefore, transforms Laura, making her wear a girdle, box suit, brim hat and glasses and in so doing makes her conform to notions of respectable femininity. Thus, these films, while involved in some complicated negotiations with the meaning of femininity, are ultimately not about *trans*forming but about *con*forming; they are about positioning and fixing their female characters within established and accepted feminine roles. Nevertheless, in the figure of Laura, who encompasses both the good and the bad female character of previous films, we can begin to see an ambivalence towards the different meanings of femininity and an inability to completely define and control it, as Laura changes back into her old clothes and remains enigmatic to the end.

Not surprisingly there is no equivalent female intervention on the rare occasions that it is the male protagonist who undergoes some form of transformation. Nevertheless, for both male and female characters transformation is shown to arise out of the violation of rape. In other words, for female characters rape is represented as both a result of, and a violation of, their femininity and for male characters as a violation of their masculine ability to protect women. Yet, while women's responses to rape are often shown to result in an unnatural rejection of femininity that must be rectified, men's responses to rape are shown to arise out of nothing more than natural and normal masculine behaviour. Thus, in *Broken Blossoms*, *Rancho Notorious* and *The Virgin Spring*, rape is shown to transform peaceful and religious or law-abiding men into violent and vengeful ones, a transformation which, unlike those of their female counterparts, is never subject to question, intervention or further change. Indeed, whether the hero is transform*ed* or transform*ing*, it is his role to bring about narrative resolution and restore the status quo and his actions are consequently rarely open to criticism or debate. This becomes particularly apparent when we look at the way in which these films articulate the motif of revenge.

Revenge

To what extent, then, is it fair to categorize these films as rape-revenge narratives? Clearly, the death of the rapist in all but one (*Outrage*) of these films would certainly seem to suggest the presence of an element of revenge. However, an analysis of by whom the rapist is killed, why and with what consequences yields some interesting and significant results. To start with, it is possible to divide the films into three categories – primary, secondary and displaced revenge. Primary revenge refers to instances in which the rapist is killed by his victim, while secondary revenge refers to those cases in which he is killed by someone other than his victim, most usually a family member or loved one. The final category, displaced revenge, covers instances in which, while the rapist is not killed, another man or men is made to suffer in his place (for example, *Outrage*, in which the heroine assaults a man she mistakes for her rapist). As this example suggests, moreover, displaced revenge is, in most cases, a sub-category of primary revenge. However, in the films discussed above, examples of primary revenge are also in a sense displaced, cast either as self-defence (*The Wind*, *Blackmail*) or as defence of a child (*Johnny Belinda*). It is only in the films in which revenge is secondary (*Birth*, *Broken Blossoms*, *Rancho Notorious*, *The Virgin Spring* and *Anatomy*) that it is also represented as genuine. Moreover, while as a category, secondary revenge can include revenge taken by a woman on behalf of another woman, the absence of the victim's mother in all but one of these films functions to deny the possibility of a secondary female avenger. Indeed, even in *The Virgin Spring*, where the mother is present, she is not involved in the killing of the rapists and it was not until *Last House on the Left* (Wes Craven, 1972) that the mother of the victim was shown to participate in the revenge. In all of the cases cited above, then, revenge is taken by men.

While, by its very nature, the family or conjugal relation involved in secondary revenge helps to legitimate it, in these cases one cannot help but feel that the fact that acts of violence and retribution are naturally associated with masculinity lends additional justification. Consequently, while in films featuring secondary revenge, the rape of a loved one is shown to be sufficient justification for male violence to go unexplained and unpunished,[37] in those featuring female violence or revenge, the presence of additional extenuating circumstances or punishment suggests that rape is not seen as sufficient justification for such unnatural behaviour. For example, in the original ending of *The Wind*, Letty runs out into the desert to die after shooting the man who raped her. In *Blackmail*, Alice is punished both for her forwardness with the artist and for his murder by finding herself threatened by a blackmailer (and in Hitchcock's intended ending, by imprisonment). Finally, in both *Johnny Belinda* and *Outrage*, the heroines are brought to trial for their acts of violence against men, which are subsequently explained not in terms of rape itself but in terms of Belinda's attempt to defend her child and Ann's 'temporary insanity'.[38] Moreover, as the 'happy' endings of the latter two films suggest, when female violence or revenge is cast in terms of feminine identity (motherhood, emotional instability) it tends to be more legitimate and less punishable than when it represents a deviation from that identity, for example, in *Blackmail* where Alice's rape and her revenge are cast as a consequence of her occupation of the role of the new woman.

In 1977, the radical feminist Robin Morgan wrote: 'Knowing our place is the message of rape – as it was for blacks the message of lynchings. Neither is an act of spontaneity or sexuality – they are both acts of political terrorism.'[39] Whether Morgan's analysis is true of rape in general, it would certainly seem to be applicable to the representations of rape discussed above. Emerging at key points in the history of US gender relations, at times when women were beginning to step outside their designated positions within society, deployments of the rape-revenge structure in the pre-1970 period functioned in various and complex ways to put women in their place by endorsing and upholding traditional conceptions of femininity. Central to the ideological project of these rape-revenge narratives was the articulation of various rape myths – for example, that rapists are insane; that when a woman says 'no' she really means 'yes'; that the rapist is inherently different from the average male; that 'bad' girls are 'asking for it'; that most rapists are black. As I have suggested, in films such as *The Birth of a Nation*, the myth of the black male rapist functioned to construct rape as a fate worse than death (insofar as it suggested that it was better to die than be despoiled) and, thus, to uphold the myth of white womanhood. The equation of rape with death in films such as *Birth*, *Blossoms*, *Rancho Notorious* and *The Virgin Spring* also contributed to making rape, quite literally, unspeakable, while in films such as *Johnny Belinda* and *Outrage* its manifestation in physical or psychical symptoms put the articulation and interpretation of rape firmly into the hands of the male doctor. Finally, in constructing rape as not only equivalent to, but as frequently resulting in, death, these films worked to deny the possibility of a female avenger (elsewhere, as I have suggested, this possibility was denied by the displacement and/or punishment of female revenge). In the 1970s, however, feminists such as Susan Griffin, Susan Brownmiller and Robin Morgan began to challenge the male definitions of rape and gender inscribed in these rape myths. In the process, they contributed not only to making rape speakable but to the construction of the female avenger herself.[40] As Carol Clover argues, one of feminism's main donations to popular culture is 'the image of the angry woman – a woman so angry that she can be imagined as a credible perpetrator … of the kind of violence on which … the status of full protagonist rests'.[41] The way in which subsequent deployments of the rape-revenge structure have attempted to articulate and make sense of these discourses, and of feminist discourses in general, will be the subject of the following chapters.

Notes

1 Sandy Flitterman-Lewis, 'The Blossom and the Bole: Narrative and Visual Spectacle in Early Film Melodrama', *Cinema Journal*, 33:3 (Spring 1994), 3–15 (p. 11).

2 Julia Lesage, 'Artful Racism, Artful Rape: Griffith's *Broken Blossoms*', in *Jump Cut: Hollywood, Politics and Counter Cinema*, ed. by Peter Steven (Toronto: Between the Lines, 1985), pp. 247–68.

3 According to Richard Schickel, the visual power of the closet scene is such that Griffith was said to have exclaimed after Gish's performance, 'My God, why didn't you warn me you were going to do that?'. Richard Schickel, *D. W. Griffith and the Birth of Film* (London: Pavilion, 1984), p. 392.

4 I include *Blackmail* as an example of a silent film since, while it was later partly reshot and dubbed to make it a sound film, it was originally made as a silent.

5 Richard Dyer, 'A White Star', *Sight and Sound*, 3:8 (August 1993), 22–4 (p. 24).

6 According to Gish in her introduction to a television broadcast of the film, the exhibitors disliked the original 'unhappy' ending and it was consequently replaced with a 'happy' ending in which Gish's estranged husband returns and they declare their love for each other.

7 *Frenzy*, for example, features the rape and murder of several women, while the bird attack in *The Birds* has been described by Pam Cook as a 'symbolic "rape"'. Pam Cook, 'Authorship and Cinema', in *The Cinema Book*, ed. by Pam Cook (London: BFI, 1985), pp. 114–206 (p. 128).

8 Schickel, *D. W. Griffith*, p. 233.

9 Cook, 'Authorship and Cinema', p. 127.

10 Selim Eyüboglu, 'The Authorial Text and Postmodernism: Hitchcock's *Blackmail*', *Screen*, 32:1 (Spring 1991), 58–78 (p. 73).

11 Ibid., p. 73.

12 Nancy E. McGlen and Karen O'Connor, *Women's Rights: The Struggle for Equality in the Nineteenth and Twentieth Centuries* (New York: Praeger, 1983), p. 20.

13 Molly Haskell, *From Reverence to Rape: The Treatment of Women in the Movies* (London: New English Library, 1975), p. 44.

14 Ibid., p. 44.

15 Molly Haskell argues that the flapper was nevertheless an ambiguous figure, 'a woman torn ... between Old World propriety and the new morality' (Ibid., p. 81), between the asexual virgin and the emancipated new woman. This ambiguity is articulated, in particular, through the outfit Alice changes into – a ballerina's tutu. As Richard Dyer has argued: 'The Romantic ballet constructed a translucent, incorporeal image. Yet the ballerina was also always a flesh and blood woman showing her legs'. Richard Dyer, *White* (London: Routledge, 1997), p. 131.

16 Alfred Hitchcock, 'Direction', in *Focus on Hitchcock*, ed. by Albert J. LaValley (New Jersey: Prentice-Hall, 1972), pp. 32–9 (p. 33).

17 Jackie Byars, *All That Hollywood Allows: Re-reading Gender in 1950s Melodrama* (London: Routledge, 1991), p. 79.

18 *Doña Barbara* (Fernando de Fuentes, 1943) represents a particularly interesting example of this combination. Unfortunately, as a Mexican film, it is outside the scope of this book.

19 Mary Ann Doane, 'The "Woman's Film": Possession and Address', in *Re-Vision: Essays in Feminist Film Criticism*, ed. by Mary Ann Doane, Patricia Mellencamp and Linda Williams (Los Angeles: American Film Institute, 1984), pp. 67–82 (p. 76).

20 Ibid., p. 74.

21 It is worth mentioning here the similarities with another melodrama of the period, *Now Voyager* (Irving Rapper, 1942). Like Belinda, Charlotte Vale (Bette Davis) is an unloved 'ugly duckling' transformed both physically and psychically by a doctor, the famous psychiatrist Doctor Jacquith (Claude Rains).

22 Pam Cook, 'Outrage', in *Queen of the 'B's: Ida Lupino Behind the Camera*, ed. by Annette Kuhn (Trowbridge: Flicks Books, 1995), pp. 57–72 (p. 60).

23 Ibid., p. 60.

24 Ibid., p. 66.

25 Ibid., p. 66.

26 That Ann needs to be 'cured' is further underlined by the fact that at her trial for assaulting Frank, a man she believes is going to rape her, it is recommended that she undergo psychiatric treatment for the period of

one year. Ann's transformation, unlike the physical transformation that occurs in *Johnny Belinda*, is, therefore, largely psychical.

27 Cook, '*Outrage*', p. 62.

28 Ibid., p. 61.

29 Ibid., p. 61.

30 Despite being a Swedish film, I include a discussion of *The Virgin Spring* here because of its huge influence on subsequent deployments of the rape-revenge structure. The film, for example, provided the inspiration for one of the first, post-1970s articulations of the structure, *Last House on the Left* (Wes Craven, 1972).

31 See, for example, Otto Preminger's *Laura* (1944) and Hitchcock's *Marnie* (1964).

32 This is suggestive of a further similarity with *The Accused*, in which the legal case also rested on a rare legal precedent (criminal solicitation).

33 Richard Lippe, '*Anatomy of a Murder*', in *International Dictionary of Films and Filmmakers*, ed. by Nicholas Thomas, 2nd edn, 5 vols (Chicago: St James Press, 1990), Volume I, 38–40 (p. 40).

34 For example, the Kinsey Report on male sexuality was published in 1948, with the report on female sexuality following in 1953. *Playboy* magazine also appeared for the first time in 1953. It was ten years, however, before the first feminist investigation into femininity and female sexuality was published – Betty Friedan's, *The Feminine Mystique* (1963). For an extremely interesting discussion of the way in which the discourses about sexuality circulating in the 1950s were embodied in the star persona of Marilyn Monroe, see: Richard Dyer, *Heavenly Bodies: Film Stars and Society* (Basingstoke: Macmillan, 1987).

35 As I have pointed out in my discussion of *Broken Blossoms* above, however, the characterization of Burrows as rapist similarly relies on comparing his violence and womanizing unfavourably with the Yellow Man's gentleness and chastity.

36 It is worth noting here, as Robin Wood does in his analysis of *The Virgin Spring*, that 'goats are traditionally symbolic of lust, and [are] used as such in association with the goatherds'. Robin Wood, *Ingmar Bergman* (London: Studio Vista, 1969), p. 102.

37 For example, in *The Virgin Spring*, while Töre (Max von Sydow) atones for his revenge by promising to build a church on the spot where his daughter was raped and murdered, he is also rewarded by the miraculous appearance of the virgin spring.

38 In *Anatomy of a Murder*, Lieutenant Manion is also brought to trial for his act of revenge, but, despite the irresistible impulse plea, his behaviour is explained solely in terms of his wife's rape and 'normal' masculine behaviour.

39 Robin Morgan, 'Theory and Practice: Pornography and Rape', in *Take*

Back The Night: Women on Pornography, ed. by Laura Lederer (New York: William Morrow, 1980), pp. 134–40 (p. 135). First published in Robin Morgan, *Going Too Far: The Personal Chronicle of a Feminist* (1977).

40 Susan Griffin, 'Rape: The All American Crime' (1970) reprinted as 'The Politics of Rape' in Susan Griffin, *Made From This Earth: Selections from her Writing, 1967–1982* (London: The Women's Press, 1982); Susan Brownmiller, *Against Our Will: Men, Women and Rape*, 2nd edn (Harmondsworth: Penguin, 1976); Morgan, 'Theory and Practice'.

41 Carol Clover, *Men, Women and Chainsaws: Gender in the Modern Horror Film* (London: BFI, 1992), p. 17.

Part III

Feminism

Chapter 4

Popular film/popular feminism: the critical reception of the rape-revenge film

'The issues surrounding the film are feminist. But the film itself is not.' Thus argued Callie Khouri, writer of *Thelma and Louise*.[1] Despite Khouri's claims, the critical reception of the film, nevertheless, centred quite explicitly on assessing the film's status as a feminist text, therefore suggesting that it is not, in fact, possible to separate the textual ('the film itself') from the extra-textual ('the issues surrounding the film'). Indeed, as Richard Dyer's work on film stars illustrates, extratextual material such as star personas, reviews and publicity material play an important part in the construction of any particular text's meanings, particularly its dominant or preferred meanings.[2] Traditionally, feminist analyses of mainstream texts have read against the grain of these dominant or preferred meanings in order to produce resistant feminist readings. Here, however, I want to read *with* the grain of these dominant meanings as they are inscribed in reviews of *The Accused* and *Thelma and Louise* in order to explore the ways in which they might produce popular, common-sense understandings of feminism. Of course, that both films were the subject of fierce controversy and debate would appear to militate against a reading of the reviews as constitutive of a set of dominant meanings. What I want to argue, however, is that the controversy both films engendered and which was played out in reviews of the films can be seen as symptomatic of the wider struggle over meanings that characterized the hegemonic project of the New Right during the 1980s and early 1990s. Within this context, therefore, the dominant meanings the reviews produced were always, in a sense, negotiated. Thus, against accepted understandings of this period as one in which feminism was simply rejected or over (as evidenced by the prevalence of the terms 'post-feminism' and 'backlash'), I will argue that feminism instead underwent a process of redefinition and negotiation; that this process was, in fact, a *part of* the wider hegemonic project of the New Right; and, that the meanings the reviews of *The Accused* and *Thelma and Louise* constructed were particularly illustrative of these processes.

The Accused

While the controversy surrounding the release of *The Accused* in 1988 circulated around its depiction of perhaps the quintessential feminist issue, and while the language and ideas voiced in reviews were clearly borrowed from feminism, the debate about rape the film engendered was not explicitly cast in terms of feminism (only six of the twenty-five reviews I surveyed directly referred to feminism). Furthermore, although almost half the reviews referred to the controversy the film had engendered, they actually revealed a remarkable consensus and consistency in their assessments of the film, suggesting that what was at stake here was the production of a set of dominant or preferred meanings. What I want to explore, then, in my analysis of reviews of *The Accused* is the way in which the meanings of feminism they produced can be read as constituted by, and constitutive of, the wider hegemonic project of Thatcherism and Reaganism.

The reviews clearly relied on and articulated feminist discourses of rape. However, these discourses were rarely explicitly identified as feminist or contextualized in terms of a broader feminist politics. Thus, almost all the reviews in one form or another quoted from the pioneering work on rape undertaken by radical feminists such as Susan Griffin, Robin Morgan and Susan Brownmiller in the 1970s.[3] This work centred largely on attacking various rape myths and on a definition of rape as being about power or violence rather than sex. Sean French's claim that, 'contrary to the myth peddled in films like "Straw Dogs"', *The Accused* represents rape as 'an act of deliberate violence and violation that no victim would ever ask for or enjoy', was paradigmatic of the way in which reviews of the film tended to reproduce almost verbatim these central tenets of feminist thinking on rape.[4] Virtually all the reviews, for example, commented on the way in which the film exploded the myth that victims of rape are 'asking for it' or that when a woman says no she really means yes. Thus, Sue Heal, writing in *Today*, suggested that the film was 'a powerful de-bunking of the adage that when a woman says No she usually means Maybe', claiming that the rape scene 'blasted out of the water any myths that [Sarah] got what she deserved'.[5] Similarly, Roger Ebert of the *Chicago Sun-Times* claimed that 'the argument of the movie is that although a young woman may act improperly … she should still have the right to say "no" and be heard'.[6] Some also commented on the way in which the film challenged the idea that men are simply unable to control their sexuality. As Margaret Walters argued in the *Listener*: 'The rapists clearly aren't driven by uncontrollable lust (that surprisingly insistent excuse for brutality) they're *angry*. Sarah's blatant sexiness is a challenge, which they can only extinguish by humiliating and hurting her.'[7] Finally, of the reviews that offered a definition of rape, half, like Walters, defined it as about power or violence rather than sex, while the other half categorized it as spectator sport committed by men for men. John Marriott of the *Daily Mail*, for example, argued that the film successfully conveyed 'the essence of rape as an act of violence',[8] while Roger Ebert went so far as to suggest that the film revealed even 'verbal sexual harassment' to be 'a form of violence'.[9] Thelma Agnew, on the other hand, claimed that the film represented rape as 'a macho exercise, a display by men for men'.[10]

What I want to argue, then, is that while the language of feminism is clearly in evidence in these reviews, it is a language that has been divorced from the politics from which it originated, not least because the language and ideas used here are rarely attributed to feminism or identified as specifically feminist. Moreover, despite the definition of rape as a matter of violence and power rather than sex, the reviews show little concern for the wider power relations that underpin and make rape possible. Thus, while Suzanne Moore, in one of the few reviews to explicitly identify the film as feminist, claimed that *the film* 'makes the smugness of the "post" in post-feminism look decidedly questionable, if not downright stupid', *the reviews* of the film can actually be read as constructing an understanding of post-feminism, one that is rather different from that which Moore employs here.[11] In other words, while the way in which the reviews depoliticize feminism is suggestive of a departure from traditional feminism and, thus, of *post*-feminism, their obvious *reliance* on feminism nevertheless counters Moore's understanding of the term post-feminism as implying that feminism is somehow over. Indeed, the absence of debate about the film's status as a feminist text suggests not so much that feminism is no longer an issue – as we have seen it clearly was, even if it was not identified as such – or even, in the words of Janice Winship, 'that the feminist case has been won', but rather 'that it goes without saying that there is a case'.[12] Consequently, reviews of *The Accused* construct an understanding of post-feminism that refers not to a break with feminism, but to the way in which, as Winship suggests, the 'boundaries between feminists and non-feminists have become fuzzy'.[13] Moreover, according to Winship, this is largely due to the way in which 'with the "success" of feminism some feminist ideas no longer have an oppositional charge but have become part of many people's, not just a minority's, common sense'.[14] This understanding of post-feminism as a depoliticized and popularized version of feminism is very much in evidence in reviews of *The Accused*.

The absence of debate about the film's politics and the common-sense meanings it engendered may also be attributed to the film's perceived 'transparency'. In other words, almost all the reviews referred to the film's apparent realism, to its pertinence to 'real life'. Consequently the meanings of the film were understood as unmediated reflections of popular consciousness, rather than as specifically political constructions, and were thus presented as self-evident or common sense. This process is particularly apparent in Hilary Bonner's discussion of the film.[15] Opening her review with the observation that opinions about the film are deeply divided, she continued by pointing out that 'some who see it say the girl was asking for trouble – and dismiss it as a feminist diatribe against men'.[16] Her next sentence (and, indeed, the rest of the review) suggests, however, that the film was simply realistic rather than specifically feminist: 'But Jodie Foster was so affected by merely acting the rape that she says: "I blacked out, just as if it was for real."'[17] In many of the reviews, references to the film's realism simply took the form of noting that the film was inspired by a real incident or of a reference to the rape statistics quoted at the end of the film. Elsewhere, realism was identified as a quality of the film itself. Iain Johnstone writing in the *Sunday Times*, for example, was among those who felt that the rape scene was 'vigorously real', while Nigel Andrews of the *Financial Times* and Adam Mars-Jones of the *Independent* both commented on the film's documentary style.[18] Others referred more generally to the film's 'uncompromising honesty',[19] 'undoubted sincerity',[20] or 'honest, low-key intensity'.[21] More specifically, Dorothy Wade suggested that the film was 'a fair and honest attempt to convey the grim reality of rape',[22] and Stephanie Calman claimed it to be 'a truthful film about violence against women'.[23] Critics also frequently referred to events in the lives of the film's stars in order to point up its realism. Kelly McGillis's much-publicized admission of her own rape six years earlier was most often cited in this respect, although John Hinckley's pathological obsession with Jodie Foster also became an issue. Perhaps the most interesting example of this process is the way in which the headline of the *Today* review – 'This is My Revenge Against the Animals Who Raped Me' – used McGillis's rape to construct the film as a real-life rape-revenge story.[24]

Clearly, this blurring of fiction and reality is likely to be as much a product of the film's publicity machine as of the reviews themselves. Certainly, it is a line that was toed by the film's stars, as witness Foster's aforementioned claim: 'I blacked out, just as if it was for real'.[25] What I want to suggest is that this emphasis on the film's realism, on its apparently transparent and unproblematic reflection of social reality, functioned to preclude the need for further questioning of (the representation of) that reality or the politics it articulated. This, in turn, worked to support the preferred meanings that the film's publicity put into circulation, meanings that actually had little to do with feminism (but which can perhaps be seen as a product of the way in which feminist characterizations of rape as a symbolic expression of power have tended to open it up to metaphorical appropriations). References to John Hinckley, for example, functioned to equate the rape of Jodie Foster in the film with Hinckley's assassination attempt on President Reagan seven years earlier. This had the effect of constructing rape not simply as a crime against women, but as part of a wider threat to the social and political order.

The film's production notes and video jacket are illustrative of these processes.[26] The video's front cover, for example, reproduces the film's publicity poster and features close-ups of Foster's and McGillis's faces shot in grainy black and white, a traditional signifier of realism. The text on the back cover, however, quite clearly demonstrates that the real issues that the film will deal with are not concerned with feminism or even rape. Instead it asks:

> What are the limits of justice? Of social responsibility? The Accused takes a powerful and thought-provoking look at human nature and

individual moral conscience, and a judicial process that treats the victim like a criminal.

Jodie Foster gives a critically-acclaimed performance as the hard-living, fiercely independent Sarah Tobias, who is gang raped in the back of a neighbourhood bar. But that is only the beginning of her ordeal. Now Sarah finds herself battling the legal system, not once but twice, as she and her attorney (Kelly McGillis) go after both her attackers and the onlookers whose cheering fuelled and encouraged the assault.

Similarly, the film's production notes ask: 'What is the responsibility of someone who witnesses a violent crime?'

> Sarah Tobias is assaulted and nobody helps her. When she cries for justice, nobody hears her. Except one lawyer. Together, Sarah and Assistant District Attorney Katheryn Murphy bring to trial the people as dangerous as the men who committed the crime – the witnesses who let it happen.[27]

This is clearly not the language of feminism. Rather it is the language of popular morality that emerged in both Britain and the USA during the Thatcher and Reagan administrations of the 1980s and that was part of the broader political agenda of the New Right. As Elizabeth Traube observes, this agenda involved 'shaping a style of right-wing populism designed to appeal to popular resentment of bureaucratic authority'.[28] This resentment was channelled, in particular, into a critique of liberal institutions such as the criminal justice system, which, as Jane Feuer points out, was seen as placing 'the rights of criminals above the rights of victims'.[29] This critique was, moreover, part of wider attacks on the liberalism and permissiveness of the 1960s and 1970s, attacks that functioned to invoke fears of moral breakdown, of crime and delinquency, in order to assert the need for individual morality and responsibility. Stuart Hall's work on Thatcherism provides a succinct summary of these processes:

> The 'cry from below' for the restoration of moral regulation took, first, the immediate symptoms of disturbance – rising crime, delinquency, moral permissiveness – and constructed them, with the help of organized grassroots ideological forces, into the scenario of a general 'crisis of the moral order'. In the later phases, these were connotatively linked with the more politicized threats, to compose a picture of a social order on the brink of moral collapse, its enemies proliferating 'within and without'. This is 'the crisis' experienced at the popular level in the universal, depoliticized, experiential language of popular morality.[30]

This language was, thus, also the language of traditional common sense, which, according to Hall, is 'a massively conservative force, penetrated thoroughly ... by religious notions of good and evil, by fixed conceptions of the unchanging and unchangeable character of human nature, and by ideas of retributive justice'.[31] As we have seen, these are also the themes that *The Accused's* publicity material promoted.

What I want to argue, then, is that in taking up the preferred meanings suggested by the film's publicity, reviews of *The Accused* frequently worked to construct the representation of rape in the film not as a specifically feminist issue, or even as an issue about gender, but as a matter of popular morality, of depoliticized common sense. Indeed, this is hardly surprising, given the ease with which the issues feminist discourses of rape have put into circulation can slide into questions of morality and responsibility – is the victim 'asking for it'?; do men have a responsibility to control their sexuality? This process became particularly apparent in Dorothy Wade's review of the film, which, despite being unusual in that it devoted a significant amount of space to the views of a feminist social worker, ultimately downplayed the specificity of rape and its significance in terms of feminism. Discussing our tendency to turn a blind eye to crime, she claimed that 'the best thing about *The Accused* is the spotlight it turns on these passive roles that any of us may play. When we hear screams in the street at night and decide to do nothing, how much responsibility do we bear if a crime, *perhaps a rape*, is committed?'[32] Adam Mars-Jones made a similar point, arguing that the film was 'only secondarily about rape', the real issue being 'the extent of a citizen's responsibility'.[33] These understandings of the film's representation of rape clearly echo those put into circulation by the film's publicity. The production notes, for example, repeatedly describe Sarah's ordeal not as a rape but as an 'assault' or a 'violent crime'.[34] Thus the film is constructed as dealing with moral, rather than specifically feminist issues, as the film's screenwriter, Tom Topor, observes in the production notes: 'The moral questions that this film raises could have been achieved by a different violent crime, a suicide or robbery.'[35] These sentiments were reproduced almost verbatim in Tom Hutchinson's review, which also glossed over the gender politics specific to rape, identifying it instead as 'a *moral* concern' and claiming that the film 'touches a disturbing nerve in *both men and women* – that of a common humanity. Or lack of it'.[36] Likewise,

Stephanie Calman credited the film with reopening 'the debate about society's collective responsibility for crime',[37] and Victoria Mather of the *Daily Telegraph* proposed that the film was an indictment of a society 'that is all too guilty of not "getting involved"'.[38] The emphasis of US reviews was similar. Rita Kempley of the *Washington Post*, for example, argued that 'Sarah's lack of good sense isn't on trial here, nor for that matter is male aggression. "The Accused" addresses the accountability of the bystander'.[39] Roger Ebert of the *Chicago Sun-Times* claimed that the responsibility of bystanders in a rape case 'may be the most important message this movie has to offer'.[40] Indeed, Ebert even went so far as to suggest that Sarah too must 'start taking responsibility for herself'.[41] Thus, the reviews can be read as effecting a kind of ideological slippage whereby a feminist politics of rape is transformed into a Reaganite politics of individual morality and responsibility. As I will illustrate in chapters 6 and 7, this slippage between feminism and the politics of the New Right is paradigmatic of articulations of the rape-revenge structure in the late 1980s and 1990s.

That the reviews constructed a discursive context understandable in terms of right-wing populism rather than feminism is further evidenced in the way in which they tended to downplay both the relationship and class differences between Sarah and Katheryn, thus emphasizing a Reaganite ideology of individualism and anti-elitism over the collective politics of feminism. Very few reviews, for example, referred to the different class backgrounds of the two female leads (the most decisive comment appeared, unsurprisingly, in *Marxism Today*), while those reviews that referred to the relationship between the two women tended to downplay any suggestions of solidarity between them.[42] Suzanne Moore argued that the film 'refuses the easy option of setting up a false sisterhood' between Katheryn and Sarah;[43] Stephanie Calman claimed that their relationship is not 'sentimentalized';[44] and Beatrix Campbell suggested that the film illustrated 'the difficulty of solidarity'.[45] What I think the representation of Katheryn and Sarah and their relationship does articulate, however, is the dialogue between popular understandings of the 1960s and the 1980s, between popular conceptions of collective political movements such as feminism and the politics of Reaganism. Sarah, for example, is clearly constructed as representative of the 1960s. In other words, she is an independent, sexually liberated hippy who smokes marijuana, has crystals in her car, practices astrology and lives in a trailer park. Katheryn, on the other hand, is a power-dressing, yuppie career woman. Not only was this dialogue taken up and played out in more general terms in reviews of the film, it was, as David Glover and Cora Kaplan have pointed out in their discussion of 1980s male crime fiction, 'part of a general struggle in the eighties as to what should constitute the public memory of popular politics'.[46] As Glover and Kaplan go on to argue:

> Though searching for an objective truth about this past against which to measure present deformations is no longer a viable political or theoretical project, thinking politically and historically about the many versions of it now in circulation certainly is.[47]

In the following section I want to use an analysis of reviews of *Thelma and Louise* to illuminate and expand on this argument.

Thelma and Louise

While the relationship of Katheryn and Sarah in *The Accused* was seen as representing 'the difficulty of solidarity', there was no such equivocation about the relationship between the two female protagonists in *Thelma and Louise* – the film was almost universally categorized as a female buddy movie. Thus, unlike the controversy surrounding *The Accused*, the debates that circulated around *Thelma and Louise* tended to gloss over the film's representation of rape in favour of an emphasis on the women's relationship and their revenge. Moreover, the reviews explicitly set out to address the question of the extent to which this depiction of female violence and sisterhood could be seen as an articulation of a feminist politics. The question was, nevertheless, a contentious one. As Sharon Willis observes:

> Within this framework, objections emerging from feminist and anti-feminist quarters took several forms. A range of critics took issue with the film's depiction of men. In a rhetoric clearly borrowed from feminism, but crudely reduced, they found the film guilty of male-bashing.[48]

As a result, the question of the film's status as a feminist text tended to be posed in one of two ways: either in terms of popular conceptions of feminism, as in Charles Bremner's 'Is *Thelma and Louise* a male-bashing movie?',[49] or in terms of popular conceptions of film, as in Joan Smith's 'Can *Thelma and Louise* be billed a feminist tub-thump, the most right-on of road movies, or is it merely a masculine revenge fantasy whose buddies happen to be female?'[50] The latter question, then, was not posed in terms of feminism *per se*, but in filmic terms. In other words, what was at stake here was the extent to which male-defined paradigms of filmmaking such as the road movie or buddy film were successfully appropriated for feminism.

Those that found the film not to be feminist tended to take the latter approach, appearing more interested in the filmic rather than social context of the film. Particularly indicative of this type of review was the way in which many of the critics took a distinctly *auteurist* approach to the film, commenting not only on Scott's visual style but placing *Thelma and Louise* in the context of the rest of Scott's *oeuvre*. More significantly, however, they also assessed the film against an implied but never defined conception of what constitutes a political or feminist film; namely, seriousness and realism combined with a rejection of the generic, structural and commercial constraints of Hollywood. Thus, the film was frequently criticized for merely 'copying male ways of doing things', for failing to depart from patriarchal paradigms, both in terms of the women's behaviour and particularly in terms of the film's use of Hollywood genre conventions.[51] For such critics, then, the film was a straight copy of the male road/buddy movie, which 'simply spruces up a well-worn genre, placing repressed females where you expect macho males',[52] and in which 'it is doubtful whether they play any roles that haven't been explored by men in buddy pictures'.[53] What appeared to be at stake in such responses to the film was a conception of feminism as about difference rather than sameness, both in terms of male and female behaviour and the representation of that behaviour and in terms of filmmaking itself. Therefore, those that found the film not to be feminist, such as the *Guardian's* Joan Smith, argued that neither violence nor revenge films were the preserve of females or feminism and that the film was 'little more than a masculine revenge fantasy in which the gender of the leading characters has been switched'.[54]

Yet, a favourite criticism of *Thelma and Louise* was also to liken it to what is perhaps one of the most feminine of genres, the fairy-tale. Adam Mars-Jones of the *Independent* claimed that 'this is fairytale territory, with a little social comment thrown in, and the logic is not strong'.[55] Iain Johnstone of the *Sunday Times* suggested that 'it's about as newsworthy as Goldilocks and slightly more so than Peter

Pan'.[56] So, while the film's similarities with the road/buddy movie suggested that the film was too masculine to be taken seriously as a feminist statement, the comparison with fairy-tales and their perceived lack of logic or social importance suggested, somewhat contradictorily, that the film was also too feminine to be feminist. Furthermore, fairy-tales were invoked to suggest that the film was not feminist because it did not deal with real, everyday life. As Lynda Hart points out: 'The *Time* cover story sought out feminist scholars to reassure readers that the film was "not ... a cultural representation but ... a fairy tale"'.[57] This issue of the film's lack of verisimilitude was also taken up by several British critics. While Joan Smith of the *Guardian* argued fairly generally that 'the dilemmas faced by the women in the film have ... little to do with real life',[58] many critics took particular exception to what they saw as Thelma's (Geena Davis) irrational and unrealistic behaviour in consenting to sleep with a perfect stranger such as J. D. (Brad Pitt) so soon after having been brutally sexually assaulted.[59]

Thus, in an attempt to circumvent the feminist label, *Thelma and Louise* was categorized both as a straightforward copy of the male road/buddy movie and as an unrealistic fairy-tale. However, it was also argued that the film could not be taken seriously as a feminist statement because it was simply a comedy. For Adam Mars-Jones, then, the film was merely a 'genial, slightly over-extended comedy' that was 'very far from hard-line'.[60] For Shaun Usher of the *Daily Mail* it was 'too commercial, not to mention funny and exciting, for a mere sermon'.[61] The suggestion here, therefore, is that for the film to be taken as a genuine piece of feminist political filmmaking it would not only have to be serious, it would also have to be 'hard-line' or a 'sermon', in other words, didactic.

While those that argued that the film was not feminist because it was no different from male paradigms, those that *did* take the film's feminism seriously responded by arguing that the film was feminist precisely *because* it was different. In other words, arguing that the film turned the conventions of the male buddy movie 'neatly on their head',[62] such critics claimed that this was more than a simple inversion of roles since the variations were made very clear. For example, Hugo Davenport argued that 'the contrast with the competitive psychology of male friendship in buddie-movies is neatly pointed up when, halfway through, Louise weakens and Thelma grows stronger',[63] while Charles Bremner suggested that Thelma and

Louise (Susan Sarandon) are different because they 'operate by female logic, independent of men'.[64] Furthermore, against those that claimed the film was not feminist because it was unrealistic and/or failed to deal with the problems faced by women in the real world, such reviews argued that, despite the sensational aspects of the film's depiction of violence, it dealt with 'real, everyday sexual politics'.[65] For example, Mick Brown pointed out that Thelma and Louise's violence serves to exact revenge 'on behalf of womankind for years of sexual harassment',[66] while Manohla Dargis argued that the film's depiction of male violence was not simplified but 'pointedly woven right into the fabric of everyday life in the form of crummy jobs, oppressive marriages, injurious laws, and ubiquitous police'.[67]

Those that found the film to be feminist also often referred to its impact on the extradiegetic world. For example, it was frequently pointed out that the film's reversal of gender roles functioned to consign men 'to the parts that Hollywood usually leaves for women',[68] while the male stereotyping answered the way in which 'women are routinely stereotyped in films every week of the year'.[69] Furthermore, Mick Brown in the Daily Telegraph argued that 'it is a tribute to the skill of Thelma and Louise that it should have provoked so much debate while remaining so funny, charming and utterly devoid of any heavy-handed polemic'.[70] Hugo Davenport, also in the Telegraph, claimed that 'the film is exciting, emotional, funny, beautifully acted, even liberating, and it never allows the drag factor of feminist dogma to slow it down'.[71] These latter comments, however, while suggesting that the film articulated a form of popular feminism, shared with reviews that found the film not to be feminist the assumption that traditional feminism was didactic, dogmatic and polemical.

Thus, despite the debate over Thelma and Louise's status as a feminist text, the conceptions of feminism on which this debate rested proved to be remarkably similar. For example, both sides of the debate constructed a version of feminism that emphasized 'women's essential difference from men'.[72] They also relied on an understanding of feminist culture as that which resists 'the male-stream definitions of art and culture'.[73] Both, moreover, saw feminism as focusing on 'the reality of women's experiences'[74] and on 'material instances of women's subordination' rather than on theoretical issues.[75] Finally, they frequently constructed feminists as 'extremist',[76] or as 'terrorists, trading in dogma',[77] who saw men as 'the enemy'.[78] While

Thelma and Louise itself may not articulate any identifiable branch of academic/theoretical or movement/political feminism, the critical responses to the film, whether they found it feminist or not, appeared to rely for their assessments on the language of the radical feminism of the early 1970s. All the quotes cited above, for example, are taken from discussions of radical feminism. It is not insignificant that since this branch of feminism eschewed theoretical interventions in favour of direct action and campaigning that it was most ripe for bastardization and popularization, becoming part of the discourse of everyday life. As Imelda Whelehan points out: 'Most people if asked to define feminism today would produce a definition which vaguely resembles the radical feminist agenda.'[79]

In relying on a definition of feminism that 'vaguely resembles the radical feminist agenda', the press were able to align what they perceived to be the film's male-bashing with feminism, while simultaneously denouncing it for being too extreme or for not being extreme enough. Certainly, *Thelma and Louise* was widely criticized for its perceived male-bashing. Joan Smith of the *Guardian*, for example, invoked a comparison between the film and Valerie Solanis's SCUM (Society for Cutting Up Men) Manifesto,[80] while John Leo's now infamous *US News and World Report* review suggested that the film's anti-male bias constituted a fascist form of feminism.[81] When, however, such man-hating was seen to be compromised by the women's heterosexuality or the inclusion of 'nice' men, the film's feminism was also considered to be compromised. Thus 'Daws' in *Variety* argued that the film is not about 'women vs. men' (that is, feminism) because the women 'can't seem to stay away from men'.[82] In another register, however, a popular version of radical feminism was invoked to support the film's status as a feminist text. For example, Manohla Dargis interpreted Thelma and Louise's trajectory through the narrative as a consciousness-raising experience that leads them to a brief lesbian encounter (their final kiss), female solidarity (their clasped hands) and separatism (their drive into the abyss).[83]

Somewhat contradictorily, then, in reviews of *Thelma and Louise* a popular version of 1970s feminism was invoked both to assert and deny the film's status as a feminist text. What I want to propose is that this simultaneous assertion and denial of the film's feminism, combined with the way that individual reviews frequently both depended on, and disavowed, the tenets of 1970s feminism, suggests that what was as stake here was not an authentic feminist politics, but a negotiated version of 1970s feminism in which sisterhood and heterosexuality, angry women and nice men could coexist. Indeed, that the film relies on, and constructs, a popular version of feminism is actually implicit in Dargis's claim that 'Thelma and Louise have *reinvented* sisterhood for the *American screen*'.[84] What is more interesting, however, is the way in which, in her *Village Voice* review of the film, she situates the production of this popular version of feminism within the specific historical and political context of the 1980s. Here Dargis asks:

> What kind of feminism are we talking about anyway? *The Second Sex*? bell hooks? Andrea Dworkin? Susie Bright? Granted, *Thelma and Louise* sells a kind of feminism *brut*, inarticulate and inchoate. Yet after more than 10 years of Reagan, Bush, and the murky chimera of post-feminism how many can still speak the language of liberation with any assurance? ... If feminism is ever to be more than a historical artifact or lost utopia, it not only has to be reclaimed, it must be reinvented.[85]

These are, of course, rhetorical questions, to which, therefore, it is assumed we already know the answers. Dargis's argument reproduces the standard feminist understanding of the 1980s and the politics of the New Right as inaugurating a backlash against feminism, and of post-feminism as a period in which feminism is somehow over. The reinvention of feminism we find in films such as *Thelma and Louise* is consequently understood as representing a response to this backlash against feminism and as a way of countering 'the murky chimera of post-feminism'.[86] Against these accepted understandings of the relationship between feminism and the New Right as essentially antagonistic and mutually exclusive, I want to argue that the popular redefinition or negotiation of feminism we find in films such as *Thelma and Louise* and *The Accused* and in the discourses surrounding them, was, in fact, a part of the wider hegemonic project of the New Right and that it is in this context that the term post-feminism is best understood.

Reviews of *The Accused*, then, simultaneously invoke *and* suppress feminism. They invoke a common-sense, popular feminism and suppress a collective, political feminism. The reviews can thus be read as part of the struggle which took place in the 1980s to (re)define and appropriate the popular meanings of the politics of the 1960s and 1970s. As David Glover and Cora Kaplan have argued:

> Today the fate of the sixties-within-the-eighties is a notoriously important issue in the struggle for cultural and political meaning ... The hegemony of the New Right has involved a sustained attempt to monopolize the complex terrain of the popular, and in particular to drastically overhaul the social significance of the sixties.[87]

The production of common-sense meanings is a vital aspect of this project. According to Gramsci, common sense 'holds together a specific social group, it influences moral conduct and the direction of the will'.[88] Thus, as Stuart Hall has observed: 'To a significant extent, Thatcherism is about the remaking of common sense: its aim is to become the "common sense of the age".'[89] It is, moreover, within the field of popular culture that the representation of common sense, of the taken-for-granted, finds its clearest articulation. Reviews of *The Accused* and the meanings of feminism they construct must be understood, therefore, within the context of the hegemonic project of Thatcherism and Reaganism. In other words, they view feminist discourses of rape through the lens of the individual populism of the Reagan era and, in so doing, construct a depoliticized, individualized, popular feminism, which is then situated as part of a broader, hegemonic common sense.

Tania Modleski has defined post-feminism as the appropriation of feminist ideas for non-feminist ends and this definition would certainly seem to be applicable to my analysis of the way in which reviews of *The Accused* articulate feminist discourses.[90] Implicit in this definition, however, is the assumption that these discourses then simply become anti-feminist. In other words, post-feminism is understood in terms of the backlash against feminism, which, it has been argued, began to emerge in the late 1980s. While the belief that the 1980s and the patriarchal politics of Thatcher and Reagan helped inaugurate such a backlash is widespread, I think this represents a somewhat simplistic cause-and-effect approach to the relationship between post-feminism and Thatcherism/Reaganism. It also fails to acknowledge the way in which the meanings that circulate around these concepts are rarely fixed, unitary and without contradictions. In some anti-Thatcher discourses, for example, Thatcher became the *object* rather than the originator of a backlash against feminism. In other words, she was constructed as a *product* of feminism and thus of the danger of giving women too much power. As Jane Feuer has argued:

> The eighties are emerging more and more as an incredibly hegemonic period; and yet we are also more and more able to sense contradictions that were played out in the culture ... It is the contradictions that enable us to see what Stuart Hall and others mean when they characterize 'hegemony' as a struggle over meanings, a process that is always ongoing even when (as during the mid-eighties) it seems as if one side has won a decisive victory. This is why it is important to look at the meanings under discussion as always being contested.[91]

In other words, although ideas about post-feminism have been produced and constructed within the context of Reaganism and Thatcherism and must be understood within this context, this does not mean that they simply reflect these ideologies. What, for example, does it mean when post-feminist icons such as the Spice Girls declare Margaret Thatcher as their heroine or when writer Natasha Walter claims Thatcher as the heroine of the new feminism described in her recent book of that name?[92] Does it mean that post-feminism or new feminism simply endorse or reflect the intricacies of Thatcher's politics or policies? Or does it mean that ideas about post-feminism and new feminism have been formed in the wake of popular understandings and representations of Thatcher and Thatcherism, understandings that have to do with individual female power and strength, the coupling of feminism with femininity ('The Iron *Lady*'/'*Girl* Power'), populism and the break with traditional ideologies that occurred under the New Right. These questions were, in fact, recently the subject of a fierce debate raging around Natasha Walter's book, *The New Feminism*. In a discussion between Walter and Hilary Cottam over whether Thatcher is indeed a heroine of the new feminism, Cottam retorts to Walter:

> In embracing Margaret Thatcher you, like her, have merely substituted the individual for politics. You want to separate the personal from the political, but are we not then left with just an empty form of celebrity feminism facing a political vacuum?[93]

According to Jennifer Wicke, however:

> Things look different ... if the celebrity sphere is not immediately vilified as a realm of ideological ruin or relegated to aberrant or merely

'popular' practices. Rather, we must recognize that the energies of the celebrity imaginary are fueling feminist discourse and political activity as never before.[94]

The debate over Thatcher's status as a feminist icon is, of course, a case in point. As Cottam concludes her case against Walter: 'We must agree to differ and I will celebrate that you have opened this space because there is so much more to be done'.[95] Far from suggesting that feminism is somehow over or past, the struggle over the meanings of feminism apparent both here and in the debates surrounding *The Accused* and *Thelma and Louise* suggests, as Janice Winship has observed, that 'feminism no longer has a simple coherence around a set of easily defined principles ... but instead is a much richer, more diverse and contradictory mix than it ever was in the 1970s'.[96] This is partly due to the way in which, as Julia Hallam points out in her survey of reviews of *Working Girl*, 'feminism as a (contradictory and unfixed) subject position is widely circulating as an interpretative strategy amongst ... journalists'.[97] However, I think it is also to do with the way in which those interpretative strategies have intersected in complex and unexpected ways with the hegemonic project and popular construction of Thatcherism and Reaganism. Suzanne Moore's feminist appropriation of the Katherine Parker (Sigourney Weaver) character in *Working Girl* (Mike Nichols, 1988), for example, could equally be referring to popular constructions of Margaret Thatcher: 'My sympathies were with Katherine – so completely set up as a male fantasy of a ball-breaking career bitch – that it's hard not to fall in love with her.'[98] To view the late 1980s and 1990s as simply a period of backlash against feminism or as a period in which feminism is over is thus to fail to address or understand the complicated and often contradictory ways in which the popular, the political and the critical intersect.

As the controversy surrounding *Thelma and Louise* shows us, a film's politics exists as much in the discourses surrounding it and its impact on the social world as in the formal and thematic content of the text itself. Thus, against Callie Khouri's insistence that 'the issues surrounding the film are feminist. But the film itself is not', I hope to have shown that the issues surrounding the film cannot, in fact, be separated from the film itself.[99] Eleanor J. Bader's *Spare Rib* review of *Thelma and Louise* is revealing in this respect, since her argument that the film's status as a feminist text was problematic because it relied on stereotypes of 'feminists (they all hate men and wish them dead)' seemed to be hopelessly entangled in discourses outside of the film.[100] In other words, it can never be entirely clear whether the equation of feminism and male-bashing is a product of the film itself or of the critical and media discourses surrounding the film. The controversy also demonstrates the way in which feminism is always discursively constructed; is never available in some pure or unmediated form. Therefore, both the reviews that attempted to read the film as an articulation of some authentic feminism and those that attempted to detach the film from its discursive context and shift attention to the film as film missed the point – neither film nor feminism exists in a vacuum. Consequently, their attempts to conclusively evaluate the feminism of the film against some fixed, authentic notion of either feminism or political filmmaking were doomed to failure. Rather, as the reviews themselves illustrate, film is one of the sites on, through and against which the meanings of feminism are produced. In order to fully understand these meanings and the way in which they are produced, we need to read films historically through the discourses surrounding them and to explore the complex ways in which such discourses intersect and negotiate with each other.

Notes

1 Cited in Lizzie Francke, 'Interview with Callie Khouri', *Guardian*, 9 July 1991, p. 17.
2 Richard Dyer, *Stars* (London: BFI, 1979); Richard Dyer, *Heavenly Bodies: Film Stars and Society* (Basingstoke: Macmillan, 1987).
3 Susan Griffin, 'The Politics of Rape', in Susan Griffin, *Made from this Earth: Selections from her Writing, 1967–1982* (London: The Women's Press, 1982), pp. 39–58; Robin Morgan, 'Theory and Practice: Pornography and Rape', in *Take Back The Night: Women on Pornography*, ed. by Laura Lederer (New York: William Morrow, 1980), pp. 134–40; Susan Brownmiller, *Against Our Will: Men, Women and Rape*, 2nd edn (Harmondsworth: Penguin, 1976).
4 Sean French, 'A Flirt with Danger', *Observer*, 19 February 1989, p. 42.
5 Sue Heal, '*The Accused*: Review', *Today*, 17 February 1989, p. 26.
6 Roger Ebert, '*The Accused*: Review', *Chicago Sun-Times*, 14 October 1988.
7 Margaret Walters, 'Silent Witness', *Listener*, CXXI: 3101 (16 February 1989), 32.

8 John Marriott, 'The Film That Puts Men in the Dock', *Daily Mail*, 17 February 1989, p. 30.

9 Ebert, '*The Accused*: Review'.

10 Thelma Agnew, '*The Accused*: Review', *Spare Rib*, 199 (March 1989), 36.

11 Suzanne Moore, 'Asking for It?', *New Statesman and Society*, 17 February 1989, pp. 16–17 (p. 16).

12 Janice Winship, '"A Girl Needs to Get Street-wise": Magazines for the 1980s', *Feminist Review*, 21 (1985), 25–46 (p. 37).

13 Janice Winship, *Inside Women's Magazines* (London: Pandora, 1987), p. 149.

14 Ibid., p. 149.

15 Hilary Bonner, 'Asking For It?: The Provocative Question Raised by Jodie Foster's New Movie', *Daily Mirror*, 10 February 1989, p. 13.

16 Ibid.

17 Ibid. ·

18 Iain Johnstone, '*The Accused*: Review', *Sunday Times*, 4 December 1988, p. 10; Nigel Andrews, 'Bearing the Rape Victim's Cross', *Financial Times*, 16 February 1989, p. 31; Adam Mars-Jones, 'Unmoving Violation', *Independent*, 16 February 1989, p. 15.

19 Victoria Mather, 'Guilty Witnesses to a Violent Crime', *Daily Telegraph*, 16 February 1989, p. 18.

20 Derek Malcolm, 'The Lust Picture Show', *Guardian*, 16 February 1989, p. 21.

21 Iain Johnstone, 'Doing Justice to the Victim', *Sunday Times*, 19 February 1989, p. 7.

22 Dorothy Wade, 'Why this Violence is Justified', *Sunday Times*, 12 February 1989, p. 5.

23 Stephanie Calman, 'Shocking Truth of How Men Turn Beast', *Sunday Express*, 19 February 1989, p. 18.

24 Terry Willows, 'This is My Revenge Against the Animals Who Raped Me', *Today*, 21 October 1988, p. 29.

25 Bonner, 'Asking For It?', p. 13.

26 Clearly, *The Accused's* press book would be a better indicator of the preferred meanings the film's publicity machine attempted to put into circulation. Unfortunately, at the time of writing, there was no copy of the press book available in this country.

27 Paramount Pictures Corporation, 'Production Information for *The Accused*' (1988), p. 1.

28 Elizabeth G. Traube, *Dreaming Identities: Class, Gender, and Generation in 1980s Hollywood Movies* (Oxford: Westview Press, 1992), p. 18.

29 Jane Feuer, *Seeing through the Eighties: Television and Reaganism* (London: BFI, 1995), p. 27.

30 Stuart Hall, *The Hard Road to Renewal: Thatcherism and the Crisis of the Left* (London: Verso, 1988), p. 137.

31 Ibid., p. 142.

32 Wade, 'Why this Violence is Justified', p. 5 (my emphasis).

33 Mars-Jones, 'Unmoving Violation', p. 15.

34 Paramount, 'Production Information for *The Accused*'.

35 Ibid., p. 3.

36 Tom Hutchinson, 'How One Girl's Ordeal Put Humanity on Trial', *Mail on Sunday*, 19 February 1989, p. 36 (my emphasis).

37 Calman, 'Shocking Truth of How Men Turn Beast', p. 18.

38 Mather, 'Guilty Witnesses to a Violent Crime', p. 18.

39 Rita Kempley, '*The Accused*: Review', *Washington Post*, 14 October 1988.

40 Ebert, '*The Accused*: Review'.

41 Ibid.

42 Beatrix Campbell, '*The Accused* On Release', *Marxism Today*, March 1989, pp. 42–3.

43 Moore, 'Asking for It?', p. 17.

44 Calman, 'Shocking Truth of How Men Turn Beast', p. 18.

45 Campbell, '*The Accused* On Release', p. 43.

46 David Glover and Cora Kaplan, 'Guns in the House of Culture?: Crime Fiction and the Politics of the Popular', in *Cultural Studies*, ed. by Lawrence Grossberg, Cary Nelson and Paula A. Treichler (London: Routledge, 1992), pp. 213–26 (p. 216).

47 Ibid., p. 216.

48 Sharon Willis, 'Hardware and Hardbodies, What Do Women Want?: A Reading of *Thelma and Louise*', in *Film Theory Goes to the Movies*, ed. by Jim Collins, Hilary Radner and Ava Preacher Collins (London: Routledge, 1993), pp. 120–8 (p. 120).

49 Charles Bremner, 'Giving as Bad as they Get', *Times* (Saturday Review), 20 June 1991, p. 6.

50 Joan Smith, 'Road Testing', *Guardian*, 9 July 1991, p. 17.

51 Shaun Usher, 'Men Get the Bullet from Tough Girls', *Daily Mail*, 12 July 1991, p. 30.

52 Geoff Brown, 'Bosom Buddies Take to the Road', *Times*, 11 July 1991. Iain Johnstone makes an almost identical criticism in 'Buddy Can You Spare a Dame?', *Sunday Times*, 14 July 1991.

53 Adam Mars-Jones, 'Getting Away from It All', *Independent*, 12 July 1991, p. 18.

54 Smith, 'Road Testing', p. 17.

55 Mars-Jones, 'Getting Away from It All', p. 18.

56 Johnstone, 'Buddy Can You Spare a Dame?'.

57 Lynda Hart, *Fatal Women: Lesbian Sexuality and the Mark of Aggression* (London: Routledge, 1994), p. 73.

58 Smith, 'Road Testing', p. 17.

59 See for example: Nigella Lawson, 'Furore Triggered by Women on the Loose', *Sunday Times*, 7 July 1991; Alexander Walker, 'A Letter from Thelma's Hide-Out', *Evening Standard*, 11 July 1991, p. 26.

60 Mars-Jones, 'Getting Away from It All', p. 18.

61 Usher, 'Men Get the Bullet from Tough Girls', p. 30.

62 Mick Brown, 'Revenge of the Abused "Accessories"', *Daily Telegraph*, 5 July 1991, p. 15.

63 Hugo Davenport, 'Taking to the Refuge of the Road', *Daily Telegraph*, 11 July 1991, p. 14.

64 Charles Bremner, 'Giving as Bad as they Get', *Times* (Saturday Review), 20 June 1991, p. 6.

65 Davenport, 'Taking to the Refuge of the Road', p. 14.

66 Brown, 'Revenge of the Abused "Accessories"', p. 15.

67 Manohla Dargis, 'Guns N' Poses', *Village Voice*, 16 July 1991, p. 22.

68 Bremner, 'Giving as Bad as they Get', p. 6.

69 Davenport, 'Taking to the Refuge of the Road', p. 14.

70 Brown, 'Revenge of the Abused "Accessories"', p. 15.

71 Davenport, 'Taking to the Refuge of the Road', p. 14.

72 Imelda Whelehan, *Modern Feminist Thought: From the Second Wave to 'Post-Feminism'* (Edinburgh: Edinburgh University Press, 1995), p. 67.

73 Robin Rowland and Renate D. Klein, 'Radical Feminism: Critique and Construct', in *A Reader in Feminist Knowledge*, ed. by Sneja Gunew (London: Routledge, 1991), pp. 271–303 (p. 296).

74 Ibid., p. 275.

75 Whelehan, *Modern Feminist Thought*, p. 79.

76 Ibid., p. 78.

77 Ibid., p. 12.

78 Leeds Revolutionary Feminist Group, 'Political Lesbianism: The Case Against Heterosexuality', in *The Woman Question: Readings on the Subordination of Women*, ed. by Mary Evans (London: Fontana, 1982), pp. 63–72 (p. 65).

79 Whelehan, *Modern Feminist Thought*, p. 86.

80 Smith, 'Road Testing', p. 17.

81 See: Bremner, 'Giving as Bad as they Get', p. 6.

82 'Daws', '*Thelma and Louise*: Review', *Variety*, 13 May 1991. See also: Mars-Jones, 'Getting Away from It All', p. 18.

83 Manohla Dargis, '*Thelma and Louise* and the Tradition of the Male Road Movie', in *Women and Film: A Sight and Sound Reader*, ed. by Pam Cook and Philip Dodd (London: Scarlet Press, 1993), pp. 86–92.

84 Ibid., p. 92 (my emphasis).

85 Dargis, 'Guns N' Poses', p. 22.

86 Suzanne Moore, for example, produces a similar reading of *The Accused*. See above, p. 105.

87 Glover and Kaplan, 'Guns in the House of Culture?', p. 222.

88 Cited in Hall, *The Hard Road to Renewal*, p. 8.

89 Ibid., p. 8.

90 Tania Modleski, *Feminism Without Women: Culture and Criticism in a 'Postfeminist' Age* (London: Routledge, 1991).

91 Feuer, *Seeing through the Eighties*, p. 16.

92 Natasha Walter, *The New Feminism* (London: Little Brown, 1998), p. 175.

93 Hilary Cottam, 'Blessed Margaret', *Guardian* (The Week), 17 January 1998, p. 4.

94 Jennifer Wicke, 'Celebrity Material: Materialist Feminism and the Culture of Celebrity', *South Atlantic Quarterly*, 93:4 (Fall 1994), 751–78 (p. 758).

95 Cottam, 'Blessed Margaret', p. 4.

96 Winship, *Inside Women's Magazines*, p. 149.

97 Julia Hallam, '*Working Girl*: A Woman's Film for the Eighties', in *Gendering the Reader*, ed. by Sara Mills (Hemel Hempstead: Harvester, 1994), pp. 173–98 (p. 190).

98 Cited in Hallam, '*Working Girl*', p. 189.

99 Francke, 'Interview with Callie Khouri', p. 17.

100 Eleanor J. Bader, '*Thelma and Louise*: Review', *Spare Rib*, July 1991, 19–20 (p. 20).

Chapter 5

Frontier femmes:
rape-revenge and the western

Although rape may be the act around which the plot sometimes pivots, Westerns don't examine the experience, or the consequences except in one respect: rape is the occasion for the outraged to seek revenge.[1]

Not only are rape and revenge standard motifs in the western, they are intimately connected. In the traditional western, however, the outraged who seek revenge for rape are typically the husbands or fiancés of the victim rather than the raped women herself.[2] Thus, as Janet Thumin has observed, stories of the west are traditionally 'stories of the masculine'.[3] What I want to argue here, however, is that the rise of second-wave feminism in the early 1970s, and the concomitant emergence of specifically *female*-centred deployments of the rape-revenge structure, resulted in a movement of women from the margins of the western's symbolic world to its frontier. The western myth thus became one of the arenas in which the changing relationship between men and women could be articulated and made sense of, in which stories of the west could become stories of feminism and femininity. Indeed, the western myth's ability to transcend its roots in history perhaps make it the ultimate narrative of transformation. For example, in his seminal study of the western, Will Wright attempts to demonstrate how changes in the western's plot structure relate to changing conceptions of contemporary society, particularly the transition from a market economy to a corporate economy.[4] As Wright argues:

> Except as a setting, the Western myth is not concerned with the actual events and people of the West; rather it uses the western setting to code *kinds* of people in fundamental relationships that exist and are problematic in modern life.[5]

Thus, with specific reference to gender, Pam Cook has observed:

The frontier has often been seen in symbolic terms as a boundary or barrier between opposing ideas ... This formulation has both a relationship to actual events (the breaking down of the barrier between East and West under pressure from eastern expansion), and also a link with psychic and social reality (the loss of boundaries of sexual difference, as eastern 'feminine' values came into contact with the 'masculine' Wild West). Not surprisingly, then, many Westerns work away at the problem of re-establishing sexual boundaries: it's unusual for the woman who starts out wearing pants, carrying a gun and riding a horse to be still doing so at the end of the movie. Suitably re-clad in dress or skirt, she prepares to take her place in the family, leaving adventure to the men.[6]

What I want to argue, however, is that the rise of second-wave feminism demanded a fundamental realignment of these oppositions and of the myths or stories the western articulates. My analysis of the way in which the rape-revenge structure has been mapped over the western genre in the post-1970 period will offer a continuation of Will Wright's structural analysis of the western.[7] In the first section of this chapter, then, I will trace the differences and similarities between two female rape-revenge westerns – *Hannie Caulder* and *Handgun* – and Wright's 'vengeance variation'.[8] In so doing, I will explore the extent to which the introduction of new functions such as the rape-avenging woman brings about changes at the level of narrative structure, the oppositions it articulates and the meanings it generates.

In the second section of this chapter, I will look at a range of rape-revenge westerns from the 1990s and my analyses here will involve supplementing the preceding emphasis on the formal and thematic content of the texts themselves with an emphasis on the discourses surrounding them. In particular, I will argue that the rape-revenge narrative's move into the mainstream during this period has meant that the role played by stars has become increasingly significant to an analysis of the way in which these narratives articulate changing conceptions of masculinity and femininity and, by extension, to the way in which they produce a set of meanings around feminism. In so doing, I will begin to explore the extent to which popular understandings of the 1990s as a period of post-feminism and backlash are articulated in these films. Finally, I will also suggest that such an analysis must take account of the increasing influence of postmodern aesthetics on genre, gender and the deployment of the rape-revenge structure.

Variations on vengeance: Frontier femmes and the vengeance variation

Despite limitations in the construction of his corpus, Will Wright's structural analysis of the western represents one of the most consistent and coherent attempts to map the genre.[9] It is for this reason that I use his work here as a template against which to analyse *Hannie Caulder* and *Handgun*. Wright identifies four main plot structures: the classical plot, the vengeance variation, the transition theme and the professional plot. It is the vengeance variation, however, that I will be concerned with here. In order to guide the reader through the following comparative analysis of the vengeance variation and the female rape-revenge western, Wright's functions for the vengeance variation and the narrative sequences that structure the action are outlined in table 1, while table 2 summarizes the ways in which *Hannie Caulder* and *Handgun* depart from this model.

Table 1 The vengeance variation

Narrative sequence	*Functions*
Weakness	1 The hero is or was a member of society.
	2 The villains do harm to the hero and to the society.
	3 The society is unable to punish the villains.
	4 The hero seeks vengeance.
Status	5 The hero goes outside of society.
	6 The hero is revealed to have a special ability.
	7 The society recognizes a difference between themselves and the hero; the hero is given special status.
Commitment (to social values)	8 A representative of society asks the hero to give up his revenge.
	9 The hero gives up his revenge.
Fight	10 The hero fights the villains.
	11 The hero defeats the villains.
Equality/ Acceptance	12 The hero gives up his special status.
	13 The hero enters society.

Note: Functions are listed in numerical order rather than according to the sequence in which they occur in any particular film.

Table 2 The female rape-revenge western

Narrative sequence	Functions
Rape	1 The heroine is a member of society but occupies a marginal, private sphere therein.
	2 The villains do harm to the heroine but not to society.
	3 The society is unwilling to punish the villains.
	4 The heroine seeks vengeance.
Rejection (of social values)	8 A representative of society asks the heroine to give up her revenge.
	9 The heroine does not give up her revenge.
Transformation	5 The heroine attempts to move from the margins of society to its centre by rejecting its standards of feminine behaviour.
	6 The heroine learns a special ability but it is not revealed.
	7 The heroine moves from the private femininity of the wife/teacher to the public femininity of the female avenger.
Revenge	10 The heroine fights the villains.
	11 The heroine defeats the villains.
Equality/ Acceptance	12 The heroine gives up her special status.
	13 The heroine takes her place within the public sphere.

Note: Functions are listed according to the sequence in which they occur in *Hannie Caulder* and *Handgun*.

Of the female rape-revenge westerns under discussion here, *Handgun* most closely approximates Wright's schema. Despite its contemporary setting, the film makes its reliance on the western myth clear not only by placing its central protagonists in the traditional and, more to the point, antagonistic roles, of eastern schoolteacher and western cowboy, but by locating its action in Texas where 'more Westerns have been set ... than in any other state'.[10] Kathleen's (Karen Young) position as a schoolteacher thus also fulfils function 1 of Wright's schema by situating her as a member of society. However, while Kathleen's rape at the hands of Larry (Clayton Day) also fulfils function 2, it does so only partially. In other words, although Larry does harm to Kathleen, he is not shown to do any direct harm to society. Indeed, whereas in the vengeance westerns Wright analyses the villains are *already* criminals (thieves, killers, gunrunners, bank robbers), here Larry is constructed as an apparently upstanding member of society.

Handgun also conforms to function 3 of the vengeance variation – 'the society is unable to punish the villains' – but it does so for different reasons. In the vengeance variation while it is generally recognized that the villains are evil, society is simply unable to punish them. However, in *Handgun*, an albeit sympathetic policeman tells Kathleen that successful prosecution of Larry is unlikely. While he cites lack of evidence as a reason for this, the subtext is that since society does not recognize Larry as a criminal it will, therefore, be unwilling to punish him. Indeed, as he points out, because Kathleen was not a virgin at the time of the rape, the defence is likely to construct her as the criminal of the case; that is, as a whore (positioning her within another of the limited roles traditionally allocated to women in the western). Consequently, while function 2's pairing of individual and social crimes suggests that crimes against men are also necessarily crimes against (a patriarchal) society, *Handgun* points up how crimes against women have little currency in such a society. The exceptions to this rule, however, are revealing. The westerns in which the individual crime of rape and crimes against society are paired are frequently those in which the raped woman is engaged or married. More significant is that the crime against society is usually robbery, thus contributing to a reading in which rape and theft are conflated. Here, then, rape is not a crime against women but the 'theft' of the hero's 'property', a crime whose social resonance to a patriarchal society is symbolized through the villains' robbery (usually of the community's bank). In films, such as *Rancho Notorious*, where the hero's fiancée is raped and murdered during a bank robbery, male society is mobilized to avenge these crimes but is simply unable, rather than unwilling, to do so. While in *Rancho Notorious* the hero's revenge is predicated on a patriarchal understanding of rape as the theft of male property, in *Handgun* the construction of rape as a crime specifically against women necessitates the introduction of a female avenger.

Hannie Caulder, unlike *Handgun*, nevertheless, apparently fulfils the requirements of function 3, since Hannie (Raquel Welch) is a rancher's wife who is raped by three outlaws as they flee from a robbery. However, while this too would appear to suggest the conflation of rape and the theft of male property, the film, in fact, disrupts such a reading by having the robbery fail and the outlaws kill Hannie's husband. Thus Hannie's rape, like Kathleen's, is constructed neither as a crime against individual male property or male society at large and, as I have suggested, it is for this reason that society is unwilling rather than unable to punish the perpetrators and that both women must seek their own revenge (function 4). These functions comprise what Wright calls the weakness sequence. In terms of the rape-revenge structure, however, they might more properly be described as constituting the rape sequence.

In both *Hannie* and *Handgun* the weakness or rape sequence is followed by a set of functions Wright labels the commitment sequence, the first of which is function 8 – 'a representative of society asks the hero to give up his revenge'. In *Handgun*, this representative takes the form of a priest and, in *Hannie*, it is a bounty hunter, aptly named Thomas Price (Robert Culp). Although Thomas repeatedly asks Hannie to give up her revenge throughout the film, in comparison to the vengeance variation, this function occurs at an unusually early point in the narrative of both *Hannie* and *Handgun*. In particular, in Wright's structure, before the hero is asked to give up his revenge, he is usually 'revealed to have a special ability' (function 6). In other words, he is proved capable of carrying out his revenge and is thus able to give it up (function 9) with no subsequent loss of masculinity. For example, in *Stagecoach* (John Ford, 1939), Ringo (John Wayne) is an outlaw who has broken out of jail and his ability to help protect the stagecoach from Indian attacks is frequently remarked upon. In *One-Eyed Jacks* (Marlon Brando, 1961), Rio (Marlon Brando) is a thief whose reputation alone is enough to make Harvey (Sam Gilman) think twice about engaging in a violent confrontation with him early on in the film and, in *Nevada Smith* (Henry Hathaway, 1966), Max (Steve McQueen) kills two men before being asked to give up his revenge. Even in *The Man from Laramie* (Anthony Mann, 1955), in which function 8 also occurs early on in the narrative, Lockhart's (James Stewart) ability to carry out his revenge is assured by intimations that he is, or was, a member of the army.

In *Hannie* and *Handgun*, however, the heroines are asked to give up their revenge before proving their ability to carry it out. Thus, whereas in Wright's vengeance variation the representative of society tries to convince the hero to give up his revenge by pointing out 'the uselessness of vengeance or the fact that the hero is becoming like the men he hunts', in *Hannie*, in particular, Thomas's attempts to get Hannie to eschew revenge are based on his belief that she is incapable of it.[11] More significantly, this incapability is cast exclusively in terms of Hannie's perceived femininity. In other words, Thomas argues that Hannie is too caring to kill a man since, having merely knocked him unconscious, she was unable to leave him 'on the cold ground last night' but instead covered him with a blanket, built a fire and watched over him. Furthermore, he claims that she is also physically incapable since 'if I was to teach you the gun, you'd then go out and get your ass blowed off', adding that it would be a 'shame to get it shot full of holes – it is as pretty a one as I ever laid eyes on'. Thus, if the redefinition of rape as a crime against women in the female rape-revenge western suggests the possibility of a female avenger, conventional conceptions of femininity simultaneously work to deny this possibility. Consequently, if Hannie and Kathleen are to move from the margins of the western's symbolic world to its frontier – are to become frontier femmes – then these conventional conceptions of femininity will also need to be redefined.

Unlike their male counterparts in Wright's vengeance variation, who subsequently give up their revenge (function 9), thus stressing their 'fundamental commitment to social values', Hannie and Kathleen do not give up their revenge and this function, therefore, is absent in the female rape-revenge western.[12] In these films, then, the vengeance variation's commitment sequence becomes instead the rejection sequence in which the heroine turns her back on the values of society. While this is largely because a commitment to social values would also entail a commitment to the patriarchal ideology that engenders rape and protects rapists, it is also because, having not yet been allowed to prove their special ability, to give up revenge would mean remaining in the position of passive victim, which those social values construct for women. Thus, whereas in the vengeance variation Wright's weakness sequence is associated largely with society, rather than the hero, since 'the villains harm both the hero and society, but society can do nothing about it', in the female rape-revenge western the weakness of society accrues largely to the heroine herself.[13] In other words, although both the hero of the vengeance variation and the heroine of the female rape-revenge western are both initially constructed as part of society, the heroine's attachment to that society is stronger because of the perceived connection between femininity and civilization in the western. While this is apparent in Hannie's role as a wife, it is perhaps even more so in Kathleen's position not only as a schoolteacher, but as a schoolteacher specifically from the east (Boston). Indeed, the motif of eastern schoolteacher as civilizing force is perhaps nowhere more apparent than in a classic of the genre, *My Darling Clementine* (John Ford, 1946). As Christine Gledhill has observed, here 'the hero's quest for personal revenge is translated into the establishment of law and order for the nascent township of Tombstone, under the influence of the heroine schoolteacher from the East'.[14] Moreover, whereas the hero is 'accepted as an equal' within that society, the heroine's weakness is compounded by her unequal status within that society and by its indifference to her plight.[15] Indeed, if the vengeance variation constructs society as 'simply a momentary victim', the western as a genre goes further by constructing women as always already victims.[16] Thus, in these films, it is the heroine rather than society that is constructed as weak, and this is subsequently reinforced by the early occurrence of function 8 and by the concomitant change in its ideological work. Consequently, the following sequence, which Wright labels status (functions 5, 6 and 7) – in which the hero is defined against the weakness of society as 'a man with special status, a gunfighter outside of society' – holds a rather more central and complex position within the narrative of the female rape-revenge western. Against Wright, but in line with my more limited structural analysis of the rape-revenge narrative, I will call this sequence transformation.

Describing the oppositions in the vengeance variation, Wright claims that 'the inside/outside distinction separates the hero from society ... The strong/weak opposition separates men from women ... the individuals are strong the society is weak'.[17] In other words, the central opposition in the vengeance variation operates around individuals against values; the hero is defined as strong and masculine against the society which is defined as weak and feminine, while the villains 'have an ambiguous location on this axis'.[18] In the female rape-revenge western the oppositions must necessarily be redefined since if, as in the vengeance variation, the feminine and society are conflated there would be no opposition. Indeed, the individual against society opposition becomes particularly problematic in the female rape-revenge western because of women's ambiguous relationship to society. In other words, while in their private roles as wives, mothers and moral guardians women are integral to society, they are simultaneously excluded from it in terms of their access to public positions of power and status. Consequently, instead of an opposition between individual and society, society itself becomes the site of opposition between the female protagonist and the male villain. While there is an implicit gender politics written into the vengeance variation through the way in which the opposition is gender coded – individuals (masculine) against society (feminine) – the female rape-revenge western makes this gendered opposition explicit. What I want to argue, then, is that in attempting to work through what is essentially a crude formulation of feminism (women versus men), these films engage with and attempt to make sense of some of the more sophisticated and complex debates and oppositions put on the agenda by feminism, specifically the sameness/difference debate and the public/private opposition. Thus, the individual against society opposition is recast as a conflict within society not simply between men and women, but between a feminine private sphere and a masculine public sphere.

It is for these reasons that the female rape-revenge western's transformation sequences are rather more complex than the vengeance variation's status sequence. For example, the first function in this sequence – 'the hero goes outside of society' – is only possible if the hero/ine was fully inside that society in the first place. So, while Hannie and Kathleen's apparent rejection of the accoutrements of femininity can be interpreted as an attempt to step outside of the feminine identities sanctioned by society, there is also a sense in which this represents an attempt to gain a fuller purchase on that society by embracing masculine identities. While not wholly a female rape-revenge western, *The Ballad of Little Jo* (Maggie Greenwald, 1993) explicitly foregrounds this problem. The film's heroine, Jo(sephine) (Suzy Amis), is cast out of society for rejecting its standards of feminine behaviour – she displays an active female sexuality by getting pregnant out of wedlock – and finds that the only way she can re-enter that society is as a man. Jo's transformation is, however, also a response to an attempted rape at the beginning of the film and, as such, like the female avenger, her transformation includes an element of eroticization. As Stella Bruzzi points out, Jo's masculine clothes 'are at once functional and an eroticizing agent'.[19] Similarly, in *Hannie*, Hannie spends the early part of the film wearing nothing but a man's poncho, which, while functional in that it just covers her nakedness, is also erotic for the same reason. What I want to suggest, then, is that the trajectory of the female rape-revenge western is not towards masculinity (that is, sameness), but towards a renegotiation of difference as it is articulated around the public/private opposition, towards, in other words, public femininities.

As with the vengeance variation, both *Hannie* and *Handgun* include scenes before the final fight in which the protagonists are given the opportunity to demonstrate their special ability. However, although this would appear to fulfil function 6 of Wright's schema, there are some significant differences. In particular, 'the hero is revealed to have a special ability' becomes 'the heroine *learns* a special ability but it is *not* revealed'. In many of the films Wright uses to illustrate his discussion of the vengeance variation the hero's acquisition of his special ability is not depicted. In *Hannie* and *Handgun*, however, it becomes the central narrative focus. Consequently, while the former would appear to embrace an essentialist politics in which it is suggested that the hero's special ability is an innate part of his masculinity, the latter would seem to embrace a constructionist politics in which gendered behaviour can be acquired or learnt. This does not mean, however, that Hannie and Kathleen are simply masculinized. In *Hannie*, in particular, Hannie's transformation is punctuated by repeated attempts to guarantee her femininity (in a sense, always already guaranteed by the casting of archetypal sex symbol Raquel Welch in the title role). For example, at various points during Hannie's transformation, she is shown playing with children, bottle-feeding a baby goat and walking hand in hand with Thomas on the beach, wearing a dress. Furthermore, when they are attacked by a band of Mexican's after Thomas has taught Hannie to shoot, she does shoot one of their attackers but is unable to deliver the fatal bullet and has to be saved by Thomas. The shooting competition in *Handgun* similarly compromises Kathleen's acquisition of a special (masculine) ability. In other words, while Kathleen makes a good start she is ultimately disqualified because she shoots one of the friendly targets. Here, however, it is suggested that Kathleen's failure is deliberate – as one of the male spectators comments: 'It looks like she did it on purpose.' What I want to suggest is that, because this friendly target is represented by a policeman, in shooting it Kathleen not only signals her rejection of society and its laws, but her refusal to play by the rules of masculinity (in this case, competitiveness). Like the fight sequence in *Hannie*, then, this sequence ultimately functions to point up Kathleen's femininity rather than her acquisition of a special (masculine) ability. This is achieved, in particular, through one of the male spectators, who comments: 'Jesus, look at her tits...Gosh, she moves just right... Wow, look at them bounce.'

The final function in Wright's status sequence is function 7: 'The society recognizes a difference between themselves and the hero; the hero is given special status.' Yet, because in the female rape-revenge western the opposition is not based around individual/society but male/female, the difference already exists and is, indeed, the narrative's main motivating force. However, as I have been arguing, this does not mean that the narrative trajectory is, therefore, towards sameness, that is, masculinity. Rather, the issues of difference and sameness are articulated not around the binary masculinity/femininity but around femininity itself. This is particularly evident in the various transformations Kathleen undergoes in *Handgun*. At the beginning of the film, before the rape, Kathleen is represented through what one might describe as typical feminine codes: that is, strappy, flowery sundresses and long hair. After the rape, however, she makes the transition to a plain, high-necked, long-sleeved smock dress and short hair, in which guise a male colleague comments that she 'looks terrible', implying that what she is wearing is 'not feminine'. Nevertheless, 'not feminine' here is not necessarily masculine either (as the next transformation indicates); it just does not conform to the standards of femininity set by the sundresses and long hair. Furthermore, while Kathleen's subsequent and final transformation from smock dress to trousers would seem to secure and complete her movement from femininity to masculinity, here too, despite her occupation of the masculine public space of the gun club, she remains feminine, as the comments about her breasts by a male spectator during the shooting competition (cited above) indicate.

Similarly, in *Hannie Caulder*, despite Thomas's initial claim that Hannie 'wants to be a man', a later conversation between the two reveals that she simply does not want to be 'the same person'. Thus, Hannie moves from being described by Bailey (Christopher Lee) as 'a fine looking woman' to being described by the sheriff as 'a hard woman'. Furthermore, the absence of other female characters, notably Bailey's wife, against which Hannie's transformation can be measured, ultimately functions to emphasize Hannie's difference from the male characters. Indeed, the only time Hannie appears in

the same frame as another woman is shortly before she kills the first
rapist when, walking up the stairs in the saloon, she bumps into two
finely dressed prostitutes. At this crucial structural juncture between
transformation and revenge we are thus reminded both of the distance Hannie has travelled from such representations *and* her continuing proximity to them, as the Madame (Diana Dors) comments,
'I don't remember hiring you'. Hannie, however, rejects the implied
designation whore by replying curtly, 'You didn't'. Thus, while Kathleen and Hannie remain feminine, their movement from the margins
of the western's symbolic world to its frontier – articulated, in particular, through their occupation of the public spaces of the gun club
and the saloon – necessitates the development of what Hilary
Radner describes as 'new categories and structures of femininity' or
public femininities to replace the marginal, private femininities of
the schoolteacher and wife. In this way, then, the frontier femme
can be read as an attempt to articulate and make sense of the changing shape and status of heterosexual femininity in the post-1970
period.

In *Handgun*, the structural juncture between transformation and
revenge is particularly illustrative of what is at stake in this movement from the margins to the frontier of the western's symbolic
world. This juncture occurs during the scene in which Kathleen is
getting dressed ready for her final confrontation with Larry. The
scene opens with the camera tracking up her body from her feet to
her face, so that initially we do not know to whom, or indeed to
what gender, the boots and trousers belong. Moreover, from the
position of the camera and Kathleen's facial expressions we can tell
that she is looking in a mirror and, in fact, the shot appears to be
taken from the point of view of her mirror-image. We do not, however, ever see her mirror-image. The scene then cuts to an over-the-
shoulder shot of Larry's mirror-image as, naked from the waist up,
he lifts weights. Thus, in an interesting variation on the shot/reverse-
shot structure, Kathleen's mirror-image is replaced with Larry's.
While the juxtaposition of these two shots could be read as an
attempt to contrast and, therefore, point up the difference between
the 'fake' male (as it is constructed through clothes) and the 'real'
male (as it is revealed through the natural body), it could also be
argued that the suturing of the two shots into one shot structure
attempts to point up the similarities between Kathleen and Larry
(the latter as the mirror-image of the former).

Clearly, then, this shot structure invites analysis in terms of Lacan's mirror-stage where the mirror-image is both 'me' and 'not me', similar and different. While this project has, as a whole, eschewed psychoanalytical paradigms, in this instance, I think a Lacanian-influenced analysis delivers an interesting and revealing reading, particularly insofar as Lacan's distinction between the imaginary and the symbolic can be read as metaphorically articulating some of the oppositions that have concerned me here (sameness/difference, private/public). What I want to argue is that in order to move from the margins of the western's symbolic world to its frontier, from the private sphere to the public sphere, Kathleen must pass from the realm of the imaginary and sameness, through the mirror-stage, into the realm of the symbolic and difference. Thus, Kathleen moves through closeness to the image of woman as victim, through identification with the other, more coherent and unified masculine (mirror) image. However, in order to create the potential for the signification of the self, in order to designate rather than to be designated, Kathleen must separate herself from both these images. In other words, if access to the symbolic is marked by the loss of self-identification, it is also afforded by the recognition of sexual difference. Consequently, while Larry represents the more coherent and unified self, he also represents the image, the object to which Kathleen must become subject if she is to enter the (symbolic) realm of institutions, law, sociality and, most importantly, signification, from which she has been excluded. Thus, shortly after the scene depicting the mirror-stage, Kathleen telephones Larry from the gun club and effectively plays out the image of woman as victim, asking Larry to come and save her. In so doing, she distances herself both from this image and from the masculine mirror-image represented by Larry. It is this recognition of sexual difference that allows Kathleen to enter the symbolic realm of signification. Indeed, as Kathleen tells Larry, 'it's just as though I'm just waking up'. It is this coming to consciousness, this entry into language and designations, that enables Kathleen to effect her revenge by positioning herself as subject and aggressor and Larry as object and victim. However, such access to signification has a price. The symbolic is the realm of no return and, consequently, while Kathleen will perhaps never again occupy the private femininity of the victim, she has entered the realm of sexual difference where, for better or worse, she will always be a woman – as the film's final shot, cemented by the freeze-frame, of Kathleen wearing a dress and earrings and holding a child in her arms, testifies.

Like the classic western, described by Pam Cook, then, *Handgun* would appear to 'work away at the problem of re-establishing sexual boundaries'. However, the introduction of a female avenger into the western's symbolic world means that those boundaries must be negotiated and redefined. In particular, the distinction between the private feminine sphere and the public masculine sphere comes under pressure as Kathleen increasingly moves into the public space of the gun club. Thus, despite the absence of function 9 – 'the hero gives up his revenge' – through which, in the vengeance variation, the hero demonstrates his commitment to the values of society, the narrative trajectory of *Handgun* is similar to that of the vengeance variation. The movement of both is towards the hero/heroine's entry into society (function 13) or, more accurately in the case of the female avenger, towards her entry into the specifically public sphere of society. However, because of women's marginal position within the western's symbolic/social world, the way in which this function is accomplished in the female rape-revenge western, and hence its ideological meaning, is somewhat different. For the hero of the vengeance variation this is achieved through his willingness to give up his revenge and the subsequent accidental or compromised nature of his defeat of the villains (hence in Wright this sequence is labelled fight rather than revenge). In contrast, for the heroine of the female rape-revenge western, revenge is the very pre-requisite that will enable her to move from the private sphere to the public sphere, from the margins of the western's symbolic/social world to its frontier – hence her reluctance to give it up. Kathleen's accession to citizenship through revenge can thus be seen as undermining the assertion of the ideology of the separate spheres that frequently accompanies the vengeance hero's entry into society (in both *The Man from Laramie* and *One-Eyed Jacks*, for example, the heroes ride off into the masculine public sphere of action and adventure, leaving the heroine to the feminine private sphere of home and family). Nevertheless, Kathleen's revenge, although deliberate and calculated, is similarly compromised. While she had previously rejected the law by shooting the 'friendly' policeman target, she now finds that in order to take her place within the public sphere through revenge she must show her acceptance of that law by simply humiliating Larry rather than killing him and by disposing of her gun –

thus complying with function 12 ('the hero gives up his special status'). Like the vengeance variation, then, the narrative trajectory of the rape-revenge western is towards both equality and acceptance. Yet, if for the vengeance hero the former involves a movement towards sameness (he becomes 'an equal among equals'),[20] for the female avenger, it involves a movement towards difference (she becomes 'equal but different' to use a feminist formulation). In this way, *Handgun* can be seen as attempting to articulate and make sense of feminist discourses of equality and the changing shape and status of heterosexual femininity in the post-1970 period. As I have suggested above, however, it does so within a framework that ultimately endorses and accepts existing aesthetic and social structures.

The ending of *Hannie Caulder* is slightly more ambiguous, concluding with Hannie riding off into the desert. While this would seem to concur with Wright's argument that 'three of our vengeance heroes reject their status and power by leaving town', what is not so clear is whether Hannie will also change her 'ways, enter society, and settle down'.[21] What is clear is that she is still only competent in the private feminine spaces (the prostitute's bedroom, the perfume shop) where she kills the first two rapists. These are, however, also the spaces in which heterosexual femininity is traditionally reproduced and transformed. It is perhaps fitting, therefore, that it is in these spaces that Hannie's transformation from the private femininity of the wife to the public femininity of the frontier femme/female avenger is made manifest. Nevertheless, in the public masculine space of the prison she needs male help, which comes in the form of the mysterious stranger who has haunted her progress. Thus, while demonstrating that she is no longer a victim by cutting to a flashback of the rape at the moment Hannie delivers the final, fatal bullet, Hannie's revenge, like Kathleen's, is also compromised, not least because the three rapists are largely portrayed as inept buffoons. Furthermore, at the end of the film, Hannie is still chaperoned, as she has been throughout, by a male character. In this case, it is the mysterious 'man with no name', an oblique reference to the star persona of Clint Eastwood and to the spaghetti westerns of the period; a man whose presence, according to Pam Cook, 'is a reminder of a final boundary Hannie can never cross. For women can never really be heroes in the Western: that would mean the end of the genre.'[22]

Hard women and soft men: Post-modernism, post-feminism and backlash

As the recent coining of critical terms such as Clover's 'female victim-hero' and Tasker's 'action heroine' testify, women are increasingly being positioned as the hero(in)es of traditionally masculine genres.[23] This is perhaps partly due to the way in which, under the increasing influence of post-modern aesthetics, the codes and conventions of established genres have been subject to hybridization, parody and ironic quotation, thus opening up a space in which the traditional gender identities those genres construct can be revised and negotiated. In relation to *Bad Girls* (Jonathan Kaplan, 1994), for example, Yvonne Tasker has argued that:

> making use of a range of conventions and images drawn from the genre, the film parodies the Western without explicitly becoming comic. Elements of parody partly stem from the 'role-reversal' involved in casting four women at the centre of the Western action, given the conventional roles typically assigned to women in the genre. Perhaps in an attempt to legitimate the central female roles, *Bad Girls* also looks to the women's film, and takes certain images of sexualized violence against women and their vengeance from the rape/revenge cycle.[24]

While *Bad Girls* relies on a fairly straight deployment of the rape-revenge structure to legitimate its central female roles, other female-centred westerns of the period subject the rape-revenge structure itself to post-modern articulations. *The Quick and the Dead* (Sam Raimi, 1995), for example, does away with rape and transformation and leaves only the figure of the vengeful woman. This foregrounding and legitimation of heroic female roles within traditionally masculine genres is not, however, simply a product of post-modern aesthetics. Rather, as Susan Jeffords points out, this revision and negotiation of traditional gender roles can also be read as 'U.S. gender culture's response to feminism, civil rights, and a declining Cold Warrior validation'.[25] Thus, as women become harder, men, according to Jeffords, are apparently becoming softer:

> 1991 was the year of the transformed U.S. man. There's hardly a mainstream Hollywood film from that year with a significant male role that does not in some ways reinforce an image that the hard-fighting, weapon-wielding, independent, muscular, and heroic men of the eighties – Rambo (Sylvester Stallone), Colonel Braddock (Chuck Norris),

Dirty Harry (Clint Eastwood), John McClane (Bruce Willis), Martin Riggs (Mel Gibson), Indiana Jones (Harrison Ford), Superman (Christopher Reeve) – have disappeared and are being replaced by the more sensitive, loving, nurturing, protective family men of the nineties.[26]

Jeffords, however, does not explore how these transformed family men might function within a context that has been widely defined, amidst calls for a return to family values, as one of backlash against feminism. Moreover, despite the reference here to Clint Eastwood, an actor whose star persona is intimately connected to the western, she does not explore how her argument might relate to the current resurgence of interest in this, most masculine of genres. While the credit for this revival lies largely with *Dances with Wolves* (Kevin Costner, 1990), the recent spate of female-centred westerns – *The Ballad of Little Jo*, *Bad Girls* and *The Quick and the Dead* – are perhaps best understood in relation to the films and star persona of Clint Eastwood. Indeed, the female rape-revenge western's debt to Eastwood is apparent not only in the reference to 'the man with no name' in *Hannie Caulder*, but in its construction of the heroines themselves. For example, in *Hannie Caulder*, Hannie herself borrows Eastwood's style of dress, the poncho and flat-topped, rigid-brimmed hat made famous in his first Italian western, *A Fistful of Dollars* (Sergio Leone, 1964). Furthermore, as Christopher Frayling argues, Burt Kennedy's films owe 'much to the narrative structure of the "Dollars" trilogy', with *Hannie Caulder* 'closest in impact to Leone's early westerns'.[27] In *The Ballad of Little Jo*, Jo again sports the Eastwood hat, while *The Quick and the Dead* is, as Ben Thompson observes, full of 'Spaghetti Western quotes – blind boy, coffin maker measuring up the hero etc.'.[28] Ellen (Sharon Stone), for example, wears the dirty long overcoat of the spaghetti hero and at one point chews on a trademark Eastwood cigarillo. That such stylistic borrowings continue throughout the female revenge westerns of the period suggest that the confluence between Eastwood's star persona, particularly as it was constructed in his Leone westerns, and these frontier femmes is more than accidental.

The clue to this confluence can perhaps most obviously be found in Leone's resistance to the classic western, in the fact that his westerns, like the female rape-revenge western, are essentially revisionist. However, it can also be found in Christine Gledhill's suggestion that Eastwood's westerns 'are liable to be discussed as much in terms of the Eastwood image and how it speaks to a post-68, "post-feminist" crisis in male identity as in terms of its contribution to and development of western traditions'.[29] Indeed, *Hannie Caulder* explicitly foregrounds this post-1968 transformation in the western's preoccupations in Hannie's comment to the sheriff: 'Like the man says, there aren't any hard women, only soft men.' Of course, this preoccupation is not confined to Eastwood's westerns, but is, in fact, a central motif in much of his work, one that is particularly apparent in his directional debut *Play Misty for Me* (1971) and his subsequent involvement in the vengeful woman tradition, *Sudden Impact*. According to Adam Knee, *Play Misty for Me* is 'indicative of a passing moment of progressive questioning of traditional constructions of male identity prior to the conservative reaction which launched [Eastwood] to greater macho stardom'.[30] It is, therefore, in one of Eastwood's most recent films, *Unforgiven* (Clint Eastwood, 1992), in which both the vengeful woman and the western traditions are combined, that the working through of a '"post-feminist" crisis in male identity', gains its fullest expression.

The action of *Unforgiven* is ostensibly motivated by an incident at the beginning of the film in which a prostitute's face is slashed by one of her clients. The sheriff of the town, 'Little Bill' Daggett (Gene Hackman), at first elects to whip the perpetrator and his friend, but then decides to make them pay a fine in the form of horses, which, significantly, is due to the brothel-owner rather than the mutilated woman. In an attempt to critique such sexual politics – in which women are treated as little more then men's property – the film has the outraged prostitutes pool their savings in order to put a price on the men's heads. Yet, while it is the prostitutes' desire for revenge and the bounty-hunters this attracts that apparently motivates the film's action, I would argue that it is motivated instead by the fact that the mutilated prostitute (Anna Thompson) precipitated the attack by giggling at her client's 'teensy little pecker'; a slight against masculinity that is compounded when the prostitutes deliberately undermine the sheriff's authority. In other words, the opening sequences of the film represent a world in which men are, or have been, 'unmanned' by women. Lest we need any confirmation of this, it is worth noting that the prostitute's name is Delilah, a name which evokes the Old Testament story in which Samson was robbed of his strength when Delilah cut off his hair.

It is not just the villains who are emasculated by women, however, but the hero too.[31] In the film's prologue we learn that William Munny (Clint Eastwood) was 'a known thief and murderer, a man of notoriously vicious and intemperate disposition'. Yet, when we first meet him, he is the embodiment of the transformed US man of the early 1990s described by Jeffords. As Christopher Frayling observes: 'It is made clear that Munny has become a sensitive single parent to his two children, dislikes cruelty to horses as well as to women, and has generally turned New Age.'[32] The credit (or blame) for this transformation is, moreover, placed firmly with Munny's dead wife, Claudia, who, he is fond of saying, 'cured me of drinking and wickedness'.[33] Thus, unlike the vengeance variation's emphasis on tracing the hero's status in relation to society, *Unforgiven*, like the female rape-revenge western, is concerned with mapping the hero's transformation in relation to sexual politics. However, the film is far from a homage to the transformative potential of feminism, not least because one only has to scratch the surface of the film's apparent critique of sexual politics to see that, underwriting the motivating face-slashing incident, is the age-old myth that a prostitute cannot be raped (which is the usual motivation for revenge where women are concerned in the western). Furthermore, as Frayling writes: '*Unforgiven* reverses the progression of the earlier films by having its central character gradually revert to type as a gunfighter, instead of settling down in a little house on the prairie.'[34]

It is this transformation that Mark Simpson traces in his analysis of *Unforgiven*.[35] Examining the film alongside Robert Bly's *Iron John*, he attempts to demonstrate not only 'the permeation of Bly's ideas in American popular culture but also ... their remarkable *symmetry* with the work of Eastwood (a masculinity "guru" from an age before the men's movement)'.[36] Bly is the leader of the US men's movement and his philosophy, briefly, is that men have been feminized or made soft (explicitly) by women and (implicitly) by feminism in particular. He crusades, through his publications, conferences and weekend workshops, to restore men to the position of warrior or wild man. This, according to Simpson, is also the project of *Unforgiven's* narrative trajectory. At the film's end, William Munny 'is finally restored as "William Munny" ["the meanest sonofabitch in the West"] ... and for Bly he is a soft man made hard'.[37] More importantly, however, for my purposes, he is also 'Clint Eastwood again, a reassuring Good Bad Guy, replacing the tormented, ineffectual, *embarrassing* Good Good Guy'.[38] The film, then, is

essentially about 'becoming Clint Eastwood' and the conflation of
the man and the myth into one, coherent star persona. While in the
film's prologue William Munny is simply a mythical character, by
the film's epilogue he has disappeared to San Francisco, Eastwood's
birthplace, and become 'Clint Eastwood'. Indeed, the Munny/East-
wood myth is curiously exempt from what, elsewhere in the film,
appears to be an attempt to expose the mechanisms of myth – the
deconstruction of the 'Duke of Death' myth is one example, the
exaggeration of the face-slashing incident into a full-scale rape and
mutilation is another. Eastwood's purpose in deconstructing the
western myth, therefore, seems to have been to reconstruct himself
as the western's only myth. As Christopher Frayling observes:

> *Unforgiven* goes against the grain of recent Westerns (*Silverado*, *Young
> Guns*) by eschewing irony and hipness and fashionable post-mod-
> ernism. The references seem to be there to anchor Eastwood's odyssey
> within a hallowed tradition, rather than to show off about the hollow-
> ness of that tradition.[39]

The film not only articulates a backlash against feminism (not least
in its formulation of a conservative family values agenda in which it
is suggested that the only effective father is a powerful, authoritarian one), but it articulates a backlash against the revisionist tendencies of the Leone westerns. As Paul Smith observes, 'what is at stake
in [Eastwood's] post-Leone westerns is a determination to reverse
the effects of the spaghetti westerns: in short, the restitution of a
genre'.[40] For this reason, I would argue that Janet Thumin's claim
that *Unforgiven's* fascination for the female audience lies in the way
in which 'in deconstructing the myths of the west the film is also
obliged to deconstruct the myths of the masculine', is perhaps more
applicable to Sam Raimi's spaghetti-influenced female revenge western *The Quick and the Dead*.[41] Indeed, the film's obvious debt not
only to the spaghetti western and the Eastwood persona but to
Unforgiven, suggest that it can, in part at least, be read as an attempt
'to reverse the effects' of the earlier film.[42]

Gene Hackman, as John Herod, for example, reprises his role in
Unforgiven as the sadistic, despot ruler of a small western town and,
as the biblical reference suggests, names and the myths surrounding
them are similarly significant. For example, in *Unforgiven*, English
Bob (Richard Harris) is constructed by his biographer, W. W.
Beauchamp (Saul Rubinek), as 'The Duke of Death' and, in *The*

Quick and the Dead, men are similarly, and perhaps more consistently, defined through their relation to violence. Scars (Mark Boone, Jr), for instance, adds a scar to his arm every time he kills a man, while Ace Hanlon (Lance Henriksen) adds an ace to his deck of cards. Herod, of course, is the figure who, in the New Testament story, was responsible for the 'massacre of the innocents'. Like *Unforgiven*, *The Quick and the Dead* also attempts to deconstruct these myths. Indeed, in a scene remarkably similar to the one in *Unforgiven* where Daggett exposes the 'Duke of Death' myth, Herod challenges the myths Ace has constructed around himself:

> HEROD I wanted to ask you about Indian Wells. Did that fight really take place?
> ACE Sure did.
> HEROD Then it's true that you gunned down four men?
> ACE Two with my left hand, two with my right. See the truth is that I'm just as good with either.
> HEROD You must be the fastest gun in the west.
> ACE It's a pity you weren't there to find out.
> HEROD (*laughs*) Oh, but I was Ace. You see, I was the one that really killed the Terence Brothers. I doubt whether a lying little shit like you was even in the same state.
> *Herod shoots Ace in the right hand*
> HEROD How about that left hand Ace, how about that left-handed draw?
> *Herod shoots Ace in the left hand and then kills him.*

The Quick and the Dead, however, goes further than *Unforgiven* towards undermining these myths of masculinity. The film is peopled with men boasting of their ability and their exploits, but one by one they become the victims of their own myths. Spotted Horse (Jonothon Gill), for example, repeatedly claims that he 'cannot be killed by a bullet' and then is, while the Kid (Leonardo DiCaprio) boasts that, unlike Herod, he has just reached his peak, before, of course, being gunned down by him. *The Quick and the Dead* thus represents a world in which men are resoundingly the victims. Moreover, unlike *Unforgiven*, these soft men are largely shown to be the victims, not of women, but of each other, their own masculinity and the western myth itself. Whereas, in *Unforgiven*, and in the western in general, women are characterized as the problem or the source of disruption to be solved by the narrative, in *The Quick and the Dead* it is the conservative, patriarchal family, as it is symbolized by the figure of the repressive, authoritarian father, which is shown to be problematic.

The narrative suggests, for example, that Herod is the man he is because one day his father, a judge, took a bullet, put it in his gun, spun the chamber, then took it in turns clicking it at Herod, his wife and himself until he finally blew the back of his own head off. Thus, with his annual quick-draw competition, Herod becomes his father by making the townspeople play a similar game of Russian roulette. In turn, the Kid is like he is because his father, Herod, disowns him and Ellen is like she is because of what Herod did to her father. Finally, Cort (Russell Crowe) has renounced violence and become soft not, as in *Unforgiven*, because of a woman but because Herod made him kill a padre (derived from the Latin *pater* meaning 'father'). Furthermore, we learn that Cort was initiated into violence by Herod himself, who, therefore, becomes something of a father-figure to Cort. Despite Herod's repeated claims that violence is in Cort's blood, the film's emphasis on the influence of fathers on their children and on deconstructing myths of masculinity would seem to support a constructionist rather than an essentialist reading of iden-tity formation. Indeed, at the beginning of the film it is revealed that Cort has been working in a mission with orphan children and that he has thus reinvented himself as a preacher or good father who, moreover, stands in opposition to Herod's bad father. The good fathers of the film are, however, wholly ineffectual. For example, in the film's brief rape-revenge sub-plot, Katie (Olivia Burnette) the daughter of the bartender, Horace (Pat Hingle), is raped by Eugene (Kevin Conway). While Horace clearly thinks about trying to shoot Eugene, he is unable to and it is thus left to Ellen to avenge Katie's rape by aptly shooting Eugene in the genitals. Furthermore, Ellen's father is unable to protect himself from Herod and his men and it is Ellen who must try and save him, while Cort, as preacher/father, would rather die than take a stand against Herod. Moreover, while Ellen is unable to save her father she does save Cort from a similar fate who, thereafter, becomes a stand-in for her father (to whom he bears a remarkable resemblance).

While in one sense the film is a critique of a corrupt and/or inef-fectual patriarchal order, in another, it is about the recuperation or transformation of that order and, by extension, of the western's symbolic world. At the end of the film, then, although the law of the father is, quite literally, reinstated when Ellen gives Cort her father's marshall badge and tells him 'the law's come back to town', the symbolic world that those laws govern is transformed. In other words, it is Cort rather than Ellen who is positioned in the traditional feminine role of civilizing force, and it is Cort as 'father', rather than Ellen, who is left to look after 'the family' of townspeople. Consequently, while *The Quick and the Dead* also parallels *Unforgiven* in its inclusion of a hard-man-turned-soft, unlike *Unforgiven* its project is, as Elizabeth Traube argues in relation to the representation of the domestic man in the films of the 1980s, the rehabilitation of 'patriarchal authority along nontraditional lines'.[43] Unlike the films Traube discusses, however, the film does not effect a concomitant recuperation of the nondomestic woman. For example, although as a reformed-outlaw-turned-preacher, Cort recalls Eastwood's preacher in *Pale Rider* (Clint Eastwood, 1985), unlike Eastwood, he is unable to save the town from the tyranny of the robber-baron. Instead it is Ellen, who like the preacher in *Pale Rider*, rides into town, redeems Redemption, then rides back to the horizon. In an obvious reversal of the end of *Unforgiven*, then, where Delilah looks yearningly after Munny as he rides out of town, Cort is left standing in the street watching Ellen gallop into the distance. Thus, *The Quick and the Dead*, like *Unforgiven*, eschews heterosexual romance as a containing device for the hard (wo)man and, therefore, is unable to imagine a place or function for the hard (wo)man within the immediate social world of the film. What I want to suggest is that, in order to begin to think about the way in which the hard woman might function within the wider social and historical context, and particularly the way in which, in articulating changing conceptions of femininity, she produces a set of meanings around feminism, we need to look beyond the world of the film to the star persona of Sharon Stone.

Although Ellen clearly has affinities both with Eastwood's pale rider and his 'man with no name' persona – not only because Herod repeatedly asks her 'Who are you?', but also because she is only once, towards the end of the film, referred to by name – unlike Munny in *Unforgiven*, she does not 'become Clint Eastwood'. This is partly because what is essentially a parody of a parody – as Yvonne Tasker points out, 'there is more than a little irony in Eastwood's persona, as the Man with No Name' – tends to question rather than reinforce Eastwood's macho star persona.[44] However, it is also, I think, due to the strength of Stone's star persona. Thus, if

Unforgiven can only be fully understood in terms of the star persona of Clint Eastwood, then *The Quick and the Dead* can perhaps only be fully understood in terms of the star persona of Sharon Stone. What I want to argue, in particular, is that if in *Unforgiven* the process of transformation, of 'becoming Clint Eastwood', can be read as articulating a backlash against feminism, in *The Quick and the Dead*, Sharon Stone comes to us as a fully formed articulation of a post-feminist sensibility. Thus, this is the only female (rape-) revenge western under discussion here that does not feature the obligatory transformation sequence, largely, one assumes, because, after the success of *Basic Instinct*, Stone has effectively 'become' Catherine Tramell and is thus always already believable as a hard woman. Indeed, the critical and commercial failure of her post-*Basic Instinct* film *Sliver* (Philip Noyce, 1993) is perhaps partly attributable to the fact that it cast her in the role of victim rather than villain – as one profile of the star argued, 'the public was not interested in Stone as an actress, but as a character'.[45] Ben Thompson implicitly points up the continuities between *Basic Instinct* and *The Quick and the Dead* as they are articulated around Stone's star persona, when he observes that the latter film has 'Sharon Stone striking *another* blow for womankind by shooting male chauvinists with her big gun'.[46] Of course, Stone's depiction of a psychopathic lesbian killer in *Basic Instinct* was more widely read not as 'striking a blow for womankind', but as constitutive of a wider backlash against feminism. At the very least, the film's engagement with feminism was seen to be compromised by Tramell's sexiness and apparent heterosexuality. Similarly, Thompson argues that *The Quick and the Dead's* 'feminist credentials could hardly be less convincing. Stone's Ellen has a mysterious tendency … to forget to do up her shirt buttons when she leaves the house.'[47] In other words, Stone's construction as a sex symbol was seen as an implicit rejection of feminism. Yet as Suzanne Moore asks:

> What is a symbol of sex meant to be doing in the nineties, I wonder? Selling herself to Robert Redford for a million dollars? … Crawling around in head-to-toe rubber a la Pfeiffer or flogging herself to her richest client like Julia Roberts in *Pretty Woman*? In this context, it's no wonder Stone made it on the basis of just one movie. What she sold us was far sexier than mere sex. It was the ultimate aphrodisiac – a fantasy of power.[48]

What I think Moore articulates quite neatly here is the way in which Stone's star persona, as it has been constructed through her portrayal of Catherine Tramell, is post-feminist not in the sense that it rejects feminism, but in the sense that, to use Charlotte Brunsdon's definition, it marks historically specific 'changes in popularly available understandings of femininity and a woman's place that are generally recognised as occurring in the 1980s'.[49] Particularly indicative of these shifts, and of Stone's articulation of them, is the emergence of figures such as the 'lipstick lesbian' (Tramell is the obvious example, but examples also include Madonna, Susan in *Friends* and Beth in *Brookside*), a figure who is post-feminist insofar as she is both dependent on and dismissive of traditional feminist identities. Thus, while *Basic Instinct* may have been read simply as a rejection of feminism, as Moore observes:

> What caught the public imagination – and particularly the female imagination – was the Katherine Tramell character, a beautiful, sexy, clever woman who does what the hell she likes and gets away with it. Stone was established, like Madonna, as a sex symbol for women as well as for men. And she has been trading on this particular sexual persona ever since. In interviews, she is sharp, sassy, full of bold one-liners such as: "Since becoming famous, I get to torture a better class of man." Meanwhile the tabloids have rushed to print stories about how hard and heartless she really is ... Stone was by now where we wanted her to be: firmly in control.[50]

Again, Moore's description neatly illustrates Brunsdon's definition of the post-feminist woman. According to Brunsdon, this figure

> has a different relation to femininity than either the pre-feminist or the feminist woman ... Precisely because this postmodern girl is a figure partly constructed through a relation to consumption, the positionality is more available. She is in this sense much more like the postmodern feminist, for she is neither trapped in femininity (pre-feminist), nor rejecting of it (feminist). She can use it. However, although this may mean apparently inhabiting a very similar terrain to the pre-feminist woman, who manipulates her appearance to get her man, the post-feminist woman also has ideas about her life and being in control which clearly come from feminism. She may manipulate her appearance, but she doesn't just do it to get a man on the old terms. She wants it all.[51]

In the first part of the following chapter, I want to explore how this notion of 'having it all' is articulated in a recent deployment of the rape-revenge structure, *The Last Seduction*. In so doing, I want to pick up on what is implicit in Brunsdon's reference to consumption here – the way in which notions of 'having it all' are understandable not simply in terms of feminism, but in terms of a Reaganite yuppie culture of consumption and success. In the second half of the chapter, I will turn my attention to another recent deployment of the rape-revenge structure, *Batman Returns*, and explore how the film attempts to make sense of feminism within the context of increasing calls for a more morally restrained capitalism centred around family values. I will, thus, be expanding upon and contextualizing some of the issues that have been raised in this discussion of the Stone star persona as it was constructed through her role in *Basic Instinct*, particularly the relationship between post-feminism, postmodernism and the contemporary neo-noir.

Notes

1 Edward Buscombe, ed., *The BFI Companion to the Western* (London: Museum of the Moving Image, 1991), p. 209.
2 See for example: *Rancho Notorious* (Fritz Lang, 1952), *The Bravados* (Henry King, 1958) and *Last Train from Gun Hill* (John Sturges, 1959).
3 Janet Thumin, '"Maybe He's Tough But He Sure Ain't No Carpenter": Masculinity and In/competence in *Unforgiven*', in *Me Jane: Masculinity, Movies and Women*, ed. by Pat Kirkham and Janet Thumin (London: Lawrence and Wishart, 1995), pp. 234–48 (p. 242).
4 Will Wright, *Six Guns and Society: A Structural Study of the Western* (Berkeley: University of California Press, 1975).
5 Ibid.
6 Pam Cook, 'Women', in *The BFI Companion to the Western*, ed. by Edward Buscombe (London: Museum of the Moving Image, 1991), pp. 240–3 (p. 241).
7 For the purposes of clarity and brevity, female-centred deployments of the rape-revenge structure across the western genre will hereafter be described as female rape-revenge westerns.
8 A further example of the female rape-revenge western can be found in *Shame* (Steve Jodrell, 1988). As an Australian film, however, it falls outside the parameters of this book and for this reason I do not include a discussion of it here. In addition, its relationship to the western, and particularly to the classical plot described by Will Wright, has already been discussed at some length by Stephen Crofts in 'Identification, Gender and Genre in Film: The Case of *Shame*', *The Moving Image*, 2 (1993), 3–88.

9 Wright, *Six Guns and Society*. Wright's corpus is limited by his decision
   to confine his study to films which grossed $4,000,000 or more.

10 Edward Buscombe, 'Cowboys', *Sight and Sound*, 6:8 (August 1996),
   32–5 (p. 34). This debt is made explicit in the film's US title, *Deep in the
   Heart*. It is perhaps also worth mentioning here that Kathleen is a
   teacher of specifically frontier history, while Larry is a collector of guns
   from the period.

11 Wright, *Six Guns and Society*, p. 67.

12 Ibid., p. 158.

13 Ibid., p. 155.

14 Christine Gledhill, 'The Western', in *The Cinema Book*, ed. by Pam
   Cook (London: BFI, 1985), pp. 64–72 (p. 67).

15 Wright, *Six Guns and Society*, p. 156.

16 Ibid., p. 162.

17 Ibid., p. 154.

18 Ibid., p. 154.

19 Stella Bruzzi, *Undressing Cinema: Clothing and Identity in the Movies*
   (London: Routledge, 1997), p. 180.

20 Wright, *Six Guns and Society*, p. 160.

21 Ibid., p. 68.

22 Cook, 'Women', p. 242.

23 Carol J. Clover, *Men, Women and Chainsaws: Gender in the Modern
   Horror Film* (London: BFI, 1992); Yvonne Tasker, *Spectacular Bodies:
   Gender, Genre and the Action Cinema* (London: Routledge, 1993).

24 Yvonne Tasker, 'Approaches to the New Hollywood', in *Cultural Studies and Communications*, ed. by James Curran, David Morley and
   Valerie Walkerdine (London: Arnold, 1996), pp. 213–28 (p. 224).

25 Susan Jeffords, 'The Big Switch: Hollywood Masculinity in the
   Nineties', in *Film Theory Goes to the Movies*, ed. by Jim Collins, Hilary
   Radner and Ava Preacher Collins (London: Routledge, 1993), pp.
   196–208 (pp. 197–8).

26 Ibid. p. 197.

27 Christopher Frayling, *Spaghetti Westerns: Cowboys and Europeans
   from Karl May to Sergio Leone* (London: Routledge and Kegan Paul,
   1981), p. 284.

28 Ben Thompson, '*The Quick and the Dead*: Review', *Sight and Sound*,
   5:9 (September 1995), 58–9 (p. 59).

29 Gledhill, 'The Western', p. 71.

30 Adam Knee, 'The Dialectic of Female Power and Male Hysteria in *Play
   Misty for Me*', in *Screening the Male: Exploring Masculinities in Hollywood Cinema*, ed. by Steven Cohan and Ina Rae Hark (London: Routledge, 1993), pp. 87–102 (p. 101).

31 Indeed, as Janet Thumin has pointed out: 'All the central male characters

are shown to be deficient in a skill that they themselves value and need. Their inadequacies are not just shown in passing ... they are emphatic – leitmotifs, almost: Will's falling off his horse, the Kid's near blindness, the Sheriff's diabolical carpentry.' Thumin, 'Maybe He's Tough', p. 237.

32 Christopher Frayling, '*Unforgiven*: Review', *Sight and Sound*, 2:6 (October 1992), 58.

33 The theme of men's emasculation at the hands of women can also be found in *The Beguiled* (Donald Siegel, 1970). Eastwood plays a wounded Unionist soldier taken in by the inhabitants of a women's school who, towards the end of the film, symbolically castrate him by amputating his wounded leg.

34 Frayling, '*Unforgiven*: Review', p. 58.

35 Mark Simpson, *Male Impersonators: Men Performing Masculinity* (London: Cassell, 1994).

36 Ibid., p. 255.

37 Ibid., p. 258.

38 Ibid., p. 258.

39 Frayling, '*Unforgiven*: Review', p. 58.

40 Paul Smith, *Clint Eastwood: A Cultural Production* (Minneapolis: University of Minnesota Press, 1993), p. 42.

41 Thumin, 'Maybe He's Tough', p. 245.

42 Clearly, in its exploration of what happens when a group of prostitutes take their own revenge, *Bad Girls* represents a more obvious but, I think, less sophisticated, response to *Unforgiven*.

43 Elizabeth G. Traube, *Dreaming Identities: Class, Gender, and Generation in 1980s Hollywood Movies* (Oxford: Westview Press, 1992), p. 138.

44 Tasker, *Spectacular Bodies*, pp. 68–9.

45 'Stone Cast Without Sin', *Observer* (LEA), 29 October 1995, p. 5.

46 Thompson, '*The Quick and the Dead*: Review', p. 59 (my emphasis).

47 Ibid., pp. 58–9. *Bad Girls* was similarly received. Leslie Sharman, for example, argued that '*Bad Girls* is more or less in [the] revisionist strain, featuring as it does four wronged women fighting against a patriarchal society which does not recognise a woman's right to own land or shoot a man in self-defence. Or so it seems on the surface. In actual fact, *Bad Girls* is about as politically correct as a L'Oreal hair mousse commercial.' Leslie Felperin Sharman, '*Bad Girls*: Review', *Sight and Sound*, 4:7 (July 1994), 37–8 (p. 38).

48 Suzanne Moore, 'A Sliver Off the Old Block', *Guardian* (G2), 10 September 1993, p. 11.

49 Charlotte Brunsdon, *Screen Tastes: Soap Opera to Satellite Dishes* (London: Routledge, 1997), p. 101.

50 Moore, 'A Sliver Off the Old Block', p. 11.

51 Brunsdon, *Screen Tastes*, pp. 85–6.

Part IV

Post-feminism

Chapter 6

Rape-revenge in post-modern Hollywood

The late 1980s and 1990s have witnessed a profound resurgence of interest in the codes and conventions of film noir among Hollywood filmmakers. This, in turn, has proved to be of particular interest to feminist film theorists concerned to trace the filmic manifestations and contours of the backlash against feminism that occurred in the late 1980s and 1990s. Given the apparent continuities between this contemporary backlash and the backlash film noir is said to articulate against women's changing status following World War II, such readings are clearly seductive ones. As Julianne Pidduck has observed in her discussion of the contemporary fatal femme cycle:

> The link between gender issues in classic and contemporary *film noir* is more than coincidental. For if the *femme fatale* in wartime and postwar cinema is often connected to a deep-seated unease in the shifting gender roles in that society, the fatal femme offers fertile ground for theorists to speculate on the perceived threat of feminist gains in the 1990s.[1]

Such analyses, however, are, at best, predictable, and at worst, oversimplified. In particular, they not only tend to assume that noir and neo-noir are identical and, therefore, have the same ideological function, they tend to overlook precisely those changes in the social, political and cultural context that the prefix 'neo' should alert us to. More worryingly, they work to install the backlash thesis as the only way of understanding feminism in the 1990s, a pessimistic position that can lead only to political paralysis. While I do not doubt that there has been a backlash against feminism in the 1990s, and that some aspects of this backlash are concomitant with that of the 1940s (for example, the call for a return to 'family values'), I do

think that this continuity should alert us to the fact that feminism
and changes in the position of women in society have always invited
backlashes. No ideology, moreover, even a backlash ideology, is
monolithic. Rather, within a hegemonic society, ideology will always
be subject to negotiation. It is these negotiations that I want to trace
here, particularly those that occur when the ideological conventions
of film noir meet both the rape-revenge structure and the cultural
and political discourses of the late 1980s and 1990s in two neo-noirs
of the period, *The Last Seduction* and *Batman Returns*. In so doing,
I want not so much to counter the backlash thesis, as to suggest that
the understandings of feminism these films produce are not only or
always those of backlash politics, and to look at some of the alternative ways in which they can be seen to make sense of feminism.

Before doing this, however, I want to sketch out some of the key
contextual changes that distinguish the noir moment from that of
the contemporary neo-noir and which, therefore, inform my argument. The most obvious of these changes concerns the rise of
second-wave feminism in the late 1960s. While some of the transformations in women's lives brought about by second-wave feminism are similar to those that occurred in the post-war period (for
example, the movement of women out of the home and into the
workplace), they are not simply continuous with them. Rather, the
changes second-wave feminism has effected are not only more
extensive and more sustained (concerning not only women's right to
work but women's legal, economic, reproductive and sexual rights),
they are enshrined in law (in equal opportunities, divorce, abortion
and rape laws). Moreover, these changes are increasingly being
taken for granted, are entering into our common-sense understanding of the world. The concomitant emergence of the female rape-
revenge narrative during this period is also significant for two
related reasons. Firstly, for the way in which it has legitimated the
actions of the violent and often erotic female figure, a figure who
clearly has affinities with the femme fatale of film noir. Secondly, for
the way in which the codes and conventions of rape-revenge appear
to be finding their way into the neo-noirs of the 1990s. From the
erotic thrillers of Paul Verhoeven (*Basic Instinct* and *Showgirls*) to
the neo-noirs of Tim Burton (*Batman Returns*) and John Dahl (*Kill
Me Again* and *The Last Seduction*), the narrative structure and motifs
of the rape-revenge cycle are currently being recycled alongside
those of film noir.

The third contextual change relates to the emergence and influence of the New Right on both sides of the Atlantic during this period. While the backlash against feminism has often been attributed to the right-wing ideologies of the Reagan and Thatcher administrations, many of these ideologies, particularly as they were popularly articulated through yuppie culture, can actually be seen as continuous with the goals of feminism. Jane Feuer's summary of the key elements of Reagan-era yuppie culture, as it was constructed in the media, is suggestive of some of these continuities. Yuppie culture, for example, included elements such as 'career obsessiveness, especially for women', 'emphasis on the two-career childless couple' and 'equality for women; sensitivity for men'.[2] Meanwhile, in Britain, as Julia Hallam has observed, 'Thatcher's emphasis on "enterprise" and individual success seemed to offer new opportunities for women as well as men.'[3] It is from within this context, in which upward-mobility, consumerism and acquisitiveness were not only emphasized, but legitimated, that traditional interpretations of the femme fatale's transgressive greed and ambition would seem to demand reinterpretation.[4]

The final contextual difference between the film noirs of the 1940s and the neo-noirs of the 1990s concerns the shift from a modernist to a post-modern aesthetic. Jean Baudrillard has described post-modern culture as a culture of the present made from fragments of the past: 'All that remains is to play with the pieces. Playing with the pieces – that is postmodernism.'[5] Rather than simply reproducing the codes and conventions (and, thus, the ideology) of film noir, then, neo-noirs can be seen to play with these fragments of the past, subjecting them to parody or ironic quotation. In this respect, I will be contesting the analysis of neo-noir outlined by Fredric Jameson in his seminal article on post-modernism.[6] Here, Jameson draws a distinction between pastiche and parody, arguing that pastiche is like parody in so far as it relies on imitation, but unlike parody in that it has no 'ulterior motives' or 'satiric impulse'. Pastiche is thus 'neutral' or 'blank parody' in which the mimicry of past styles is without irony or purpose.[7] Jameson's example of pastiche in contemporary culture is significantly the neo-noir or what he describes as the nostalgia film (*Chinatown*, 1974, and *Body Heat*, 1981). According to Jameson, these films represent a 'desperate attempt to appropriate a missing past'.[8] However, they do not attempt to recapture a real past but simply an image of the past, such

that 'the history of aesthetic styles displaces "real" history'.[9] Moreover, Jameson argues that nostalgia films, such as *Body Heat*, have
been carefully constructed so as to efface 'most of the signals that
normally convey the contemporaneity of the United States in its
multinational era'.[10] Consequently, he claims that 'we seem increasingly incapable of fashioning representations of our own current
experience'.[11] Linda Hutcheon, on the other hand, argues that the

> parodic reprise of the past of art is not nostalgic; it is always critical. It
> is also not ahistorical or de-historicizing; it does not wrest past art
> from its original historical context and reassemble it into some sort of
> presentist spectacle. Instead, through a double process of installing and
> ironizing, parody signals how present representations come from past
> ones and what ideological consequences derive from both continuity
> and difference.[12]

It is the ideological consequences that derive from the continuity
and difference between past and present representations that I will
be concerned to trace in this chapter. In particular, I will be exploring how the parodic reprise of film noir reconfigures the backlash
against women of the 1940s in a way that can be seen as both specific to, and an attempt to make sense of, our own current experience in the late twentieth century.

Post-modern culture is, however, characterized not only by the
parody of past representations and styles, but also by a pluralism of
styles and genres. As I have suggested, many contemporary neo-
noirs are marked not only by a self-conscious deployment of the
codes and conventions of film noir, but also by a playful recycling of
the narrative structure and motifs of the rape-revenge cycle.
Throughout I have been arguing for the historical specificity of this
cycle in relation to the rise of second-wave feminism. Janey Place
has put forward some similar arguments with regard to film noir.
Place argues that film noir should be considered not as a genre, but
as a movement which, 'in fact, touches every genre':

> For a consideration of women in film noir, this is more than a seman-
> tic dispute. Film movements occur in specific historical periods – at
> times of national stress or focus of energy … The attitudes toward
> women evidenced in film noir – i.e., fear of loss of stability, identity
> and security – are reflective of the dominant feelings of the time.[13]

This chapter, therefore, will explore the significance of this post-
modern combination of these two quite discreet, historically specific

cycles of films. What happens when the pre-second-wave feminist narratives of the film noir cycle meet the feminist narratives of the rape-revenge cycle in an era that has frequently been characterized as one of backlash against feminism? How is this combination negotiated and what meanings does this negotiation produce in terms of feminism in the 1990s? I will also be examining the relationship between these post-modern films and post-feminism. In her survey of contemporary feminism, Imelda Whelehan claims that much recent feminist thinking is marked by a 'schizophrenic viewpoint', suggesting that feminism is currently undergoing an 'identity crisis'.[14] Indeed, as Boyne and Rattansi have argued, the postmodern condition can be characterized as 'one of coincidence between "crises in representation"' in both the arts and political movements.[15] What then might the post-modern representation of both feminism and feminine identity tell us about feminism in the 1990s?

Having it all: *The Last Seduction*

As I have already suggested, John Dahl's *The Last Seduction* represents a playful combination of the motifs and narrative structures of both the film noir and rape-revenge cycles. Yet, while Dahl's interest in playing with the conventions of film noir is widely established, his perhaps more unconscious interest in the conventions of rape-revenge has yet to be remarked upon. For those familiar with Dahl's work, however, this combination should not come as a surprise, particularly since it is one that is apparent in his mainstream directorial debut, *Kill Me Again* (1989). Here, the femme fatale, Fay (Joanne Whalley-Kilmer), and her boyfriend, Vince (Michael Madsen), literally act out the rape-revenge structure (he pretends to rape her, she pretends to kill him) in order to trick the private detective, Jack (Val Kilmer), into leading them to the money he has buried. Indeed, Dahl even foregrounds the structure's nature as filmic convention by positioning Jack as the voyeuristic male spectator in the wardrobe. In this early example, however, Dahl ultimately falls back onto a traditional deployment of the conventions of film noir by violently eliminating the duplicitous femme fatale. Dahl's next two films, *Red Rock West* (1993) and *The Last Seduction* (1993), however, were financed on the Hollywood fringes (both were screened on cable television before making their theatrical debuts) and, therefore, can be seen as less constrained by the commercial and ideological imperatives and formulas of main-stream Hollywood. Indeed, in the latter film, the heroine's ability to mirror-write or write backwards functions not only as a self-conscious reference to her role as a duplicitous femme fatale, but as a marker of the film's concern with reversing conventional expectations of genre and gender.[16] In so doing, it suggests that we, like the heroine's husband (who is forced to hold his wife's note up to a mirror in order to decipher it), will need to abandon established strategies of reading if we are to make sense of the film.

In line with its deployment and combination of the discourses of both the film noir and rape-revenge cycles, *The Last Seduction* can be seen to tell two stories. On the one hand, it tells a story of female ambition and greed, which is clearly borrowed from the film noirs of the 1940s. On the other, it tells a feminist story, which is clearly borrowed from the rape-revenge narratives of the 1970s and 1980s. Within the context of the 1990s, however, these stories are given specific contemporary inflections. The film noir story of female ambition and greed, for example, is translated and updated into a Reaganite story of individual success and upward mobility, while the feminist rape-revenge story becomes a tale Bridget tells to explain and justify her behaviour. In so self-consciously foregrounding the rape-revenge story *as* story, the film expresses not only a hyper-awareness of the conventions of the rape-revenge story that is purely contemporary, but an understanding of that story's function as one of the ways in which Hollywood has attempted to make sense of feminism. The post-modern play with the conventions of film noir and rape-revenge consequently results in the intersection of a 1980s success story with a feminist story. It is this intersection and its consequences for feminism that I will be concerned to investigate here.

Elizabeth Traube has described the 1980s success story as a narrative not only in which women were marginalized, but in which they were often positively demonized:

> During the 1980s Hollywood filmmakers turned with renewed energy to stories of individual mobility and success. The scaled-down dreams of 1970s melodramas such as *Rocky I* or *Saturday Night Fever* gave way to grander, generically comic fantasies of the unrestricted triumph of desire. Only men, however, enacted the more expansive dream. Unlimited ambition in women continued to be constructed as a threat, requiring either their subordination to the appropriate men or their expulsion from the imagined community. During the Reagan era … a

fantasized threat of female power, embodied in women and in feminized enemies, became instrumental to an ongoing ideological project
of remasculinization.[17]

Traube's analysis operates broadly within the logic of the backlash
thesis and, while her conclusions are somewhat pessimistic, her pursuit of this argument in relation to her chosen films is, on the whole,
convincing. It is not my purpose here then to critically engage with
Traube's analysis. Rather, I want to explore the extent to which *The
Last Seduction's* specific take on the success story departs from the
ideological project Traube identifies with that story.

The plot synopsis that appears on the film's video jacket explicitly
identifies the film with the desires for affluence and upward-mobility characteristic of the 1980s success story. Unlike the 1980s success
story, however, it is a woman who is situated as the subject of this
fantasy of the unrestricted triumph of desire: 'Bridget Gregory
(Fiorentino) wants it all. And she wants it now. No matter what it
takes. No matter who gets hurt.' While this description could be
referring to the acquisitive femme fatale of a 1940s film noir, the use
of the specifically post-second-wave feminist notion of 'having it all'
points towards the film's updating of the noir story. This contemporary retelling of the noir story as both a feminist story and as an
1980s success story is confirmed in the opening sequence. Here two
different types of commercial transactions are juxtaposed: Clay (Bill
Pullman) selling a suitcase of pharmaceutical cocaine to two black
guys and his wife, Bridget (Linda Fiorentino), bullying a team of
telephone salespeople selling commemorative coin sets. From the
outset, then, the film is set firmly within the political context and discourses of the 1980s, a period succinctly described by Arthur Marwick as the 'era of buying and selling'.[18] It is within this context,
furthermore, that the cocaine deal also functions since, as Marwick
observes, 'cocaine was the drug of the eighties' and 'the staple of one
facet of yuppie life-style'.[19] According to Marwick, the roots of the
yuppie phenomenon lay in 'the large incomes and commissions to be
earned in finance, accountancy, law, in agencies and consultancies of
all kinds, as well as in commerce … combined with vigorous propa-
ganda on behalf of the notion that success was far more important
than social origins'.[20] In many ways, then, *The Last Seduction* sets
itself up as a drama of upward mobility and as an articulation of the
yuppie ethos of success by any means necessary. As we later learn,

the motive behind the drugs deal is Bridget's desire for new digs, specifically a penthouse; a motive that is, according to the yuppie ideology articulated by Bridget, a wholesome one. Indeed, the film is careful to point up that the selling of commemorative coin sets, while obviously legal, is perhaps no more wholesome than drugs dealing. The duplicity involved is made particularly apparent when, given the choice between a thousand dollars worth of rare com-memorative coins and a hundred dollars cash as commission for a sale, one of the salespeople unhesitatingly chooses the cash.

This opening sequence, however, is also understandable in terms of feminism and the changing position of women and, as I have sug-gested, it is within this register that the 'wanting it all' of the video synopsis also makes sense. Here the influence of feminism is dis-cernible principally through the figure of the career woman. For example, Bridget is not only a working woman, she is a saleswoman and thus occupies a position diametrically opposed to the tradition-ally feminine position of consumer. More than this, she actually supervises a team of predominantly male telesales personnel who are economically dependent on her for the cash commissions she has the power to distribute. Indeed, throughout, the film repeatedly articu-lates a common-sense discourse about women and work that simply would not have been possible without second-wave feminism ('A woman loses fifty percent of her authority when people find out who she's sleeping with'; 'A woman has to protect her standing at the office, *you know that*.'). In contrast, Clay, while similarly occupying the position of salesperson, lacks Bridget's power because he is not in control of money. Consequently, *The Last Seduction* constructs a world in which white men's power, represented as largely economic, has been usurped by traditionally oppressed groups such as blacks and women, leaving white men in the position of economic depen-dants. While, in many respects, this is simply the logical extension of the ideology of the 1980s, particularly the yuppie idea that suc-cess is far more important than social origins, it is also an index of the changing position of women and minorities brought about by the collective social movements of the 1960s and 1970s.

Toppled from their position of economic superiority, white men become demasculinized. Clay, for example, as the name suggests, is soft and malleable, while Bridget describes the male telesales per-sonnel as eunuchs. Simultaneously, however, money becomes femi-nized. For example, after the two black men empty the briefcase full of money onto the ground, Clay is forced to stuff the proceeds of the drugs deal into his shirt, giving him a pregnant-looking bulge, which he subsequently gives birth to on the sofa. Furthermore, on inspecting the bundles of notes, Bridget remarks: 'They're soft. I thought they'd be stiff.' In other words, money is no longer endowed with phallic attributes and instead begins to take on traditionally feminine characteristics.

The connection between Bridget and the ideology of the 1980s is made even more explicit when, having absconded with the money, she is forced to stop for petrol. The scene opens with a close-up of a large sign that reads 'self-serve only' from behind which Bridget emerges. The camera then follows her to her jeep, which is being filled by a male attendant. Clearly, the ironic juxtaposition of images here undermines the denotative meaning of the sign and suggests that Bridget would rather get men to do her dirty work for her. On a connotative level, however, the sign neatly encapsulates the ethos of the 1980s, while the camera work functions to position Bridget as the embodiment of that ethos. Lest we fail to make this connection, the connotative meanings of the sign are reinforced shortly afterwards when Bridget's lawyer asks whether she is 'still a self-serving bitch'.

The question that remains, however, is what all this has to do with rape-revenge and feminism? As I have already argued, the representation of Bridget as an economically independent career woman has clearly been enabled not only by the Reaganite ideology of success through individual initiative, but by feminism. More significantly, while the opening sequences function to construct the film as a 1980s success story, they also work to suggest that the film's subsequent narrative trajectory might also be understandable as a tale of female revenge. This becomes particularly apparent in the scene where Clay returns home with the proceeds from the drugs deal stuffed down his shirt. In response to Bridget's claim that he was an idiot to 'walk the streets like that', Clay strikes her hard across the face. Immediately contrite, however, he tells her: 'Hey, you can hit me, anywhere – hard.' During the course of the narrative Bridget will take up his offer to exact her revenge, but not in quite the literal way he anticipates. Indeed, the way in which this narrative of female revenge intersects with the 1980s success story also has some unexpected effects, principally on the way in which the film makes sense of feminism. In particular, at key points throughout the film,

Bridget's acquisitiveness, selfishness and greed are legitimated through recourse to feminist discourses, specifically those around violence against women, which the rape-revenge narrative articulates. For example, on two occasions during the course of the film, Bridget attributes her actions to the fact that Clay hit her:

CLAY Give me the money back.
BRIDGET It's mine. You hit me.
CLAY I slapped you.
BRIDGET It's mine.

On one level, then, the film represents the co-option of 1970s feminist discourses around violence against women to the Reaganite yuppie ideology of the 1980s. The co-option of these feminist discourses is, however, both knowing and self-conscious, as Clay and Bridget's second exchange makes explicit:

CLAY Oh Bridge, what made you do this?
BRIDGET I don't know. You slapped me.
CLAY That's just an excuse.
BRIDGET You're probably right, but I get to slap you back.

Yet, while the self-consciousness inherent in this deployment of feminist discourses works to undermine their function as a legitimating device, this is only partial. In other words, although it is recognized that the deployment of feminist discourses of domestic violence is just an excuse for Bridget's behaviour, it is nevertheless those same feminist discourses that enable Bridget to slap Clay back with impunity. Furthermore, the exchange represents an articulation of the slippage inherent in feminist discourses between domestic violence as a physical actuality ('You slapped me') and domestic violence as a metaphorical expression of power (the ways in which Bridget contrives to slap Clay back). It is this slippage, moreover, which enables feminist discourses to be appropriated for ends that are not specifically feminist.

The irony implicit in the film's deployment of feminist discourses also means that the film can rely on those discourses at the same time as it disavows or critiques them. It is worth noting, however, that the film invokes a particular type of feminist discourse, one that has been described by Naomi Wolf, among others, as 'victim feminism'. Victim feminism has recently been the subject of several feminist critiques and is defined by Wolf as 'when a woman seeks power through an identity of powerlessness'.[21] This definition would appear to be particularly applicable to the way in which feminist discourses are deployed in *The Last Seduction*. In other words, Bridget repeatedly adopts an identity of powerlessness or invokes and utilizes a discourse of victim feminism to get what she wants. For example, she tells her new employer in Beston that her husband beat her in order to convince him to conceal her true identity; she tells Mike (Peter Berg) that Lance Collier (one of the men on the 'cheating husbands' list) also beat his wife in order to convince him that killing him is justified; she explains away Harlan's (Bill Nunn) death by pretending he was about to indecently assault her; and she escapes the second private detective by phoning the police and pretending that he has indecently exposed himself to her young daughter.

As I have suggested, however, this identity of powerlessness is adopted both knowingly and self-consciously, especially since Bridget is so clearly constructed as not a victim. Indeed, the film repeatedly exposes the gap between this identity and Bridget's identity as a 'self-serving bitch' and this is, in fact, where a good deal of the film's humour comes from. Particularly noteworthy is the scene in which Mike begs her to open up and let him love her. After implying that she has been hurt by men once too often, Bridget confesses shyly, 'Maybe I could love you', then, with perfect comic timing, snarls, 'Will that do?'. In addition, Bridget's displays of feminine sweetness or helplessness are so hugely exaggerated that they are virtually parodies of feminine behaviour. These are, therefore, also the points at which the film can be seen to be most clearly engaging and negotiating with the discourses of feminism. More specifically, the film's use of parody functions to mark both its reliance on, and disavowal of, 1970s feminism. For example, in revealing how femininity is socially constructed, such parodies suggest that the film has been informed by a feminist critique of the perceived naturalness of gender roles. Simultaneously, however, Bridget's parody of feminist attempts to claim special treatment on the basis of victim status suggests an equivalent critique of victim feminism. In particular, by masquerading as a victim, Bridget questions the authenticity of that identity and of the feminist politics associated with it, particularly its claims to represent the truth of women's experience. Consequently, rather than reproducing the standard feminist distinction between a manipulative feminine identity and an authentic, truthful feminist identity, the film collapses these two identities, suggesting that the latter's adoption of an identity of powerlessness is little more than another addition to the repertoire of wiles and manipulation through which women have traditionally got their way. This is not to say that there is an authentic self behind Bridget's masquerade of powerlessness. Rather, the self behind the masquerade is itself a construction composed of fragments of media images (the femme fatale, the yuppie career woman). Indeed, as Bridget herself says to Mike: 'I work here now. Don't fuck with my *image*.' Of course, many may find *The Last Seduction's* mockery of the stereotype of woman as victim extremely problematic. Yet, as Charlotte Brunsdon has argued, 'a feminist project can only gain from a rather more provisional, attentive, even ironic, sense of self – and other'.[22]

Elsewhere, feminist ideas are treated playfully, ironically or even irreverently (as at the end of the film, where Bridget literally *asks* to be raped – a point to which I will return), and it is perhaps examples such as this that prompted Philip French to argue that the film operates 'at the point where the extremes of misogyny and feminism meet'.[23] As I have been suggesting, however, I think the film, in fact, functions at the point where the discourses of feminism and the discourses of Reaganism meet and, in negotiating this intersection, the film represents an attempt to make sense of the relationship between these two sets of discourses. The influence of Reaganism can be seen specifically in the film's construction of a world where anything can be brought or sold (sex, murder, information, time – 'I'll buy a week'), where everything is reduced to a matter of economics even, as we have seen, domestic violence. Indeed, this is a world in which even heterosexual relations are conducted in the language of the market place. For example, when Mike tells Bridget that he is 'hung like a horse', she insists on taking a look. When Mike protests, she retorts: 'I don't *buy* any things I don't see.' Moreover, when she continues by asking Mike how many lovers he has had, he replies: 'What, do I get extra *credit points* for experience.' While this exchange perhaps owes as much to AIDS as to Reaganism, it also owes something to feminism, particularly feminism's critique of the economics of marriage as a form of legalized prostitution in which women are little more than sexual commodities. Feminism itself, nevertheless, also becomes inscribed in the market place as a consumer item. Here, for example, feminism quite literally becomes an advertising fiction, as Bridget, the consummate saleswoman, sells various versions of the feminist story to a number of men who are only too happy to prove their feminist credentials by buying her product. Likewise, in order to sell the idea of murder to Mike, Bridget frequently resorts to feminist discourses either of domestic violence (she argues that killing Lance Collier is justified because he beat his wife) or equality (she claims she wants a relationship of equals based on them both committing a murder).

This emphasis on selling, and particularly on its connotations of trickery, links with Bridget's manipulation of feminist and feminine identities to position her within a lineage of representations of US success heroes, comprehensively described by Elizabeth Traube: 'The archetypal comic success hero … is a trickster who succeeds through cunning, duplicity, and the artful manipulation of images' rather than through honest hard work.[24] Traube goes on to argue that:

> If the concept of the performing self had origins in popular antebellum comedy, its future was tied to the growth of the professional-managerial class. During the twentieth century, an older delight in image-making would be incorporated into the bureaucratic and consumption ethics of late capitalist society.[25]

A term that appears frequently in Traube's discussion of this 'corporate shape-changer' is seduction.[26] Given its centrality to *The Last Seduction's* title, Traube's use of this word is illuminating since it points to the complex ways in which the seduction of the film's title might make sense. In other words, while dictionary definitions key into the film's noiresque construction of dangerous female sexuality ('charm, entice, allure (*usu* to evil)'), Traube's analysis alerts us to its corporate applications.[27] Of course, women have always had a privileged relation to dressing-up and, therefore, to both seduction and identity transformation. Indeed, image-manipulation is a key narrative motif not only of the success story, but of the film noir and rape-revenge cycles. The centrality of identity transformation to the latter has already been well-documented in preceding chapters and, thus, here I will refer only to Christine Gledhill's observations concerning the 'changeability and treachery' of the femme fatale.[28] Traube argues, however, that while success stories construct image-manipulation and 'bureaucratic seduction as a positively valued style for men', they 'simultaneously [discourage] its cultivation by women, whose career ambitions are ritually tamed in the basic plot'.[29] Indeed, she goes on to suggest that the taming of the career woman these films enact represents a means of reintroducing 'the theme of moral discipline into success stories'.[30] Perhaps the clearest example of this process is the representation and narrative trajectory of Katherine Parker (Sigourney Weaver) in *Working Girl*. Traube's description of Katherine as a 'true shape-changer' and 'predatory seductress', who 'dispassionately includes sex among the resources at her disposal for controlling others', is also a fairly accurate description of Bridget. Katherine, however, unlike Bridget, is ultimately expelled and punished for her corporate duplicity and predatory sexuality. According to Traube, this comes in the form of a 'symbolic phallic punishment' whereby the heroine's earlier disparaging reference to Katherine's 'bony ass' is appropriated by the businessman, Trask, and used 'as a metonymic transformer that deprives Katherine of her dangerous, seductive sexuality prior to her expulsion'.[31]

There is a further link here with *The Last Seduction*, where reference is also made to Bridget's 'bony ass'. Unlike *Working Girl*, however, it is the man who makes the comment, rather than Bridget herself, who is subsequently punished and deprived of his (albeit mythical) dangerous sexuality. Bridget has been trapped in her car by Harlan, the black private detective hired to find her by Clay. Realizing her only means of escape is to crash the car in the hope that Harlan will be killed while she is saved by the driver's airbag, she attempts to get Harlan to remove his seat belt by asking him if it is true that black men are particularly well-endowed. Initially refusing to take the bait, Harlan simply retorts by asking whether it is true that white women have bony asses. However, after Bridget has taunted him by suggesting that he is simply trying to hide his shortcomings, he agrees to show her his penis. While he is distracted with undoing his seat belt and trousers, Bridget accelerates and drives into a tree. Harlan goes through the windscreen and is not only killed, but suffers the additional ignominy of dying with his trousers down. Bridget, on the other hand, survives and, indeed, it is precisely her ability to shape-change, to transform herself, when questioned about the incident, into the image of desexualized white femininity – in which register the 'bony ass' comment functions – that allows her to avoid any implication in Harlan's death and escape punishment. Consequently, unlike *Working Girl*, which attempted to reintroduce the theme of moral restraint into the success story by punishing the female corporate shape-changer, *The*

Last Seduction, as one reviewer put it 'has no moral other than "bad girls win"'.[32]

This peripeteia, I think, represents an interesting example of the way in which the anti-feminist ideology the 1980s success story identified by Traube intersects with, is transformed by, and is transforming of, the discourses of the film noir and rape-revenge cycles. The scene, for example, clearly constitutes a playful and self-conscious articulation of the anxieties about masculine identity and sexuality, which were characteristic of film noir.[33] Unlike film noir, however, these anxieties are not overcome by destroying the threat to masculinity embodied in the figure of the femme fatale. On the contrary, the desire to overcome the anxiety by attempting to prove masculinity is shown to lead not to the destruction of the femme fatale, but to the destruction of masculinity itself. There are clearly continuities here, then, with the rape-revenge structure, where equivalent attempts to assert masculinity (through the act of rape) are similarly destroyed (through the act of revenge). Indeed, Bridget's explanation for Harlan's death relies on a playful deployment of the rape-revenge structure (as she says, it was 'like in the movies'), and particularly of certain rape myths (for example, those of the black male rapist and of the white female victim). Here, however, it is patriarchy, in the form of male authority figures (Harlan and the detective investigating his death), rather than women, who are shown to be the victims of such myths. Unlike film noir, then, *The Last Seduction* holds the law up as an object of ridicule rather than of authority and, in so doing, aligns itself with the rape-revenge cycle's rejection and circumvention of the law. Finally, the specific form Bridget's shape-changing takes here aligns her with the transforming female avengers of rape-revenge (although the traditional direction of those transformations – victim to avenger – is reversed).

The climax of the film invites a similar kind of analysis. The plot here clearly owes a good deal to perhaps *the* classic film noir, *Double Indemnity* (Billy Wilder, 1944). The reference, however, is both knowing and self-conscious. For example, Bridget herself refers to the film's title when explaining her plan to Mike and she also assumes the name Mrs. Neff (the surname of *Double Indemnity's* male protagonist) in order to facilitate her final escape from the second private detective. Indeed, that Bridget associates herself with Neff (Fred MacMurray) rather than the more obvious choice of the femme fatale, Phyllis Dietrichson (Barbara Stanwyck), is significant since it alerts us to the fact that, while the film's resolution may borrow from the plot of *Double Indemnity*, we should not expect it to fulfil the same ideological function in relation to gender. More explicitly, the alignment of Bridget with Neff, rather than Phyllis, would appear to have a two-fold purpose. Most obviously, it functions to privilege Bridget's role as a career woman over her role as a femme fatale, since both she and Neff, the association reminds us, have careers selling insurance. Although film noir does not entirely exclude the femme fatale from the world of work, as Christine Gledhill has observed, it specifically situates them in 'bars and night-clubs rather than in professions or factories' and, thus, in occupations that 'emphasise the sexual objectification of women'.[34] The occupational differences the film constructs between Bridget and the femme fatale, therefore, also serve to emphasize its contemporary rendition of film noir as a 1980s success story with a feminist subtext. This is made explicit in the film's particular take on the *Double Indemnity* plot. Bridget, like Phyllis, needs to convince Mike to kill her husband. Unlike Phyllis, however, she does this not by constructing herself as the sexual reward for compliance, but by appealing to Mike's desire for upward mobility ('You want to live bigger, but there's nothing you'd kill for').

What finally clinches Mike's decision to go to New York and kill Clay/Cahill – his false belief that the transvestite, Trish (Serena), he mistakenly married is coming to Beston to be near him – has the effect of setting the film firmly back within the parameters of film noir and especially those of *Double Indemnity*. As both Richard Dyer and Claire Johnston have observed, for example, the relationship between Neff and Keyes (Edward Robinson) in *Double Indemnity* can be read as implicitly homosexual.[35] The motif of Mike's marriage to Trish is, however, not only characteristic of film noir's articulation of anxieties about masculinity, it is also the film's central narrative enigma. In this respect, then, the film is constructed according to film noir's traditional investigative narrative structure: the enigma is set up early on in the film's first bar scene (Mike's sojourn in Buffalo and mysterious marriage), is subject to investigation during the course of the narrative (Bridget's visit to Buffalo) and finally resolved in the closing scenes (Mike married a transvestite). Clearly, where this structure differs from that found in film noir is in its reversal of the gendered patterns of such investigations. In other words, as Christine Gledhill has observed, in classic film noir it is 'woman' and particularly 'the secrets of female sexuality' that frequently become 'the object of the [male] hero's investigation'.[36] In *The Last Seduction*, as we have seen, those roles are reversed.[37] Indeed, that Mike is the object of Bridget's investigative gaze is established by the first shot of him, which is (indirectly) motivated by Bridget's gaze at the bar from the petrol station. This shot, moreover, uses the standard cinematic conventions usually used to represent and construct the 'feminine' (close-ups, soft-focus, slow motion and raunchy music). Bridget's 'masculinity', on the other hand, is suggested both by her association with the city (her pseudonym is New York backwards) and by Mike's belief that she represents 'a new set of balls'.

In typical noir style, however, Bridget, the bad city girl is also contrasted with Stacy (Donna Wilson), the good country girl and this partly functions to stabilize gender relations by positioning Bridget on one side of the virgin/whore dichotomy.[38] Furthermore, while it is worth noting that the country/city opposition is also a key motif of the rape-revenge cycle, here I think it marks the point at which the conventions of film noir intersect with the dynamics of the contemporary success story. It is within this register that the 'new set of balls' comment is perhaps also best understood. In other words, Mike sees women like Stacy as anchors and, thus, as blocks to upward mobility ('You get too close to one, Beston's got you for life'), while he sees women like Bridget as representing a 'new set of balls' and, thus, as a route to upward mobility. The connection is made explicit by Mike's claim that he will leave Beston when he has grown 'a new set of balls'. When Mike expresses an interest in Bridget, his friend retorts, 'That's city trash, man … what do you see in that?' Mike's reply – 'A new set of balls' – refers back to his earlier comment and situates Bridget, as representative of the city, as his means of escape from Beston. In this respect, then, the character of Mike is clearly continuous with that of Walter Neff in *Double Indemnity* who, as Sylvia Harvey explains, 'seeks an escape from the dull routine of the insurance company that he works for, in an affair with the deadly and exotic Phyllis Dietrichson'.[39]

As we have seen, however, by the end of the film it is Bridget rather than Mike who is associated with Neff. Within the context of the film's reversal of the gender conventions of film noir, this association functions to prefigure the gender reversal that occurs in the film's climactic scene where Bridget dresses up as a man (right down to the Y-fronts) and taunts Mike into raping her by pretending she is Trish. Here, then, the codes and conventions of film noir are once again transformed by the self-conscious deployment of the codes and conventions of the rape-revenge cycle. Thus, while Bridget largely conforms to the description of the femme fatale outlined by Janey Place, she also departs from it in small, but significant details.[40] For example, unlike the femme fatale, whose weapon of choice is the gun, which, according to Place, is the symbol of 'her "unnatural" phallic power', Bridget's is a can of mace (she attempts to defend herself from Harlan with it and she uses it to kill Clay).[41] Bridget's choice of weapon thus functions to situate the film within feminist discourses of violence against women, and to align Bridget with the female avenger of rape-revenge rather than with the femme fatale of film noir. It also suggests Bridget's power comes from feminism rather than from her appropriation of the phallus, and thus counters the widespread tendency to equate feminism with masculinization. As I argued in chapter 1, this tendency is particularly apparent in Clover's work on the rape-revenge film. In many ways, however, *The Last Seduction* could be seen as simply confirming Clover's argument. Certainly, the crossdressing motif is one that is continuous with certain films of the rape-revenge cycle. It is, moreover, one which, within the logic of the film's concern with transvestism, would appear to work to construct Bridget as a 'phallic woman'.

I think, however, that the self-consciousness I have identified in the film's deployment of social, political and cultural discourses, together with the playful way in which it engages with audience expectations, should alert us against assuming too conventional an understanding of this motif.[42] For example, in all other respects, the climactic scenes reverse the traditional expectations of the rape-revenge structure. On a very simple level, the rape is located at the end of the film rather than at the beginning. This, in turn, functions to reverse the conventional direction of the rape-revenge film's transformations. In other words, rather than moving from being feminized to being eroticized/masculinized, Bridget moves from being eroticized/masculinized to being feminized. This is made explicit in her taunt to Mike, 'I'm Trish, rape me' (literally, 'I'm a man, make me a woman'). While the way in which Bridget asks to be raped here represents an apparently reactionary confirmation of the myth that women are 'asking for it', its deployment is, as always, heavily ironic (it is men who are shown to be the victims of such myths since, by raping Bridget, Mike implicates himself in the murder of Clay). Moreover, in assuming Trish's identity and asking to be raped, Bridget also succeeds in symbolically displacing the traditional punishment of the femme fatale onto the film's other phallic woman (Trish). In this respect, Bridget's crossdressing can be seen as an ironic comment on the widespread belief that a powerful and successful woman is also a masculinized one. Indeed, given the ineffectuality of the phallic objects (guns, knives) with which the men in the film arm themselves, the film can clearly be seen to construct a post-modern milieu in which the phallus, once the transcendental signifier, has become unfixed from its formerly unrivalled association with power. In the film's final scenes, then, Bridget is shown to have shed the sexy but business-like clothes – stockings; short, fitted skirts; tailored trousers; shirts; waistcoats; jackets in black, white and grey – of the 'phallic' femme fatale/career woman. Instead, she wears a long, figure-hugging dress, in soft, moss-coloured material, her make-up is softer and more muted and her hair less sleekly styled. In addition, whereas, throughout the film, Bridget has been aggressively self-sufficient, here she allows her chauffeur to hold her umbrella and open doors for her; an indication both of Bridget's wealth and power and of her femininity. Thus, contrary to Clover's arguments concerning the masculinization of the female avenger, but in line with the erosion of the distinction between feminism and femininity that the film articulates, *The Last Seduction's* narrative trajectory is *towards* femininity and its reconciliation with female power and feminism. Bridget, indeed, 'has it all'.

According to Mary Ann Doane:

> The femme fatale is situated as evil and is frequently punished or killed. Her textual eradication involves a desperate reassertion of control on the part of the threatened male subject. Hence, it would be a mistake to see her as some kind of heroine of modernity. She is not the subject of feminism but a symptom of male fears about feminism.[43]

Bridget's triumph at the end of *The Last Seduction* would seem to counter the traditional understanding of film noir and, indeed, neo-noir, as representing a backlash against feminism. Does this mean, however, that she is, therefore, 'the subject of feminism'? If she is, what version of feminism does her trajectory through the narrative articulate? In privileging the feminist stories Bridget enunciates over film noir's traditional emphasis on the masculine story, *The Last*

Seduction would certainly appear to situate Bridget as the 'subject of feminism'. However, alongside these feminist stories the film also articulates a Reaganite story of success. Thus, the film can be seen as blending 1970s feminist discourses about violence against women with the Reaganite yuppie ideology of the 1980s. In this sense, the film's project is similar to that of the cable TV channel, Lifetime, which Jane Feuer has argued 'rewrites 1970s feminism as 1980s female yuppiedom' for the 1990s.[44] The traffic between discourses, however, is not simply one-way. There is consequently a case to be made for arguing that while feminism is used to legitimate the politics of Reaganism, Reaganism actually both enables and justifies feminist ambition and will to power. Elizabeth Traube articulates some of these contradictions in her discussion of women and the American Dream. The figure of the nondomestic woman she argues:

> has sources in the feminist movement and in the middle-class ideology of success through individual initiative, which liberal feminism helped to extend to women.
>
> One result of that extension is that contemporary women may not need an ideological commitment to feminist politics to launch them on a nontraditional path. Both Gerson and Rosanna Hertz have shown how the pushes of economic need and domestic isolation or instability combine with the pulls of expanding workplace opportunities to draw middle- and upper-middle-class women into corporate and professional careers, which Hertz describes as 'an intersection of feminism and the American dream'.[45]

This suggests, moreover, that the understanding of feminism the film produces is not one of backlash but one in which feminism is simultaneously invoked and suppressed. For example, as I have argued, the film depends on certain discourses of 1970s feminism (particularly those around violence against women) at the same time as it disavows or critiques the identities (particularly that of the victim) these discourses construct for women. In this respect, I think the film's critique of victim feminism must be read not as a backlash *against* feminism, but as a backlash *within* feminism. While feminists such as Imelda Whelehan have been, perhaps understandably, suspicious and critical of this backlash, arguing that it represents a form of woman blaming which is fundamentally anti-feminist, I think such criticisms are, in fact, misguided.[46] In particular, they overlook the fact that it is not feminism *per se* that is being rejected but certain aspects of 1970s feminism that, in the words of Charlotte

Brunsdon, are no longer 'adequate to the experience of young women growing up today'.[47] In this respect, the version of feminism the film articulates is best understood as post-1970s feminism rather than as anti-feminism. For example, the film's combination of a Reaganite success story and a feminist revenge story redefines the archetypal feminist notion of 'having it all' according to the exigencies of the present moment. In other words, while in traditional feminist discourse, 'having it all' more often than not meant giving things up (particularly heterosexual femininity as it is constructed through adornment and consumerism), the negotiations that occur between 1970s feminism and the 1980s culture of consumption in *The Last Seduction* suggest that it is now possible to have both femininity *and* feminism. Furthermore, in depicting a woman who not only 'wants it all' and gets it, but who succeeds in reconciling the apparent contradictions (between feminism and femininity) that this brings, *The Last Seduction* can be seen as countering the backlash rhetoric, which insisted that feminism's claim that women could 'have it all' had only succeeded in making them miserable. Of course, the understandings of feminism the film produces are not without their problems or detractors. For example, in an acerbic response to a recent US advertising campaign featuring real-life career women wearing smart business jackets on top, but nothing but Jockey's new range of hosiery below, Linda Grant accused the women who dress sexily in the workplace not of wanting it all, but of 'wanting it both ways'.[48] Moreover, like most Hollywood films, the politics *The Last Seduction* articulates are individual rather than collective while, as the conclusion of the film suggests, it is only those in positions of wealth and power that can afford to play at being feminine. In this respect, the understandings of feminism the film produces are open to criticisms similar to those levelled at Naomi Wolf's 'power feminism' – as Julie Burchill recently argued: 'Though currently posing as a universal dilemma, to have or not to have it all is, in reality, an issue only affecting middle-class western women.'[49]

Of vamps and avengers: *Batman Returns*

In her discussion of victim feminism versus power feminism, Naomi Wolf cites Catwoman (Michelle Pfeiffer) in the film *Batman Returns* as an example of a 'power-feminist avenger'. According to Wolf, Catwoman's role as a power-feminist avenger becomes clear in a scene when she saves a woman from rape, but as the woman meekly showers her rescuer with thanks, Catwoman looks her up and down with a mixture of pity and contempt and sneers, 'You make it so easy.'[50]

While Catwoman is, unlike Bridget in *The Last Seduction*, much more clearly constructed in the tradition of the female avenger of violence against women of the rape-revenge cycle, she is also, according to Wolf, 'the masked avenger of the slights and humiliations of clerical work'.[51] This interpretation, however, is not entirely accurate. Rather, I want to argue that Catwoman is constructed as the avenger of capitalist excess and greed as it is embodied in the figure of Max Shreck (Christopher Walken). In other words, while in her guise as Selina Kyle, secretary to Max Shreck, Catwoman is indeed humiliated and shown to be little more than a glorified waitress, it is her discovery of Shreck's capitalist excesses (the plans for the new power plant), rather than her humiliation, that lead to her 'death' and subsequent desire for revenge. Like *The Last Seduction*, *Batman Returns* combines the 1980s success story with the rape-revenge story, although the effects of this combination are somewhat different. The narrative trajectory, in other words, is not towards 'the unrestricted triumph of desire' but towards a more morally restrained and responsible capitalism.[52] Unlike the 1980s success story, however, which, according to Traube, 'reintroduced the theme of moral discipline' by identifying 'the dangerous, uncontrolled forces loose in society with the independent, upper-middle-class, professional-managerial woman', *Batman Returns* identifies these uncontrolled forces as masculine (Shreck) and the forces of moral discipline as feminine (Catwoman).[53] Given the way in which, as Traube observes, moral influence had since the nineteenth century 'appeared as a natural vocation of woman', this situation of Catwoman in the role of moral guardian (of capitalism) is almost as problematic as the success story's traditional demonization of women.[54] It is worth pointing out, however, that the film also explicitly, and rather playfully, sexualizes the theme of moral discipline by constructing Catwoman as a PVC-clad dominatrix complete with whip. It is perhaps significant, in this respect, then, that the film makes Catwoman's first act of revenge a specifically feminist one (saving a woman from rape) and only her second, an attack on capitalist excess as it is articulated through conspicuous consumption (blowing up Shreck's department store). From within the context of the first act, the blowing up of the department store can be read both as a moral comment on the excesses of capitalism *and* as a feminist attack on the relegation of women to the role of consumers rather than producers within a capitalist economy. In constructing Catwoman first as a feminist and then as the moral guardian of capitalism, the film juxtaposes a feminist critique of consumerism with the New Right's late 1980s call for a more morally restrained and responsible capitalism centred around family values.

That the film is not an attack on capitalism itself but on capitalist excess is made clear by the two opposing versions of capitalism the film constructs: that of a responsible capitalism embodied in the figure of Bruce Wayne/Batman (Michael Keaton) and that of a corrupt capitalism personified in the figure of Max Shreck. Interestingly, both versions of capitalism can be understood through their relation to the motif of the vampire, a motif whose cultural currency and visibility in 1992 was assured by the release of *Bram Stoker's Dracula* (Francis Ford Coppola, 1992), *Buffy the Vampire Slayer* (Fran Rubel Kuzui, 1992) and *Innocent Blood* (John Landis, 1992). Indeed, the emergence of the vampire story at key moments in the cultural and social history of the west suggests that, like Batman, the vampire represents a potent and enduring myth which can be mobilized in various ways to make sense of a changing social and political context.[55] My specific purpose here, then, is to trace how the combination of these myths in *Batman Returns* can be seen as an attempt to make sense of feminism within the wider political context of the 1990s.

The influence of the vampire myth in *Batman Returns* is particularly apparent in the figure of Max Shreck who takes his name from the actor who played the vampire in the first film adaptation of Bram Stoker's novel (*Nosferatu*, F. W. Murnau, 1922). Shreck is constructed as a contemporary vampire, a symbol of dangerous and excessive consumption, whose proposed power plant will suck not blood but power from Gotham City. Indeed, as Christopher Frayling has observed, one of the many ways of interpreting the vampire myth is as 'about a pathological form of consumerism'.[56] That Shreck represents a form of capitalism that has quite literally become monstrous and uncontrollable is made clear in his exchange with The Penguin/Oswald Cobblepot (Danny DeVito). 'I'm a business man ... but that does not make me a monster', Shreck tells The Penguin, as the latter, nevertheless, produces a whole series of evidence that, in fact, proves the connection. The power plant for Shreck is, more-over, like blood for the vampire, the route to a form of eternal life, as he tells Selina shortly before 'killing' her: 'This power plant is my legacy, it's what I leave behind, for Chip.'[57] Indeed, while Shreck actually 'kills' Selina by pushing her out of the window, as he closes in on her the film employs all the cinematic conventions traditionally used to represent the vampiric act. Framed in a close-up two-shot, Shreck moves towards Selina as if to kiss/bite her, his head inclined to one side, his lips parted and his eyes fixed on the point where her neck would be were it in frame. That the film is quite literally play-ing around with such conventions is, however, underlined when Shreck abruptly pulls back and pretends he was only joking. Shreck also is dressed according to the specifically cinematic tradition of the vampire as aristocrat. He wears white wing-collared shirts, bow ties and dark suits, with his grey hair swept back off his face. In addition, in the final sequences, he wears a long black cape and, in fact, throughout he wears his coats cape-like over his shoulders.

Bruce Wayne, however, also has associations with the vampire through his alter-ego, the caped-crusader, Batman. As Andrew Ross has observed, the bat totem was 'visually established in modern Euro-western cultural iconography as the vampiric defense of white, aristocratic blood'.[58] The origins of Bruce Wayne's vampiric vigilante alter-ego, however, stem not from the 'defense of white, aristocratic blood' but from the defence of property, as William Uricchio and Roberta E. Pearson explain:

> His childhood trauma stemmed from an incident in which attempted resistance to a petty violation of property rights (the theft of a neck-lace) gave rise to a capital crime (murder). Bruce Wayne's father was willing to give his life to defend property and uphold the law. The son followed in his father's footsteps.[59]

Like Shreck, then, Bruce Wayne/Batman represents a contemporary capitalist articulation of the vampire myth. The myth as it is articu-lated through Bruce Wayne/Batman, however, places him at the opposite pole of the capitalist moral dichotomy to Shreck (who, at one point, describes Bruce Wayne as a 'trust-fund goody-goody'). In other words, as Uricchio and Pearson have observed, Bruce Wayne/Batman's 'vast inheritance places him largely outside the con-straints of capitalist accumulation' and this disassociates him from the capitalist excess personified by Shreck.[60] Instead, as Uricchio and

Pearson elaborate, 'his inheritance and his obsession both stem from an attempt to defend property' and thus situate him not only as supportive of the capitalist economy, but as quite literally conservative.[61] As Bruce Wayne himself points out to Selina, Batman 'probably saved millions of dollars in property damage alone'.

How does Catwoman who, at first glance, would appear to owe more to the femme fatale of film noir and the female avenger of rape-revenge, function within this vampire economy? What I want to argue is that the femme fatale, the female avenger and the female vampire have more in common than might at first appear. It is in the combination and negotiation of these historically specific figurations of femininity that *Batman Returns* can be seen to be attempting to make sense of feminism past, present and future. I want to start by elucidating some fairly basic continuities between film noir and the gothic literary tradition out of which the vampire narrative emerged. The term 'film noir', for example, was derived from the term 'roman noir' used by French critics to describe the nineteenth-century British gothic novel. The similarities between the gothic novel and film noir are, however, not simply semantic but extend right through to the form of the narrative, which in both is frequently fragmentary and unstable. This lack of narrative coherence is, interestingly, also a feature of Burton's *Batman* films (a feature for which he has frequently been criticized). It is really not surprising, however, that Burton should adopt a Gothic mode of story-telling for a character whose origins so clearly lie in the Gothic world of vampires and whose home is none other than *Goth*am City.

Despite her widespread connection with the film noirs of the 1940s and 1950s, the origins of the femme fatale can also be traced to an earlier historical period. As Mary Ann Doane has observed:

> The femme fatale emerges as a central figure in the nineteenth century, in the texts of writers such as Théophile Gautier and Charles Baudelaire and painters such as Gustave Moreau and Dante Gabriel Rossetti … The femme fatale is a clear indication of the extent of the fears and anxieties prompted by shifts in the understanding of sexual difference in the late nineteenth century.[62]

Even more interesting, perhaps, is the fact that the inspiration for these representations came largely from the vampire stories that had circulated widely since the publication of John Polidori's *The Vampyre* in 1819. The evolution of the femme fatale can thus be traced to these stories and particularly to the French writers who, as Christopher Frayling has argued,

> transformed the vampire from melodramatic villain into a more personalised kind of sexy predator. Théophile Gautier's 'Clarimonde' (1836) has 'sea-green eyes and teeth of purest Orient pearl' with which she easily manages to seduce a young country priest; Charles Baudelaire's 'woman with the strawberry mouth' (1857) sucks the pith from the bones of a young poet.[63]

Thus, as Sharon Russell has observed: 'The *femme fatale* leading men to their doom is entirely a sexual image deriving from the siren and the vampire.'[64] It is perhaps not surprising, then, to find that the decadent culture described by both Doane and Frayling was one in which Bram Stoker was deeply enmeshed, or that the figure of the active and erotic femme fatale can be perceived in *Dracula* (1897) in the form of the female vampire.[65]

The femme fatale and the female vampire, moreover, are both figures who must be destroyed. This drive to punish or eradicate these dangerously active and sexual female figures has often been interpreted as a sign of the anti-feminist tendencies of the texts in which they appear. Certainly, Stoker's *Dracula* was, like the film noir cycle, produced at a time when women seemed to be threatening the established status-quo. The 1890s witnessed the rise of first-wave feminism and *Dracula* was, in fact, published in the same year that the National Union of Women's Suffrage Societies was formed under Millicent Garrett Fawcett. *Dracula*, then, like the film noir and rape-revenge cycles, has a particularly privileged relation to feminism. Like film noir and rape-revenge, however, I think it would be reductive to read *Dracula* simply as a backlash text. Rather, I think it represents an attempt to make sense of the spectre of the New Woman and a gathering women's movement.[66] For example, although signs of the sexual emancipation associated with the New Woman are violently punished in the treatment of Lucy, who becomes a female vampire, in the figure of Mina, Stoker appears to have attempted to come to some form of compromise with emergent feminism. Thus, while Mina is to a certain extent represented as a passive victim, she also plays an active part in the ultimate destruction of Dracula. As such, her characterization depends both on the Victorian ideal of compliant womanhood embodied in the 'Angel in the House' stereotype *and* on the feminist ideal of the assertive 'New Woman'. Van

Helsing articulates this combination when he says: 'Ah, that wonderful madam Mina! She has man's brain – a brain that a man would have were he much gifted – and woman's heart.'[67]

Significantly, several commentators have elucidated the Dracula story's anti-feminist tendencies by suggesting that the staking of the female vampire represents a form of symbolic rape. Both Elaine Showalter and S. S. Prawer, for example, have described the staking of the female vampire as a form of 'gang-rape'.[68] Others have likened the vampiric act itself to rape. David Ehrenstein, for example, has argued that 'the spectacle of Dracula's conquests becomes a socially acceptable form of enjoying rape'.[69] Certainly there is much to recommend a reading of the vampiric act as a violent sexual act, not least because of the similarity between the vampire's bite and a kiss and the exchange of bodily fluids this accommodates.[70] More interesting for my purposes, however, are the similarities between the effects of vampirism and the effects of rape on the representation and narrative trajectory of the woman in both the vampire story and the rape-revenge story. In other words, in both stories the effect of vampirism/rape is to bring about a transformation in the woman, a transformation that involves the movement from victim to female vampire/female avenger. This transformation, moreover, frequently involves the eroticization of the previously chaste or dowdy female victim. Eroticization is one of the key signifiers of the threat to patriarchy the female vampire/avenger represents. Firstly, it represents the liberation of female sexuality, a liberation that is threatening because it is no longer confined to providing sexual pleasure for the male. Rather, female sexuality becomes either a lure to trap and destroy the unsuspecting male or, because it has been liberated from its association with marriage and heterosexual romance, exclusive or self-sufficient. The latter is particularly apparent in the lesbian vampire films of the post-1970 period, although it is also a feature of the rape-revenge film where the female avenger, despite her new found sexuality, rejects heterosexual romance.

The final correlation between the female vampire and the female avenger requires little elaboration beyond citing Bonnie Zimmerman's observation that 'whether the woman vampire is lesbian or heterosexual, her real object of attack is always the male'.[71] Indeed, whether the female vampire is a genuine vampire or a mortal vamp/femme fatale, such as those played by Theda Bara in the 1910s, her attacks on men can be read as acts of revenge. As Bara herself claimed: 'Women are my greatest fans because they see in my [role as] vampire the impersonal vengeance of all their unavenged wrongs ... I have the face of a vampire, perhaps, but the heart of a feministe.'[72] These correlations between the vampire story and the rape-revenge story are strikingly illustrated in *The Velvet Vampire* (Stephanie Rothman, 1971) in which, according to Zimmerman, 'the vampire halts in her pursuit of the female victim to attack a rapist'.[73] Given these similarities, and the prominence of the female or lesbian vampire at key moments in the history of feminism (the 1890s and the 1970s), it is possible to argue that the female/lesbian vampire, like the female avenger of rape-revenge, represents one of the key female figures through which British and US culture has attempted to make sense of emergent feminism. Indeed, the recent surge of feminist interest in 'vampy' figures such as the contemporary femme fatale suggests that such figures might also represent a key site through which the current feminist moment can be understood.[74]

Despite their similarities, the vampire story and the rape-revenge story, nevertheless, diverge in two important ways. Firstly, the vampire story frequently shows women not only actively inviting the vampire's attack but getting lascivious pleasure from it. Thus, the spectacle of Dracula's conquests is not only, as David Ehrenstein has argued, 'a socially acceptable form of enjoying rape', it is also a way of making rape socially acceptable by suggesting that women actually want and enjoy rape. The second way in which the vampire story and the rape-revenge story differ is in their ultimate treatment of their female characters. In other words, while both stories construct liberated and threatening female figures, in the vampire story that liberation must ultimately be destroyed through the staking of the female breast; through, in other words, enacting a form of symbolic rape, which returns the woman to her original role of passive victim. In the rape-revenge story, however, there is no such return and the female figure, therefore, remains outside of masculine control and authority as the active avenger of her own rape. The female avenger does, however, have another corollary in the vampire story. This comes in the form of the morally pure woman who is able to resist vampirism and helps to bring about the destruction of the male vampire. Like the female avenger, this figure often embodies some of the traits of the feminist New Woman, but her moral purity and her role in destroying the threat to masculine sexuality and authority the vampire represents ultimately differentiates her from the female avenger of rape-revenge. Furthermore, while the vampire narrative has traditionally split the roles of vamp and avenger (respectively Lucy and Mina in *Dracula*), the rape-revenge film combines them in the figure of the erotic female avenger. This combination, therefore, necessitates a negotiation of both these roles. Given the way in which Catwoman is constructed as an erotic female avenger within a narrative that so explicitly borrows the iconography and conventions of the vampire story, she would appear to provide the ideal site through which to trace these negotiations and their consequences for feminism.

At the beginning of *Batman Returns*, Selina is, like the heroines of both the vampire story and the rape-revenge story, desexualized. This is signalled in a range of ways. Her clothes are drab and dowdy, her hair is pulled back off her face, she has no husband and her relationships with men are, by her own admission, always brief. Camera work also functions to construct Selina as non-erotic object by always positioning her at the edges or background of the frame. Perhaps the most privileged signifier of her unattractiveness, however, is her glasses, which, according to Mary Ann Doane, are 'one of the most intense visual clichés of the cinema', signifying amongst other things, 'repressed sexuality'.[75] More than this, the woman who wears glasses, is constructed as the active bearer of the look rather than as an object to-be-looked-at. Both Doane and Linda Williams have argued that this reversal of the normal gendered relations of looking is so threatening to patriarchal society that it must ultimately be punished.[76] This is, of course, exactly what happens in *Batman Returns*. That is, Shreck pushes Selina out of the window because she has been prying into protected files concerning his proposed power plant. Indeed, throughout this scene, Selina's active look is emphasized not only by her glasses, but by the use of lighting to create angular shadows that give the impression that she is, in fact, wearing two pairs of glasses.

Naturally, by the time we see Selina falling to her 'death', the glasses have disappeared, never to be seen again. To all intents, then, Selina's 'death' marks her transformation from active bearer of the look to passive object-to-be-looked-at (death being the ultimate state of passivity). Indeed, even after Selina has returned from the dead, her 'death' at the hands of the 'vampire', Shreck, is shown to have had the effect of eroticizing her and thus of repositioning her as an

object-to-be-looked-at. This transformation is signalled by changes
in the visual treatment of both Selina and her new incarnation, Catwoman. No longer situated in the background or at the margins of
the frame, Selina/Catwoman moves to the centre foreground of the
frame. That she is now situated as an erotic spectacle is, moreover,
evidenced by the frequency with which she is presented via various
framing devices. In the first shot of her as Catwoman, for example,
she is shown standing framed in her window. More often, however,
she is framed in the centre of the shot by two men standing at each
edge of the shot with their backs to the camera looking at her (for
example, in the scene with Bruce Wayne and Shreck at Shreck's
office, in the scene with the two security guards in the department
store, and in the scene outside the department store with Batman and
The Penguin). However, if the woman as bearer of the look represents a threat to masculinity, so too does the woman as spectacle.
Writing in the 1970s, Laura Mulvey claimed that:

> [The woman] connotes something that the look continually circles
> around but disavows: her lack of a penis, implying a threat of castra-
> tion and hence unpleasure ... Thus the woman as icon, displayed for
> the gaze and enjoyment of men, the active controllers of the look,
> always threatens to evoke the anxiety it originally signified.[77]

Mulvey argues that the cinema, nevertheless, constructs two avenues
of escape from this anxiety: voyeurism or fetishistic scopophilia. It
is the latter that is most significant here. For Mulvey, fetishistic
scopophilia involves 'complete disavowal of castration by the substitution of a fetish object or turning the represented figure into a
fetish so that it becomes reassuring rather than dangerous'.[78] With
her spiked heels, whip and tight-fitting, PVC suit, Catwoman clearly
represents the ultimate fetishist's fantasy, the phallic woman *par
excellence*. The unreconstructed obviousness of this representation
suggests, however, that *Batman Returns*, like *The Last Seduction*, is
very knowing about the discourses of psychoanalysis. This is particularly apparent in an early scene where Selina listens to a message on
her answering machine from her boyfriend. Excusing himself from
the weekend break they had planned together, he claims, 'Doctor
Shaw says I need to be my own person and not an appendage'.
Selina's reply – 'Some appendage. Guess I should have let him win
that last racket ball game' – not only cements the sexual connotations of the term appendage, but playfully positions Selina as the

castrating woman. Similarly, when Catwoman encounters the two security guards in Shreck's department store one says to the other, 'I don't know whether to open fire or fall in love'. 'You poor guys, always confusing your pistols with your privates', Catwoman retorts sarcastically, as she symbolically castrates them by whipping both their guns away. By mocking the notion of masculinity that psychoanalysis constructs and by showing men to be the ultimate victims of their own fetishistic fantasies, the film can clearly be seen to be poking fun at both psychoanalysis and masculinity. Within this context, the way in which Catwoman dominates the frame and dictates camera movement is suggestive not of her status as a passive object-to-be-looked-at, but of her status as the active controller, if not of the look itself, at least of the effects of her own image.

If the film can be seen to undermine its apparent construction of Catwoman as simply a passive fetish object, it can also be seen to challenge its initial punishment of the woman's active gaze. In other words, if Selina loses her glasses, she gains a symbolic pair in the form of her mask. Not only does this emphasize and frame her eyes, the very shape of the eye-holes represents a visual echo of the angular shadows her glasses cast in the scene described above. Indeed, the references to cats (particularly their curiosity) in this early scene serves to cement this interpretation by pre-figuring Selina's transformation into Catwoman. Batman's mask, on the other hand, almost totally obscures his eyes and, therefore, his power to see. The eye-holes, for example, are very small and what remains visible of his eyes is covered over by black make-up so that his eyes literally disappear. This ability to see or not is, of course, most clearly articulated through the totemic animals the two characters adopt. Cats, for example, are predators and have extremely acute vision, whereas bats are commonly (though incorrectly) associated with blindness (hence the popular expression, 'blind as a bat').[79]

Catwoman's status as both an erotic object and as the active bearer of the look, signified through her elaborately made-up eyes, also align her with the femme fatale or vamp. As Linda Williams has remarked: 'The bold, smouldering dark eyes of the silent screen vamp offer an obvious example of a powerful female look.'[80] As I have already argued, however, the origins of the femme fatale, as Williams' use of the term 'vamp' here suggests, lie partly in the female vampire. Indeed, in the film's final sequences, Catwoman is quite literally constructed as vampiric (although her remarkable recovery from certain death has, of course, already placed her within the ranks of the undead). For example, when Shreck asks her what she wants, her reply is quite explicit: 'Your blood, Max.' Furthermore, whereas earlier at the ball, while dressed in what Christine Gledhill has identified as the conventional garb of the noir femme fatale (a 'long be-sequined sheath [dress]'), Selina had favoured the noir heroine's traditional weapon of choice (the gun), here she reverts to the vamp's original weapon, the kiss/bite ('How about a kiss Santy Claus').[81] This kiss/bite is, moreover, filmed using the standard cinematic conventions usually employed to represent the vampiric act. The extreme close-up from Shreck's point of view of Catwoman's face moving rapidly towards him, mouth open, teeth bared with a stun gun held up to her mouth is particularly noteworthy in this respect. Even the stun gun, not traditionally a weapon in the vampire's arsenal, is significant since it acts as a symbolic stand-in in the absence of real vampire fangs (it has two small, sharp points which, when held up to the mouth, are positioned where the vampire's incisors would be). Finally, Catwoman's nine lives means that, like the vampire, she is difficult to kill by conventional methods (here, a gun).

That Catwoman is not killed is, of course, crucial given that both the female vampire and the femme fatale are customarily punished, often violently. That Catwoman escapes such punishment is largely due to the fact that her vampiric act is also explicitly cast as an act of revenge, as her comment, 'a die for a die', demonstrates. This comment functions to define Catwoman's revenge as specifically one of violence against women and to locate her within the tradition of the female avenger of rape-revenge. However, in carrying out her revenge Catwoman also succeeds in destroying the male vampire, Shreck, and the threat posed (particularly in the recessionary early 1990s) by his immoral and irresponsible brand of consumer capitalism. In this respect, the specific form Catwoman's revenge takes – 'kissing' Shreck while holding onto an exposed electric cable, thus killing him with the very electricity he had planned to suck, like blood, from Gotham City – is not only fitting but serves to point up the dual function of her revenge. The effect of this electrocution is, moreover, similar to the effect sunlight has on the vampire as described by Mina in *Dracula*: 'The whole body crumbled into dust'.[82] Catwoman's role as a vampire slayer, therefore, also aligns her with Mina in *Dracula*, who, as Maurice Hindle has argued, 'makes the final destruction of Dracula possible'.[83]

I argued above that the characterization of Mina can be seen as Stoker's attempt to come to some form of compromise with first-wave feminism by incorporating elements of both the Victorian 'Angel in the House' and the feminist New Woman into her characterization. In casting Catwoman as both a female avenger and as the moral guardian of capitalism, I want to suggest that *Batman Returns* represents an attempt to reach a similar compromise between the demands of feminism and the increasing call in the 1990s for a return to more traditional models of gender (otherwise known as the backlash). That the kinds of models those calling for such a return had in mind were, in fact, those established in the late nineteenth century became clear by the fact that, in Britain at least, their demands were often articulated through a call for a return to 'Victorian values'.[84] These values, popularly believed to encompass the work ethic, thrift and puritanism, were seen as the remedy to the problems besetting capitalism in late 1980s and early 1990s. More importantly, 'Victorian values' invoked a model in which women's roles in the capitalist economy were clearly defined and circumscribed, as Elizabeth Traube explains:

> Known as the ideology of the separate spheres, this belief system arose with early capitalism and provided the framework for the emergence of the middle classes in Victorian England and America. Legitimation of the new bourgeois way of life involved a redefinition of women as domestic beings, with an innate capacity for nurturance that required proper cultivation. The virtuous woman improved herself through work; but whereas her industrious mate labored in the marketplace, she was uniquely qualified for work in the home, which came to be seen as woman's proper place or 'sphere.' Thus under the influence of the gender system, the split between home and workplace that capitalism imposed took on the appearance of a natural division, adjusted to fundamental differences between the sexes. Woman's role in this scheme was to stabilize society from within by exerting a moral influence on household members.[85]

The Victorian ideology of the separate spheres, in other words, cast women in the role of the moral guardians of capitalism. Given the appeals in the 1990s for a more morally restrained and responsible capitalism after the recklessness of the 1980s, one can certainly see the attraction of such an ideology, not least because it was simultaneously able to articulate a subtle backlash against feminism by demanding women's restoration to the home in the interests of cap-

italism. As I have suggested, *Batman Returns'* specific articulation of
the Victorian vampire narrative in many ways supports this ideology
by situating Catwoman as the moral guardian of capitalism, pro-
tecting it from the immoral excesses of the vampire-consumer,
Shreck. Indeed, in choosing a form of revenge that effectively robs
Catwoman of one of her dwindling nine lives, the film also aligns her
with Victorian notions of women as self-sacrificing martyrs (notions
that are also significantly apparent at the end of *Nosferatu* where
Mina sacrifices herself in order to destroy the vampire). However, in
casting the forces of moral restraint and discipline in both sexual
(Catwoman as dominatrix) and feminist (Catwoman as avenger of
violence against women) terms, and in allowing Catwoman to sur-
vive, the film also manages to resist some of the more pernicious and
insidious aspects of this ideology (not least the belief that 'the only
good feminist is a dead one').[86] In particular, it refuses one of the
central tenets of this ideology, the call for a return to family values,
and it fails to resolve the threats to masculine power and authority
the female vampire/avenger represents. In this respect, *Batman
Returns* avoids the kind of recuperation of traditional gender roles
that occurs in the final paragraph of *Dracula*, where Van Helsing's
description of Mina gradually slips from active New Woman to nurturing mother to passive object of male protection:

> This boy will some day know what a brave and gallant woman his
> mother is. Already he knows her sweetness and loving care; later on he
> will understand how some men so loved her, that they did dare much
> for her sake.[87]

In contrast, the end of *Batman Returns* has Bruce Wayne reduced
to the role of nurturer (of Catwoman's cat), while Catwoman,
perched on the rooftops above Gotham City, not only dominates the
film's final frame but appears to have quite literally toppled Batman
from his position as the heroic vigilante protector of Gotham City.
In the concluding shot of the prequel, *Batman* (Tim Burton, 1989),
Batman is shown in an almost identical position to the one Catwoman occupies here, while below on the ground Vicki Vale (Kim
Basinger) waits patiently for him in the car with Alfred (Michael
Gough). *Batman Returns*, however, reverses these spatial relations –
here Bruce Wayne, patiently trawling the streets in the hope of finding Catwoman, occupies the same position as Vicki Vale. Thus,
while the film does not exactly deconstruct the Victorian ideology of

the separate spheres, it does invert it by positioning Batman within the traditionally feminine, private, domestic realm of heterosexual relations and Catwoman in the conventionally masculine, public, social space of action and heroism.[88] This is not to say, however, that Catwoman simply becomes masculinized – as her construction here as the object of Batman's desire suggests, she remains throughout an eroticized figure. In this way, Catwoman can be seen as an articulation of one of the new public femininities, described by Radner and discussed in chapter 1, which have emerged in response to women's movement out of the home in the twentieth century. Indeed, whereas Catwoman is never shown within the domestic space of the home after her initial transformation, Batman is frequently shown occupying this space throughout the film and, in fact, he is the only character who consistently does so. Alongside the film's articulation and exploration of public femininities, then, it is possible to discern an equivalent interest in articulating and exploring what might usefully be described as private masculinities. What I want to suggest, therefore, is that the changing inscription of femininity and feminism in popular film cannot be fully understood without a similar understanding of the contemporary construction of masculinity and particularly the emergence of these private masculinities.

I want to start, then, by suggesting that Andrew Ross's arguments concerning the superhero revival of the 1980s might need, in the context of the 1990s, some qualifications. Ross argues that:

> The superhero revival was kindled by the desperate attempts, under Reagan, to reconstruct the institution of national heroism, more often than not in the form of white male rogue outlaws for whom the liberal solution of 'soft' state-regulated law enforcement was presented as having failed.
>
> Under the cover of challenging the authority of official law enforcement, the new comics resurrect the practice of voluntarist law enforcement on the part of vigilantes at a time when the politics of the superhero tradition had long fallen into disfavour, and when advances in civil rights had stemmed the flow of 'white justice'.[89]

Batman Returns, however, refuses the logic of this nostalgic yearning for the heroic narratives of the past. Instead, it actually foregrounds the way in which heroism is often simply the construction of political publicity campaigns (for example, The Penguin's saving of the Mayor's baby is shown to be deliberately engineered in order to bolster The Penguin's own political ambitions). Simultaneously,

Batman's status as a national hero is frequently questioned or undermined. Newspaper headlines, for example, pronounce that 'Batman Blows It', while as Catwoman points out: 'It seems that every woman you try to save ends up dead or deeply resentful. Maybe you should retire.' Indeed, the most significant physical threats Batman faces come not from other men but from the vengeful Catwoman. Furthermore, Batman appears to have total faith in conventional law enforcement. For example, at the end of the film he tries to convince Catwoman to turn Shreck over to the police rather than dispense her own vigilante justice and, in response to her claim that 'the law doesn't apply to people like him or us', retorts, 'Wrong, on both counts'. The last two observations suggest some interesting continuities with the transformations that occurred in the 1990s in the characterization of perhaps *the* archetypal 1980s superhero, Arnold Schwarzenegger. As Susan Jeffords observes in relation to *Kindergarten Cop* (Ivan Reitman, 1990), by the end of the film, Schwarzenegger

> feels guilty when he punches an abusive father and promises from now on to use the law to get such men. His life is most threatened, not by another super-macho, special combat male enemy (like Mr. Joshua in *Lethal Weapon*), but by a determined mother who is out to revenge the death of her son.[90]

Thus, the hard body that Jeffords has identified as characteristic of the male action hero of the 1980s has, in *Batman Returns*, become if not exactly a soft body then a penetrable one (Batman's suit, for example, is penetrated on more than one occasion by one of Catwoman's claws).[91] The emergence of a soft, penetrable body clearly keys into contemporary anxieties about AIDS and homosexuality, anxieties which the vampire myth is well-placed to articulate.[92] Jeffords, however, relates this shift in the representation of masculine identity 'from hard-bodied heroism to a manhood divided and troubled' both to Reagan's succession by Bush and to the increasing call for a replacement of the competitive, consumer-led values of the 1980s with more morally restrained family values.[93] To take the former point first: Jefford's argues that while Bush was dependent on Reagan for his presidential nomination, 'in order to establish his own presidential image, Bush needed to differentiate himself from Reagan':

> In doing so, he chose, from the day of his inauguration, to articulate that difference as one of 'kindness' versus, by implication, meanness,

of 'gentleness' versus harshness. And by giving up Reagan's most cherished dream – Star Wars – Bush gave up as well any claim to toughness or vision.[94]

Bush, then, rejected the Reaganite hard body, a body which, according to Jeffords, would increasingly 'come to seem not only tangential to the family but antithetical to it'.[95] In the 1990s, the external hard-bodied masculinity of the 1980s was relegated in favour of a private masculinity with more internal concerns (health, emotions, families, homes). In *Batman Returns*, this shift from the politics of Reagan to those of Bush is particularly apparent in the mayor's address to the citizens of Gotham City. Although he denounces the urban chaos that is gripping the city, the mayor does not call for a tough crackdown on criminal activity. Instead, he makes an emotive appeal to the spirit of Christmas, a season that he suggests should be a time of healing. This appeal is, moreover, firmly located within a discourse of family values since it is made not simply as an official, but as a husband and father. Similarly, at the end of the film, Batman seems far more concerned with healing his fractured identity through embracing the home and heterosexual relations than with dispensing tough vigilante justice – indeed, Batman's success in thwarting The Penguin's plan to kill the first-born sons and daughters of Gotham City specifically positions him in the role of the guardian of home and family.

What I want to suggest, then, is that the film traces the source of the crisis of masculinity that occurred in the 1990s, in which masculine identity is divided and split between the hard body and family values, to the destruction of family life. Indeed, the film's concern with the effects of dysfunctional families is set up in its opening sequences, where we learn that The Penguin's fractured identity is a result of his abandonment as a child by his parents. Similarly, in the film's prequel, *Batman*, we discover that the development of Bruce Wayne's alter-ego, Batman, and his subsequent difficulty with duality, is the consequence of the murder of his parents when he was a child. Unlike many of the backlash texts of the late 1980s, however, the threat to the family here is located not in the figure of the independent woman, but in crime (Batman) and society's intolerance of difference (The Penguin). Yet, while Batman subsequently commits his life to fighting crime and The Penguin to gaining social acceptance, for both the ultimate route to resolving their identity crises is

through heterosexual romance. Thus, for The Penguin, marriage to
Catwoman not only represents a way of completing his identity as
mayor of Gotham City but, as his reference to *Beauty and the Beast*
suggests, of making sense of both their identities and achieving some
kind of (narrative) unity. Likewise, at the end of the film, Batman
entreats Catwoman to abandon her plan to kill Shreck and come
home with him, implying that since they are 'the same, split right
down the centre', together they can find some kind of unity. Consequently, although the film does not explicitly blame the breakdown
of the family and the crisis of masculine identity it has precipitated
on the non-domestic woman, these narrative moves do implicitly
suggest that the solution to this crisis lies in the reinstatement of the
family as the primary institution through which conventional and
stable gender identities are produced and secured. This becomes
particularly clear in The Penguin's vision of his and Catwoman's
future together; a future in which she would bring him his slippers
and a dry martini, in which, in other words, she is cast firmly in the
traditional nurturing feminine role. The trajectories of the male
characters in *Batman Returns* are, thus, to use Jameson's term, 'nostalgic', representing a yearning for the narrative certainties and
stable and unified gender identities of the past.

The film, however, does not follow through on these nostalgic
impulses and, in fact, on a least one occasion shows that men's failure to move with the times, especially with regard to women's
changing status and demands, is the ultimate source of their down-
fall. For example, at the end of the film, Shreck attempts to deflect
Catwoman's murderous advances by offering her jewels in return
for his life. The offer is clearly inspired by Catwoman's pre-second-
wave feminist incarnation as a jewel thief and has a two-fold purpose. On the one hand, it serves to point up the movement of
Catwoman from a figure defined by the trappings of femininity
(jewels) to one defined by feminism (the avenger of violence against
women). On the other hand, it points up the (fatal) consequences of
nostalgia, articulated here through Shreck's ignorance of these
changes. Given that nostalgia is a central precept of the backlash
against feminism, *Batman Returns'* critique of nostalgia would seem
to offer a challenge both to backlash politics and to Jameson's
understanding of post-modern culture. Indeed, Jameson's somewhat androcentric perspective causes him to overlook the way in
which the figuration of the female protagonist frequently works to

disrupt such nostalgic impulses. In particular, her rejection of traditional heterosexual romance tends to undermine any attempt to resolve the fracturing of both narrative and identity through a resolution based on such conventions. Indeed, Catwoman openly mocks the convention of the romantic narrative resolution, while implicitly linking problems of narrative with problems of identity: 'Bruce, I would love to live with you in your castle forever, just like in a fairytale. I just couldn't live with myself, so don't pretend this is a happy ending.' In rejecting a narrative resolution based on the conventions of heterosexual romance and family, Catwoman also rejects the discourses and structures through which traditional feminine identities are reproduced and secured. Instead, it is revenge that not only forms the narrative conclusion of the film but that represents the route through which the female protagonist finds meaning. The question that remains, however, is what version of female identity does this produce and what are its consequences for feminism?

I want to begin to address this question via a brief analysis of the end of *Showgirls*, since the triteness with which the conventions of the rape-revenge cycle are exploited here is revealing. The film concludes with Nomi (Elizabeth Berkley) hitchhiking out of Las Vegas after having violently attacked her best friend's rapist. Having been picked up, she is asked if she gambled: 'What did you win?' 'Me', she replies. This deployment of the rape-revenge structure allows the film to insert a feminist narrative of self-discovery into a narrative about the erotic display of female bodies. Consequently, the film simply replaces the notion of a commodified self it has relied on throughout with a notion of an authentic self, while failing to question either notions. In contrast, by giving its central female protagonist a dual identity as Selina Kyle/Catwoman, *Batman Returns* is able to pose some rather more complex questions about constructed and authentic female identities. Furthermore, the film's reliance on both the pre-second-wave feminist representations of the vampire and film noir cycles and the feminist representations of the rape-revenge cycle allows it to explore a whole range of feminine and feminist identities and the connections between them. It is in the character of Selina Kyle that the problems of contemporary feminism are most clearly articulated. At the beginning of the film Selina is represented as a dowdy and downtrodden secretary. While her status as a single, working girl, combined with her obvious desire to further her career, suggests that she is, in part at least, a *product* of feminism, I would argue that she is set up as such in order that she can be shown ultimately to be a *victim* of feminism. In other words, her independence and career are not shown to have brought her happiness or fulfilment. Rather, in the 'words' of her cat she is 'pathetic', while in terms of backlash rhetoric she is terminally single ('Well that was brief', she says after encountering Batman, 'just like all the men in my life...what men?'). Somewhat contradictorily, however, the film also relies on the discourses of victim feminism, constructing a world in which women are the victims of sexism, inequality and male violence. It is one of these acts of violence that brings about Selina's transformation into Catwoman.

The characterization of Catwoman is clearly based on both the literal female vampire and the metaphoric vamp or femme fatale.[96] Catwoman is also clearly inspired by the female avengers of the rape-revenge cycle. For example, her first act as Catwoman is to violently attack a man who is attempting to rape a young woman and, in fact, all her subsequent acts of violence can be read as acts of revenge against men who have committed violence against her.[97] More importantly, as a female avenger, Catwoman is posited as specifically the creation of second-wave feminism. This connection is most apparent in her parting comment to the woman she saved from rape: 'I am Catwoman, hear me roar.' The phrase is borrowed (with obvious modifications) from Helen Reddy's 1972 number one record, 'I Am Woman', which became one of the anthems of the American Women's Liberation Movement in the 1970s. In addition, despite her part in the plan to kidnap the Ice Princess (Cristi Conaway), Catwoman displays a solidarity with other women that clearly comes from feminism. Bonding between women is, for example, suggested through references to girl talk, by the fact that Catwoman lets the Ice Princess go and by Catwoman's anger on discovering that The Penguin has killed the Ice Princess. Finally, the last line of the film, spoken by Bruce Wayne, implicitly locates the film itself, and Catwoman in particular, within liberal feminist discourses of equality: 'Merry Christmas, Alfred. Goodwill to all men ... and women.'[98]

Given that she is the only other significant female character in the film, the Ice Princess also functions as the model of feminine identity against which Catwoman is defined. What is particularly interesting in this respect, is that in constructing the Ice Princess as a beauty queen and in contrasting Catwoman with her, the film recalls the antipathy to traditional constructions of heterosexual femininity, which has come to typify second-wave feminism. In particular, it recalls the first widely publicized expression of such antipathy, the feminist demonstration at the Miss America contest in 1968. This functioned to establish an enduring popular distinction between a constructed female identity and an authentic feminist identity, in which the former took on a set of characteristics that the latter defined themselves against. Thus, women were stupid, childish and feminine while feminists were intellectual, serious and dowdy. In the contrasts it draws between Catwoman and the Ice Princess, however, *Batman Returns* attempts to undo this opposition. While it does not really challenge the construction of the beauty queen as stupid, childish and feminine, in its construction of Catwoman as witty, sophisticated and sexy it does posit an alternative set of contrasting feminist characteristics.

What this begins to suggest is that the film's conflation of two historically specific representations of women, the vamp and the avenger, in the figure of Catwoman might have some interesting implications for feminism. Before speculating on these implications, however, I want to explore the effects of this conflation further. On the one hand, it would seem that the conventions of the rape-revenge cycle function to undermine the misogyny associated with the representation of the vamp as evil incarnate. In other words, while both the vamp and the female avenger represent a threat to patriarchal society, the rape-revenge cycle gives the vamp the justifiable motive and feminist credentials her earlier incarnations lacked. The representation of Catwoman, then, could be said to militate against the backlash against women it has often been argued representations of the vamp articulate. On the other hand, as a highly attractive and sexual figure, the vamp serves to temper the connotations of unfemininity associated with both revenge and feminism.[99] While it could, of course, be argued that the latter merely functions to construct Catwoman as an erotic spectacle for the male members of the audience, the image of the woman displayed for the erotic contemplation of the male is, as I have argued above, not without its dangers, particularly when it is combined with an active female gaze. Furthermore, as I have suggested elsewhere, sexiness is not necessarily inimical to feminism, particularly when it is so clearly to the benefit of women and the detriment of men. Indeed, given that Catwoman continually rejects the offers of heterosexual romance her new incarnation inspires, what would actually appear to be at stake here is a self-sufficient female sexuality. As Naomi Wolf has observed, Catwoman's suit is 'a second skin that cannot be raped, a manifestation of women's longing to be absolutely sexual but absolutely inviolable'.[100] Of course, the inviolability of Catwoman's suit and her rejection of heterosexual romance can also be understood in terms of contemporary anxieties about AIDS. However, the changes the disease has brought about in sexual practices (the emphasis on auto-eroticism and non-penetrative intercourse) clearly line up with feminism's demands for more of an emphasis on female sexual pleasure – as Catwoman purrs contentedly after her transformation: 'I don't know about you Miss Kitty, but I feel so much yummier.'

If the changing shape and status of heterosexual femininity Catwoman's transformation articulates owes something to both feminism and AIDS, it also owes something to punk which, as Dick Hebdige has observed, also borrowed 'the illicit iconography of sexual fetishism'.[101] Thus, like the subcultural bricoleur who changes the meaning of signs by reinserting them into a different context, the representation of Catwoman recontextualizes the identities of the vamp and avenger according to the exigencies of the present moment. Indeed, if the female punk did semantic violence to the traditional signifiers of feminine identity (for example, by wearing garish make-up and tampons as earrings), then Catwoman does literal violence to these signifiers. On returning home after having been pushed out of the window by Shreck and brought back to life by an army of alley cats, Selina/Catwoman starts to destroy her apartment. She takes a knife to her cuddly toys (before pushing them down the waste disposal) and a can of black spray paint to her pink walls and clothes. She also spray paints her doll's house – one of the primary means by which young girls are initiated into the feminine role of wife and mother. In addition, the neon sign reading 'Hello There', a substitute for her non-existent husband, is broken so that it instead bears a telling indictment of the feminine space of the home – 'Hell Here'. Indeed, Catwoman's rejection of a feminine identity based on home and family is foregrounded later when The Penguin speaks of the transformation of happy home-makers into Catwoman. Finally, Catwoman blows up Shreck's department store, the sole retailer of Gotham Lady Perfume (designed 'to make women feel like women') and in so doing destroys one of the primary means through which feminine identity is constructed – consumerism.[102]

In its place, the film posits an alternative model of consumption and identity formation – bricolage. Thus, Catwoman's suit is recycled from a plastic rain coat and other bits and pieces, while the stitches that hold it together form an irregular patchwork pattern suggesting that Selina's current identity is, like the punk's, constructed from the recycled fragments of past ones.[103] Moreover, like the punk's outfits, Catwoman's suit foregrounds the signs of its own fabrication. In other words, the viewer is not only party to its construction but, as with the punk's use of safety pins, is constantly reminded of this by the visible white stitches that hold it together and by the fact that Catwoman is continually losing her 'claws'. This is not to say, however, that Selina Kyle somehow represents, in the words of Catwoman, 'the woman behind the cat'. Rather, as I have already suggested, she is also a construction, first, of the media-led backlash against feminism and, second, of the star persona of Michelle Pfeiffer herself. The characterization of Selina as a drab and downtrodden secretary who is treated as little more than a glorified waitress by her employer, for example, clearly owes something to Pfeiffer's previous role as a depressed and dowdy waitress in *Frankie and Johnny* (Garry Marshall, 1991). Indeed, although the film is at pains to constantly remind us of Selina's dual identity (she and Bruce, for example, discuss the inaccuracies of the media construction of their alter-egos), as the film progresses it becomes more and more difficult to distinguish the 'woman' from the 'cat' as these two identities become increasingly blurred. Such double-coded identities function, in part, to signal the artificiality of identity. For example, towards the end of the film, Bruce and Selina attend a masked ball where they are the only people without masks, suggesting that their 'real' identities are themselves disguises, no more authentic than those of their mythic alter-egos. In the film's closing scenes, these identities increasingly begin to slide into one another as Catwoman, looking more and more dishevelled, prepares to exact her revenge on Shreck. Thus, when Catwoman removes her mask during the final showdown it is to reveal that the identity of 'the woman behind the cat' is not singular or authentic but a complex amalgam of contradictory identities, including the working girl ('Selina Kyle, you're fired!'), the victim of male violence ('You killed me, Batman killed me, The Penguin killed me'), the feminist avenger ('A die for a die') and the good girl ('All good girls go to heaven'), as well as the object of male desire. Consequently, whereas in *Showgirls* revenge functioned as the means by which Nomi found herself, in *Batman Returns* it is the means through which Selina finds herselves.

If, as Imelda Whelehan argues, feminism is currently undergoing an identity crisis, this is perhaps because of the impossibility of maintaining, in a post-modern society where the notion of stable, discreet, unified identities has collapsed, the distinction between constructed feminine identities and authentic feminist identities on which early second-wave feminism depended.[104] The trajectory of Selina/Catwoman through the narrative of *Batman Returns* signals the erosion of this distinction and thus marks a break with the discourses of early second-wave feminism. In this sense, the film can be seen not only as post-modern, but also as post-feminist. The film, however, offers two versions of this highly contested term and the identities associated with it. In the first version, post-feminist identity is understood in terms of a backlash politics that constructs contemporary women as depressed, dowdy and terminally single career woman, as, in other words, *victims* of feminism. In the second version, post-feminist identity is marked by the erosion of an absolute distinction between feminine and feminist identities. Thus, while the characterization of Selina/Catwoman clearly owes something to the pre-second-wave feminist representations of the vampire and film noir cycles and the hyper-feminine and sexualized representation of the vamp, it is also indebted to second-wave feminism, particularly as it has been articulated through the narratives of the rape-revenge cycle and the representation of the female avenger. In recycling these representations, the film neither wholly accepts nor wholly rejects the versions of femininity or feminism associated with each, but instead attempts to renegotiate the meaning of these terms and the relationship between them. *Batman Returns* rejects any simple elision of post-feminism with either pre-feminism (in which women are seen as the victims of *femininity*) or with backlash politics (in which women are seen as the victims of *feminism*). Indeed, if feminism is currently undergoing an identity crisis, it is perhaps merely a reflection of a new generation of young women's profound ambivalence towards both traditional feminist and feminine identities, an ambivalence the figure of Catwoman articulates. In this respect, despite her affiliations with the vamp and the female avenger of rape-revenge, Catwoman is a profoundly contemporary figure. As such, she suggests that the future of feminism might lie, not in a nostalgic yearning for the certainties of the past (this, after all, is the territory of the backlash), but in its ability to renegotiate those certainties.

Notes

1 Julianne Pidduck, 'The 1990s Hollywood Fatal Femme: (Dis)figuring Feminism, Family, Irony, Violence', *Cineaction*, 38 (1995), 65–72 (p. 65).

2 Jane Feuer, 'Feminism on Lifetime: Yuppie TV for the Nineties', *Camera Obscura*, 33–4 (1994–95), 133–45 (p. 135).

3 Julia Hallam, '*Working Girl*: A Woman's Film for the Eighties', in *Gendering the Reader*, ed. by Sara Mills (Hemel Hempstead: Harvester, 1994), pp. 173–98 (p. 176).

4 See for example: Joan Copjec, *Read My Desire: Lacan against the Historicists* (London: M.I.T. Press, 1994), p. 199; Janey Place, 'Women in Film Noir', in *Women in Film Noir*, ed. by E. Ann Kaplan (London: BFI, 1978), pp. 35–67 (p. 46).

5 Cited in Steven Best and Douglas Kellner, *Postmodern Theory: Critical Interrogations* (Basingstoke: Macmillan, 1991), p. 128.

6 Fredric Jameson, 'Postmodernism, or The Cultural Logic of Late Capitalism', in *Postmodernism: A Reader*, ed. by Thomas Docherty (Hemel Hempstead: Harvester Wheatsheaf, 1993), pp. 62–92.

7 Ibid., p. 74.

8 Ibid., p. 75.

9 Ibid., p. 76.

10 Ibid., p. 76.

11 Ibid., p. 77.

12 Linda Hutcheon, *The Politics of Postmodernism* (London: Routledge, 1989), p. 93.

13 Place, 'Women in Film Noir', p. 37.

14 Imelda Whelehan, *Modern Feminist Thought: From the Second Wave to 'Post-Feminism'* (Edinburgh: Edinburgh University Press, 1995), p. 216.

15 Cited in Angela McRobbie, 'New Times in Cultural Studies', *New Formations*, 13 (Spring 1991), 1–17 (p. 1).

16 As Janey Place has argued: 'Another possible meaning of the many mirror shots in film noir is to indicate women's duplicitous nature. They are visually split, thus not to be trusted.' Place, 'Women in Film Noir', pp. 47–8.

17 Elizabeth G. Traube, *Dreaming Identities: Class, Gender, and Generation in 1980s Hollywood Movies* (Oxford: Westview Press, 1992), pp. 97–8.

18 Arthur Marwick, *British Society Since 1945*, 2nd edn (London: Penguin, 1990), p. 325.

19 Ibid., p. 364.

20 Ibid., p. 325.

21 Naomi Wolf, *Fire with Fire: The New Female Power and How It Will Change the 21st Century* (London: Chatto and Windus, 1993), p. 147. See also: Katie Roiphe, *The Morning After* (London: Hamish Hamilton, 1993).

22 Charlotte Brunsdon, 'Pedagogies of the Feminine: Feminist Teaching and Women's Genres', *Screen*, 32:4 (Winter 1991), 364–81 (p. 381).

23 Philip French, 'Beware of Brutal Brunettes', *Guardian* (Review), 7 August 1994, p. 10.

24 Traube, *Dreaming Identities*, p. 101.

25 Ibid., p. 102.

26 See, for example, Ibid. pp. 104–5 where there are three uses of 'seductive' and two of 'seduction'.

27 *The Penguin English Dictionary*, compiled by G. N. Garmonsway, 3rd edn (Harmondsworth: Penguin, 1979), p. 655.

28 Christine Gledhill, '*Klute* 1: A Contemporary Film Noir and Feminist Criticism', in *Women in Film Noir*, ed. by E. Ann Kaplan (London: BFI, 1978), pp. 6–21 (p. 18).

29 Traube, *Dreaming Identities*, p. 105.

30 Ibid., p. 106.

31 Ibid., p. 113.

32 Jonathan Romney, 'Vital Video: Sleazy Does It', *Guardian* (G2), 2 December 1994, p. 17.

33 The self-consciousness of this articulation of the discourses of film noir is made explicit by Harlan's direct reference to Freud in his comment that 'The Freudian mind-fuck isn't going to work either'.

34 Gledhill, '*Klute* 1', p. 15.

35 Richard Dyer, 'Resistance through Charisma: Rita Hayworth and *Gilda*', in *Women in Film Noir*, ed. by E. Ann Kaplan (London: BFI, 1978), pp. 91–9 (p. 92); Claire Johnston, '*Double Indemnity*', in *Women in Film Noir*, ed. by E. Ann Kaplan (London: BFI, 1978), pp. 100–11.

36 Gledhill, '*Klute* 1', p. 15.

37 The irony, here, of course is that Mike is a claims adjuster. In other words, like Barton Keyes in *Double Indemnity*, he investigates people's insurance claims.

38 For an interesting explication of this opposition and of the country/city opposition in general, see Colin McArthur, 'Chinese Boxes and Russian Dolls: Tracking the Elusive Cinematic City', in *The Cinematic City*, ed. by David B. Clarke (London: Routledge, 1997), pp. 19–45.

39 Sylvia Harvey, 'Woman's Place: The Absent Family of Film Noir', in *Women in Film Noir*, ed. by E. Ann Kaplan (London: BFI, 1978), pp. 22–34 (pp. 26–7).

40 Place, 'Women in Film Noir', pp. 35–67.
41 Ibid., p. 45.
42 The knowingness with which the film deploys the discourses of popular psychoanalysis should, in particular, warn us against trying to produce literal psychoanalytic readings.
43 Mary Ann Doane, *Femmes Fatales: Feminism, Film Theory, Psychoanalysis* (London: Routledge, 1991), pp. 2–3.
44 Feuer, 'Feminism on Lifetime', p. 145.
45 Traube, *Dreaming Identities*, p. 127.
46 Whelehan, *Modern Feminist Thought*, pp. 216–37.
47 Charlotte Brunsdon, *Screen Tastes: Soap Opera to Satellite Dishes* (London: Routledge, 1997), p. 101.
48 Linda Grant, 'I'm Sexy. So Promote Me', *Guardian* (G2), 23 June 1998, p. 6.
49 Julie Burchill, 'To Have and Have Not', *Guardian* (Weekend), 14 March 1998, p. 7.
50 Wolf, *Fire with Fire*, p. 244.
51 Ibid., p. 244.
52 Traube, *Dreaming Identities*, p. 97.
53 Ibid., 106.
54 Ibid., p. 143.
55 *Batman* (Leslie Martinson, 1966), for example, can be seen as an attempt to work through and resolve anxieties about communism. Significantly, the threat of communism is largely articulated through the demonization of Catwoman (Lee Meriwether), who disguises herself as Kitka, a Russian journalist from *The Moscow Bugle*. At the end of the film, of course, the threat is overcome through the punishment of Catwoman.
56 Christopher Frayling, '*Dracula*', in *The BFI Companion to Horror*, ed. by Kim Newman (London: BFI, 1996), pp. 98–9 (p. 98). The similarities between vampirism and capitalism have also been noted by Richard Dyer, 'Dracula and Desire', *Sight and Sound*, 3:1 (January 1993), 8–12 (p. 10); Ken Gelder, *Reading the Vampire* (London: Routledge, 1993), p. 17; and Franco Moretti, *Signs Taken For Wonders: Essays in the Sociology of Literary Forms*, trans. by Susan Fischer, David Forgacs and David Miller, rev. edn (London: Verso, 1988), pp. 90–8.
57 This implication of the life-giving properties of electricity suggests an allusion to another gothic novel, Mary Shelley's *Frankenstein* (1818).
58 Andrew Ross, 'Ballots, Bullets, or Batmen: Can Cultural Studies Do the Right Thing?', *Screen*, 21:1 (Spring 1990), 26–44 (p. 27).
59 William Uricchio and Roberta E. Pearson, '"I'm Not Fooled By That Cheap Disguise"', in *The Many Lives of the Batman: Critical Approaches to a Superhero and his Media*, ed. by Roberta E. Pearson and William Uricchio (London: BFI, 1991), pp. 182–213 (p. 195).

60 Ibid., p. 202
61 Ibid., p. 203
62 Doane, *Femmes Fatales*, pp. 1–2.
63 Christopher Frayling, 'Vampirism (Before *Dracula*)', in *The BFI Companion to Horror*, ed. by Kim Newman (London: BFI, 1996), pp. 320–1 (p. 321).
64 Sharon Russell, 'The Witch in Film: Myth and Reality', in *Planks of Reason: Essays on the Horror Film*, ed. by Barry Keith Grant (London: The Scarecrow Press, 1984), pp. 113–25 (p. 115).
65 'Dracula', *The South Bank Show* (LWT, UK) transmitted in January 1993.
66 For specific references to the New Woman see Bram Stoker, *Dracula*, ed. by Maurice Hindle (London: Penguin, 1993), pp. 118–19.
67 Stoker, *Dracula*, p. 302.
68 Elaine Showalter, *Sexual Anarchy: Gender and Culture at the Fin-de-Siècle* (London: Virago, 1992), p. 181; S. S. Prawer, *Caligari's Children: The Film as Tale of Terror* (Oxford: Oxford University Press, 1980), p. 257.
69 David Ehrenstein, 'One From the Art', *Film Comment*, 29:1 (January–February 1993), 27–30 (p. 29). See also: Russell, 'The Witch in Film', p. 121; Bonnie Zimmerman, 'Daughters of Darkness: The Lesbian Vampire on Film', in *Planks of Reason: Essays on the Horror Film*, ed. by Barry Keith Grant (London: Scarecrow Press, 1984), pp. 153–63 (p. 156).
70 For a more detailed exposition of the similarities between vampirism and sexual intercourse see: Richard Dyer, 'Children of the Night: Vampirism as Homosexuality, Homosexuality as Vampirism', in *Sweet Dreams: Sexuality, Gender and Popular Fiction*, ed. by Susannah Radstone (London: Lawrence and Wishart, 1988), pp. 47–72.
71 Zimmerman, 'Daughters of Darkness', p. 160.
72 Cited in Andrea Weiss, *Vampires and Violets: Lesbians in the Cinema* (London: Jonathan Cape, 1992), p. 98.
73 Zimmerman, 'Daughters of Darkness', p. 155. While I have been unable to locate a copy of this film in order to check Zimmerman's claim here, *Time Out Film Guide* also refers to this incident: 'After casually sticking her stiletto into a potential rapist, Yarnall's Diane Le Fanu (or should we call her Carmilla?) slinks into the Stoker Art Gallery and invites a young married couple … for the weekend to her isolated desert home'. Tom Milne, ed., *Time Out Film Guide*, 3rd edn (London: Penguin, 1993), p. 754.
74 Camille Paglia, for example, claims that the vamp represents 'the missing sexual personae of contemporary feminism'. Camille Paglia, *Vamps and Tramps: New Essays* (London: Viking, 1995), p. ix. The currency

of such figures is also suggested by the fact that the seminal text on the femme fatale, *Women in Film Noir*, ed. by E. Ann Kaplan (London: BFI, 1978) was being revised and updated in 1999. For a more detailed discussion of feminist analyses of such figures, see chapter 1.

75 Mary Ann Doane, 'Film and the Masquerade: Theorizing the Female Spectator', in *Issues in Feminist Film Criticism*, ed. by Patricia Erens (Bloomington: Indiana University Press, 1990), pp. 41–57 (p. 50).

76 Doane, 'Film and the Masquerade', p. 50; Linda Williams, 'When the Woman Looks', in *Re-Vision: Essays in Feminist Film Criticism*, ed. by Mary Ann Doane, Patricia Mellencamp and Linda Williams (Los Angeles: American Film Institute, 1984), pp. 83–99.

77 Laura Mulvey, 'Visual Pleasure and Narrative Cinema', in *Feminism and Film Theory*, ed. by Constance Penley (London: BFI, 1988), pp. 57–68 (p. 64).

78 Ibid., p. 64.

79 See Ivor H. Evans, *Brewer's Dictionary of Phrase and Fable*, 14th edn (London: Cassell Ltd, 1989), p. 124 for an explanation of this phrase.

80 Williams, 'When the Woman Looks', p. 85.

81 Gledhill, '*Klute* 1', p. 19. The continuities between the vampire story and the film noir story and their representations of women is suggested by the fact that in both the kiss is constructed as a deadly weapon. This is particularly apparent in the title of the noir thriller *Kiss Me Deadly* (Robert Aldrich, 1955). *Batman Returns*, moreover, makes allusions both to this film and to the potentially fatal consequences of the kiss through the repetition of the line, 'A kiss can be so much deadlier if you mean it'.

82 Stoker, *Dracula*, p. 484.

83 Ibid., p. viii.

84 While, under John Major, the call for a return to 'Victorian values' was translated into a call to go 'back to basics', the ideology remained largely the same.

85 Traube, *Dreaming Identities*, pp. 123–4.

86 Ironically, given the film's attack on capitalist excess, the revelation that Catwoman has survived her confrontation with Shreck can be understood not only in terms of feminism, but in terms of the logic of the market place. Her survival, in other words, ensures her availability for potential sequels.

87 Stoker, *Dracula*, p. 486.

88 It is worth noting here that the film's use of vertical space can be understood not only in terms of gender, but in terms of class. See Peter Wollen, 'Delirious Projections', *Sight and Sound*, 2:4 (August 1992), 24–7 (p. 26).

89 Ross, 'Ballots, Bullets, or Batmen', p. 33.

90 Susan Jeffords, 'The Big Switch: Hollywood Masculinity in the Nineties', in *Film Theory Goes to the Movies*, ed. by Jim Collins, Hilary Radner and Ava Preacher Collins (London: Routledge, 1993), pp. 196–208 (p. 199).

91 Susan Jeffords, *Hard Bodies: Hollywood Masculinity in the Reagan Era* (New Brunswick: Rutgers University Press, 1994).

92 For a more detailed exposition of the relationship between vampirism and homosexuality see: Dyer, 'Children of the Night', pp. 47–72.

93 Jeffords, *Hard Bodies*, p. 97.

94 Ibid., p. 99.

95 Ibid., p. 100.

96 Hereafter, I shall use only the term 'vamp' as, unlike the term 'femme fatale', it is able to encompass the construction of Catwoman as both femme fatale *and* female vampire.

97 In this respect, the film replaces rape with a more generalized violence against women.

98 That The Penguin plans to 'punish all God's children ... male *and* female' on the basis that 'the sexes are equal' suggests, however, that equality is not without its drawbacks.

99 It also answers the criticism often levelled at the action heroine (particularly Thelma and Louise) that she simply sheds her traditionally feminine characteristics for traditionally masculine characteristics and is, therefore, not a genuine challenge to conventional understandings of gender roles.

100 Wolf, *Fire with Fire*, p. 244.

101 Dick Hebdige, *Subculture: The Meaning of Style* (London: Routledge, 1991), pp. 107–8. Moreover, one of the two songs used in the film is by archetypal female-led punk band, Siouxsie and the Banshees. The band went on to become the icons of the gothic youth culture of the early 1980s, which, significantly, explicitly borrowed the iconography of the vampire (black clothes, crucifixes, white foundation and red or black lipstick).

102 The point at which Selina begins the destruction described above and her transformation into Catwoman is also the point at which she hears the 'Gotham Lady Perfume' message on her answering machine. What is not clear, however, is whether it is the feminine stereotypes or the references to 'your boss' in the message that tip her over the edge.

103 As Dick Hebdige has argued, punk recycled 'the entire sartorial history of post-war working-class youth cultures in "cut up" form'. Hebdige, *Subculture*, p. 26.

104 Whelehan, *Modern Feminist Thought*, p. 216.

Chapter 7

From feminism to family values: the maternal avenger

In the previous chapter, I argued that, in the 1990s, the rape-revenge structure became increasingly subject to post-modern articulations, and I attempted to trace the way in which these artic-ulations of the structure represented an attempt to make sense of feminism from within the contemporary political context. I was particularly concerned here to demonstrate how post-modernism, frequently charged with being uncritically nostalgic, actually suc-ceeded in offering a challenge to dominant understandings of the 1990s as a period of backlash against feminism. Rather than press-ing for a return to a pre-feminist past, I suggested that these films reconstitute the past (both filmic and feminist), giving it inflections specific to the contemporary moment. While this often meant that feminism was co-opted to dominant political ideologies and thus robbed of its oppositional stance, it also meant that feminism was given a legitimacy and, therefore, a popular appeal it had previ-ously lacked. Consequently, far from suggesting that feminism was undergoing a wholesale *rejection* in the early 1990s, these films instead suggested that feminism was undergoing a process of *nego-tiation*. Against the tendency to equate post-feminism with back-lash, then, I would argue that we need to make proper distinctions between these two terms. In other words, as the 'back' of backlash suggests, backlash politics are driven by nostalgia and the desire to return to an idealized past. The backlash attempts to reject or cir-cumvent feminism and is, therefore, more accurately described as pre-feminist rather than post-feminist. The term 'post-feminism', on the other hand, is more contradictory since written into the term is both an acknowledgement and a disavowal of a feminist past. Post-feminism, therefore, should be understood not simply as a rejection of feminism, but as an attempt to reconcile or negotiate the contradictions of the contemporary feminist moment in which feminism is being simultaneously appropriated and rejected, popularized and subject to a backlash.

This is not to deny the existence of a backlash against feminism, but to suggest that the backlash was simply one way of making sense of feminism in the 1990s. It is to deny, however, that the backlash represented an attack on feminism in its entirety (to claim as much would be to attribute to feminism a unity and a coherence it has never possessed). Instead, the backlash targeted those aspects of feminism that represented the most serious threat to the health of the contemporary body politic: namely, feminism's critique of the family and motherhood, in particular. Thus, perhaps *the* seminal backlash text of the period, *Fatal Attraction* (Adrian Lyne, 1987), makes its villainess the single, independent woman threatening the sanctity of the nuclear family and its heroine the good wife and mother. Because the heroine of the female rape-revenge narrative, however, is precisely the single, independent and self-sufficient woman the backlash text villainizes, these films, with their implicit rejection of heterosexual romance and family, would appear to be largely unamenable to the articulation of a backlash politics. Nevertheless, the late 1980s and early 1990s – a period coincident with the emergence of the backlash – saw the decline of conventional articulations of the female rape-revenge structure. In the previous chapter, I analysed one of the forms the structure has since taken. These post-modern articulations of the rape-revenge structure have been accompanied, however, by an increase in two further types of rape-revenge: legal (*The Accused*; *Shame*, Steve Jodrell, 1988; *Without Her Consent*, Sandor Stern, 1989; *She Said No*, John Patterson, 1990) and parental (*In My Daughter's Name*; *Eye for an Eye*; *A Time to Kill*). What I want to argue is that these films not only represent an attempt to contain the feminist politics of the rape-revenge narrative but, in the case of the maternal rape-revenge film at least, can also be seen to articulate a backlash politics.

Legal rape-revenge films not only represent a turning away from violent solutions but explicitly address the futility of such solutions. For example, in *Shame*, Asta (Deborra-Lee Furness) teaches Lizzie (Fairuza Balk) how to defend herself against a potential attacker, but is unable to answer Lizzie's question 'What if there's five of them?' and, in *The Accused*, Sarah comes off worst in her vehicular confrontation with one of the men who watched her being raped. *She*

Said No, on the other hand, while similarly suggesting the inherently self-destructive nature of such solutions also marks them out precisely as fantasies. Here, the victim, Elizabeth (Veronica Hamel), dreams that she shoots her rapist and then, in an interesting twist on the female rape-revenge structure, turns the gun on herself. Such films, while critiquing legal institutions and particularly rape laws that entail putting the victim on trial (both *The Accused* and *She Said No* feature unsuccessful criminal trials of the rapists), ultimately show the legal system working in the victim's favour. In *The Accused*, for example, the spectators to the rape are found guilty of criminal solicitation, and, in *She Said No*, the victim brings a successful civil prosecution against her rapist. What is more, with the exception of a handful of films – *Positive ID* (Andy Anderson, 1987), *Thelma and Louise* and *Dirty Weekend* – subsequent articulations of the female rape-revenge structure attempt to circumvent the problem of its female avenger's evasion of the law either by situating her as an agent of that law, as in *Settle the Score* (Edwin Sherin, 1989) and *Blue Steel* or by making her subject to that law, as in *Mortal Thoughts* (Alan Rudolph, 1991) and *The Rape of Dr Willis* (Lou Antonio, 1992).[1] The latter two films also render the female avenger 'safe' by casting her revenge as 'displaced' (self-defence in *Mortal Thoughts* and non-deliberate in *The Rape of Dr Willis*).

Parental rape-revenge films, however, would seem to reverse this movement towards upholding legal solutions. In other words, in all three films the legal system is shown to be unable to adequately punish the perpetrators of rape. The rapist in *In My Daughter's Name*, for example, pleads temporary insanity and serves only a short time in a psychiatric institution while, in *Eye for an Eye*, the rapist is released on a technicality. Finally, in *A Time to Kill*, the victim's father, correctly, it is suggested, believing that a racist legal system is unlikely to convict the white rapists of his black daughter, kills the men on their way to the preliminary hearing. The failings of the legal system also drive the mothers in the previous two films to take the law into their own hands and kill their daughter's rapists. Despite the secondary nature of the revenge, these films are remarkably similar to conventional articulations of the female rape-revenge structure, particularly those such as *Handgun* and *Extremities* (Robert M. Young, 1986) in which the victims resort to violent solutions after the law has failed them. There is, nevertheless, an essential difference. In female victim-centred deployments of the structure, the legal ramifications of violent revenge are rarely, if ever, explored, tending to suggest that the female avenger has escaped legal retribution. However, in the parental-centred deployments of the structure, the parental avenger either does not attempt to escape legal retribution and is tried for their crime, as in *In My Daughter's Name*, or the legal system is shown working in the victim's favour, as in *Eye for an Eye*, in which the mother lures her daughter's rapist to her home and shoots him 'legitimately' in a breaking-and-entering situation, and *A Time to Kill*, in which the father is found not guilty by reason of insanity. Consequently, while apparently critiquing legal institutions, these films also represent their parental avengers as willing to succumb to or act within that same legal system and, moreover, show that system to be fair. As the mother in *In My Daughter's Name* argues: 'I took the law into my own hands. I'm willing to pay the price.' Thus, despite the different ways in which revenge is achieved in the legal and parental rape-revenge film, both follow similar narrative trajectories in which, after initial criticism, the legal system is succumbed to and upheld. Given these similarities in the representation of the law, I want to focus my attention on the latter group of films since they provide an additional dimension absent in both the female and legal rape-revenge films that is particularly pertinent to a discussion of feminism in the 1990s: the representation of the family and especially the mother. For this reason, I will be focusing on the maternal avengers of *Eye for an Eye* and *In My Daughter's Name* rather than on the paternal avenger of *A Time to Kill*.

The maternal avenger and the vigilante-mom made-for-TV film

What is particularly striking about both sets of films is that out of the seven I have referenced, three are made-for-television movies: *Without Her Consent*, *She Said No* and *In My Daughter's Name*. According to Jane Feuer such made-for-television movies are known in the trade as 'trauma dramas'.[2] In an excellent structural analysis of the trauma drama, Feuer identifies an eight-step plot structure and an ideological impetus common to this group of films. In particular, she argues that they represent an articulation of the 'massive loss of faith by individuals in institutions', such as the judicial system, which occurred during the 1980s, and that they function to resolve 'the

Table 3 The made-for-TV trauma drama

1   The family represents the ideal and norm of happy American family life.
2   A trauma occurs.
3   The victims/parents seek help through established institutions.
4   The institutions are unable to help them and are shown to be totally inadequate.
5   The victims take matters into their own hands.
6   They join a self-help group or form a grass-roots organization.
7   The new organization is better able to cope with the trauma, often having an impact on established institutions.
8   Normality is restored (however inadequately).

Source: Jane Feuer, *Seeing through the Eighties: Television and Reaganism* (London: BFI, 1995), pp. 25–6.

traumas of the American family in a rejuvenation of public institutions by the people'.[3] As Feuer observes, the latter was 'the same promise that got Reagan elected', and she argues that while these films 'invoked a long tradition of American populism, [they] gave it an inflection that was specific to the Reagan agenda'.[4] She also suggests, however, that 'the new populism as embodied in these films is not unambiguously right wing in sentiment'.[5] In other words, she argues that despite their critique of liberal institutions, their calls for the restoration of the old-fashioned family (which these institutions were thought to threaten) and their emphasis on individual rather than collective social action, these films' optimistic endings were not wholly believable and often left a sense of 'the fragility of the average American family'.[6] Indeed, in a footnote, Feuer suggests that 'in the nineties, the pendulum appears to be swinging back, *especially when the trauma concerns women's issues*'.[7] While Feuer's argument is useful for the detailed way in which it elucidates how popular film articulated a Reaganite vigilante agenda, her exploration of the relationship between this agenda and feminism remains underdeveloped. In particular, her claim that trauma dramas that deal with women's issues are, at the very least, ambiguous because 'feminist/women's issues [are] not amenable to placement on the usual left-right political spectrum' betrays a belief that feminism somehow exists outside of history, politics and culture.[8] As I argued in chapter 4, however, feminism is shaped both in response to and by current political ideologies, while in the sphere of popular culture and media, as well as politics, feminism, like populism, can be mobilized and appropriated for both left- and right-wing aims (the anti-pornography campaigns of Catherine MacKinnon and Andrea Dworkin, for example, can be seen as reinforcing conservative morality).

With this in mind, I want to explore what happens to the feminist stories the rape-revenge structure can be seen to articulate when it meets the vigilante and familial politics of the trauma drama in the maternal rape-revenge films of the 1990s.[9] While this will involve an analysis of the extent to which these films conform to or depart from the structure of the trauma drama, it will also involve a look back to the trauma drama's generic antecedents in melodrama. As a form, melodrama has always lent itself to the articulation of a vigilante politics. David Grimsted gives a particularly interesting account of this relationship and its influence on contemporary politics in his discussion of the vigilante chronicles of the mid-nineteenth century USA. Here he argues that 'to look at the rhetoric, structure and argument of these tales is to encounter melodramatic politics in its most theatrical guise, and to gain some clues about melodrama's more disguised role in comparatively everyday politics'.[10] Central to both the theatrical and the political melodrama, for example, is the rhetoric of the Eden myth which, according to Grimsted,

> is fitted to a politics characterised by a sense of deep moral decay that craves correction by expulsion or extermination of all evil. In Attakapas, crime, relaxation of customs, the weakening of religious beliefs, and above all 'venality, cowardice, and the impotency of justice, that triple leper', had leached society of all decency until the pure finally recognised that 'the time has come when all the nations who do not wish to die must prepare by a struggle the heroic remedies that will cure them'. What is haunting about this melodramatic rhetoric is how recently one has heard it from the mouths of Ronald Reagan, Jerry Brown, David Duke and H. Ross Perot who promise escape from black decay to daybreak so long as the virtuous follow them in crushing evil empires, evil politicians and all the evil people who resist their march to the millennium.[11]

Feuer also traces the origins of the trauma drama's vigilante politics to melodrama, although her argument is somewhat different from Grimsted's in the emphasis it places on melodrama's relationship to women's issues, especially those concerning the family and motherhood. Noting both the gendered division of labour between mothers and fathers in these films, together with their largely female audience, she suggests that:

> Perhaps these vigilante-mom made-for-TV films appealed to the same impulses as a right-wing feminism in support of the family. In this sense, they could be considered 'women's pictures' or even politicized melodramas. They delineate those forms of political activism possible for ordinary women during the Reagan years.[12]

Feuer, however, also draws a distinction between the politicized melodrama of the trauma drama and the pure or domestic melodrama of other 1980s made-for-TV movies. According to Feuer, the pure or domestic melodrama is, like the trauma drama, characterized by 'the crisis of the individual family' but, unlike the trauma drama, it offers 'no public solution' to this crisis.[13] In these films, then, functions 3–7 of the trauma drama, in which the critique and rejuvenation of public institutions by the people occurs, are omitted. The structural emphasis of Feuer's analysis, therefore, precludes a more developed exploration of the way in which the vigilante politics of the contemporary trauma drama might intersect and overlap with the aesthetics and morality of classic film melodrama. This intersection becomes particularly apparent in the maternal rape-revenge film and it provides an ideal site not only through which to develop such an analysis, but through which to assess the effects of this intersection on the way in which the feminist stories the rape-revenge films tell are negotiated. In this chapter, therefore, I want to supplement a comparative structural analysis of the maternal rape-revenge film and the trauma drama with a close textual analysis of the way in which the maternal rape-revenge film deploys the codes and conventions of classic film melodrama. Significantly, one of the central tenets of both Clover's analysis of the rape-revenge film and feminist writing on melodrama is that these films privilege a female point of view. My discussion of the relationship between melodrama and the maternal rape-revenge film, therefore, will focus particularly on relations of looking and patterns of investigation, especially the way in which 'the look' works to construct distinctions between public and private space, guilt and innocence. Because it is the more visually and textually sophisticated of the two films, this discussion will concentrate mainly on *Eye for an Eye*. First, however, I want to explore the extent to which the maternal rape-revenge film can be seen to conform to the structure and ideology of the trauma drama.

Here, I will be particularly concerned to evaluate both Feuer's claim that it is the films that depart from the usual eight step plot structure that can be 'read against the grain of the more hegemonic films that contain all eight-steps', and her suggestion that in the 1990s the politics of the trauma drama became less unambiguously right-wing 'especially when the trauma concerns women's issues'.[14]

In chapter 5, I analysed the way in which the rape-revenge structure has been mapped over the genre of the western or, more specifically, the vengeance variation identified by Will Wright in his structural analysis of the genre.[15] Here, I argued that feminism and the introduction of new functions and variations into the western brought about changes at the level of narrative structure, the oppositions it articulated and the meanings it generated. Feuer seems to be arguing a similar point in relation to the trauma drama, and clearly the rape-revenge film would seem to be one of the primary sites for the explication of the women's issues she refers to. In fact, there is a remarkable similarity between the structure and functions of the trauma drama and Wright's vengeance variation, not least in their overarching themes of individuals against institutions (the trauma drama) and individuals against values (the vengeance variation). The crucial difference, however, lies in the fact that whereas the films which most closely approximated the structure and functions of the vengeance variation were specifically female rape-revenge films, those that most closely approximate the structure and functions of the trauma drama are specifically maternal rape-revenge films. What I am suggesting, in other words, is that the maternal rape-revenge film's coupling of a discourse of rape with a discourse of maternity complicates attempts to read these films against the grain of the right-wing politics of the trauma drama. Against Feuer's claim that when the trauma concerns women's issues the politics of the trauma drama are less unambiguously right-wing, then, I want to argue that the maternal rape-revenge film mobilizes women's issues largely in the service of both patriarchal and right-wing ideologies, particularly those inherent in backlash politics.

Both *In My Daughter's Name* and *Eye for an Eye* appear to conform with functions 1-5 of Feuer's trauma drama structure. Both films open with preparations for the birthday party of a family member (the father in *In My Daughter's Name*, the younger daughter in *Eye for an Eye*) and, therefore, suggest 'the ideal and norm of happy American family life' (function 1).[16] These scenes are, however, undercut not, as Feuer suggests is the case in *Friendly Fire* (David Greene, 1979), by the impending trauma, but by a sense of fissure and frictions within the family itself. In *In My Daughter's Name*, for example, the mother, Laura (Donna Mills), and her teenage daughter, Carly (Ari Meyer), are constantly arguing. Although the film suggests that this is the normal pattern of mother–daughter relations, there is also a sense in which the finger of blame for this state of affairs is pointed clearly at lack of paternal authority embodied by the weak father, as Laura complains to her husband, Michael (John Getz), 'Why do I always have to be the bad cop?' Likewise, in *Eye for an Eye*, the mother, Karen (Sally Field), is a divorcee with a similarly ineffectual second husband, Mack (Ed Harris). Similarly, the films that Feuer argues are 'easily interpreted as left-wing or at least subversive inversions of the formula', also tend to undercut 'the ideal and norm of happy American family life'. In *The Burning Bed* (Robert Greenwald, 1984) this is achieved through the way in which 'the scenes of normative family life … are narrated from the perspective of its abysmal failure', while, in *An Early Frost* (John Erman, 1985), the presence of a gay son is 'so disruptive of the idealized nuclear family that the film is unable to complete the pattern'.[17] Finally, in *Unnatural Causes* (Lamont Johnson, 1986), as in *Eye for an Eye,* the sanctity of the American family is undermined by the presence of a divorced parent.

What I want to argue, however, is that in the maternal rape-revenge film it is not the traditional conservative ideal of the American family that is being subverted or critiqued. Rather, as in the right-wing trauma drama *Toughlove* (Glenn Jordan, 1985), it is the permissive, liberal family of the 1960s and 1970s. *In My Daughter's Name*, for example, explicitly identifies the parents with a liberal sensibility rooted in the 1960s through references to the music of James Brown. In fact, *In My Daughter's Name* and *Eye for an Eye* go one further than *Toughlove* in locating the origins of the permissive family in specific liberal discourses, particularly those of feminism. For instance, in *In My Daughter's Name*, the problems threatening the family are traced to the loss of paternal authority (indicated by the father's abdication of his role as disciplinarian), a state of affairs that can in turn be traced to feminist attacks on both the family and male authority. Indeed, here the feminist politics of rape-revenge are specifically constructed as constituting an attack on the family. This is made explicit in Michael's comment to Laura after she has shot and killed her daughter's rapist: 'You're destroying us, our family.' Laura's retort (while looking pointedly at Michael) – 'I did what had to be done. *Somebody* had to' – functions to undermine the feminist connotations of her actions while simultaneously further implicating feminism in the destruction of the family. In other words, it suggests that Laura has usurped the traditionally masculine role of avenger and defender of the family not out of feminist principle, but because feminism has alienated men from their proper masculine roles within the family. Michael's business, a plant nursery, is significant in this respect since it expressly associates him with the traditional feminine role of nurturer.

In contrast, in *Eye for an Eye*, Karen's divorce and the absence of her daughter's biological father would appear to function not only to undermine the conservative ideal of the normal, happy American family, but also to legitimate her maternal revenge. In *Eye for an Eye*, however, unlike the apparently subversive *Unnatural Causes*, the divorced parent is both female and remarried. In this way, the film is able to lay the blame for the disruption of family life on women (and, by extension, on feminism), while simultaneously containing such disruption through the motif of remarriage. It is in this way, I think, that we also need to read the film's articulation of the Eden myth.[18] That the family live on Eden Street is suggestive both of the melodramatic 'Edenic home and family' described by Christine Gledhill and of the 'ideal and norm of happy American family life' found in the trauma drama.[19] In both forms, moreover, as in the original myth, the sanctity of the Edenic family is apparently threatened by external forces. The rape in *Eye for an Eye* would appear to fulfil a similar function. Yet, as David Grimsted points out, in melodrama, as in the Eden myth, '*the evil within* [is] ... externalised into the villains who bedevil the virtuous'.[20] With this in mind, it is possible to argue that in *Eye for an Eye*, as in the original myth, it is not the rapist or serpent that brings about the destruction of Eden, but the woman who, through her refusal to be satisfied with her allotted role as man's helpmate within the Edenic home, tempts man to transgress. In other words, as J. C. J. Metford points out: 'Sin entered the world through Eve's disobedience to the divine command not to eat of the fruit of the Tree of Knowledge of Good and Evil.'[21] The contemporary implications of the Eden myth as it is articulated in *Eye for an Eye* should be clear: it is the woman who 'wants it all', that is, the feminist, who is responsible for male crimes, such as rape. Closer analysis of the film not only bears out this interpretation, but suggests that the narrative trajectory of the film is, like that of the Eden myth, towards relocating women as wives and mothers in the home (Eve's curse for her transgression was, as Joan Comay observes, 'to bear children in pain and sorrow, and to be ruled by her husband').[22] Feminism, then, can clearly be added to Feuer's list of the liberal institutions that the trauma drama identifies as a threat to the American family.

Both *In My Daughter's Name* and *Eye for an Eye* follow functions 2–5 of the trauma drama almost exactly. The failure of the judicial system to properly punish the rapists in both these films would appear not only to conform to the trauma drama's critique of liberal institutions, but to suggest a feminist critique of a patriarchal legal system that is complicit with rapists, not least because the rapist's trial in *In My Daughter's Name* is dominated by male judges and lawyers. In both films, however, the characterization of the rapist helps to distance him from identification with the legal system and patriarchal society as a whole. For example, *Eye for an Eye* uses the stereotype of the rapist as psychopath in order to differentiate him from the majority of normal men. In particular, the rapist, Robert Doob (Kiefer Sutherland), is consistently associated, both visually and verbally, with dogs (for example, he is described as marking 'his territory like a dog' and as a 'piece of dog shit'), an association that works to construct him as little more than an animal, as sub-human. There is, however, also an important class dimension to this canine characterization. According to Grimsted, the kinds of terms the vigilante chroniclers of the mid-nineteenth century used to describe their victims were those 'that reek of low social status' such as *canaille*, derived from the Latin *canis*, meaning 'dog'.[23] Like the villains of the vigilante chronicles, then, Doob's association with dogs also functions to differentiate him from the rest of normal society on the basis of class.[24]

Similarly, in *In My Daughter's Name*, despite the fact that the rapist's insanity plea is deliberately constructed as far-fetched and unbelievable, any suggestion that he is, in fact, normal is undermined when Laura tells his mother: 'When I look at your son, I see a monster.' More interestingly perhaps, the rapist, Peter Lipton (Adam Storke), is also characterized as a spoilt only child, the license plate of his brand new BMW, for example, bears the registration

'RICH KID'. In contrast, Laura's car is old and continually breaking down. As with *Eye for an Eye*, the distinction between rapist and victim is also understandable in terms of class. Unlike *Eye for an Eye*, however, *In My Daughter's Name* relies not on the conflict between the proletariat and the bourgeoisie found in the vigilante chronicles, but on that between the aristocracy and the bourgeoisie found in the traditional melodrama. Indeed, according to Thomas Elsaesser, this conflict is frequently interpreted metaphorically 'as sexual exploitation and rape'.[25] The scene in *In My Daughter's Name* that reveals the graffiti Laura has daubed on Lipton's car, makes this connection explicit through the way in which the camera tracks from the 'RICH KID' of the car's license plate to the words 'killer' and 'rapist' spray-painted across the car's bonnet and windscreen. While this could be interpreted as a subversive critique of the class system and particularly white, male privilege, I want to suggest another interpretation. Peter Lipton is not simply a member of the upper-class, he is a 'rich kid', a spoilt only child, a 'mummy's boy'. He is, in other words, the product of an over-indulgent, liberal mother and an absent father; of the permissive, anti-authoritarian family of the 1960s and 1970s. In fact, the absence of a patriarchal authority figure suggests that the burden of guilt for Lipton's behaviour lies not simply with the permissive family, but with his mother and, more specifically, feminism. The issue of maternal guilt is, furthermore, raised again at the end of the film where it is posited as the reason for Laura's violent revenge on her daughter's rapist (rather than the public act of rape prevention she claims it to be). In contrast, the motivation for the New-Right zealotry found in the trauma drama is, according to Feuer, 'often maternal love':

> This motivation creates a contradictory position for the mothers portrayed in these films. In the deepest sense of New Right ideology, these are traditional women left behind by feminism. And yet, as in the case of many New Right ideologues, these mothers are the only people left in the culture who retain the moral righteousness necessary to the task. Therefore they (always reluctantly) take on a masculine role for the sake of their victimized children.[26]

Certainly, the substitution of morally justified mothers for female victim-avengers would seem the obvious way not only to insert a new right ideology of family values into the rape-revenge cycle, but also to militate against or divert its potentially subversive feminist politics. However, this would still leave the issue of male complicity in rape largely unresolved. What I want to suggest, therefore, is that when the rape-revenge narrative's feminist stories meet a New Right ideology of family values in the maternal rape-revenge film, the politics Feuer identifies in the trauma drama become rather more complex and sinister.

Nevertheless, like those trauma dramas that Feuer identifies as interpretable as left-wing or subversive inversions of the formula, *In My Daughter's Name* omits function 6 ('they form a self-help group or join a grass-roots organization'), and neither *In My Daughter's Name* or *Eye for an Eye* include function 7 ('the new organization is better able to cope with the trauma, often having an impact on established institutions'). Thus, it is not the judicial system that the mothers in both these films attempt to take on or change. Rather, hers is an intensely private and personal battle waged against another individual and, although she may try to enlist the help of other victims or potential victims or join a self-help group (as in *Eye for an Eye*), these sources of support either reject or are rejected by her. What I want to suggest, then, is that while functions 6 and 7 are clearly crucial to the trauma drama's right-wing message of 'the rebirth of America through right-wing individualist populist activity', their omission or variation does not necessarily make the films left-wing or subversive in sentiment.[27] Instead, the omission of these crucial functions can also have the effect of tipping the balance of these films away from the politicized public solutions of the trauma drama towards the depoliticized private solutions of the domestic melodrama, a movement that has important consequences for the way in which these films make sense of the feminist stories inscribed within the rape-revenge narrative.

Melodrama and the maternal avenger

The question posed by *Eye for an Eye's* publicity poster – 'What do you do when justice fails?' – would nevertheless appear to invite a reading of the film as an articulation of the same kind of vigilante politics Feuer identified in the trauma drama. This is certainly the framework within which the film was understood by reviewers.[28] The film's opening credit sequence, however, rephrases this question and asks more specifically: 'Do you kill for your child?' A moth flutters around a child's bedroom, the child, terrified, calls for her mother. When the mother arrives the child pleads, 'Kill it mummy. Please kill it'. The mother, disregarding her daughter's pleas, gently catches the moth in her hands and carefully puts it out of the window. Here, then, the mother is clearly constructed as the pre-server rather than the taker of life. This sequence also sets up a distinction between internal and external spaces and situates the window as the interface between those spaces. This internal, domestic scene is immediately followed by an external tracking shot of the house, which is accompanied by the sound of footsteps and breathing on the soundtrack suggesting that it is also a point-of-view shot. However, the film withholds the initial establishing shot of the shot/reverse-shot structure, thus posing another question: 'Who is looking?' Over this shot the film's title appears suggesting that we read this title, and hence the film, not only literally, as a revenge drama, but also metaphorically, as a drama of seeing. This interpretation is reinforced in the next shot, a close-up of a mirror in which Karen's eye is reflected and magnified. While this shot does not provide an answer to the previous one, it does suggest, through the magnification of Karen's eye, that she has an active and powerful gaze and, therefore, a privileged relation to seeing. She is, however, using the mirror to apply make-up and this shot, to use Mulvey's terms, positions her not only as 'bearer of the look' but as an object 'to-be-looked-at'. Indeed, Karen's status as erotic spectacle is assured when, having completed her make-up, her husband, Mack, attempts to seduce her. Here then the magnification of Karen's eye functions to construct the female gaze not as powerful but as narcissistic.

Although, as the film progresses, Karen's gaze appears to become more active (she follows and watches Robert Doob, the man who has raped and murdered her daughter), the process of looking is still sexually differentiated by means of the window. The topography of spaces the film employs and their relation to processes of specular-ization are thus remarkably similar to those found in the woman's film. As Mary Ann Doane observes in her discussion of such films:

> Within the 'woman's films' as a whole, images of women looking through windows or waiting at windows abound. The window has special import in terms of the social and symbolic positioning of the woman – the window is the interface between inside and outside, the feminine space of the family and reproduction and the masculine space of production. It facilitates a communication by means of the look

between two sexually differentiated spaces. That interface becomes a potential point of violence in the paranoid woman's films.[29]

In *Eye for an Eye*, then, Karen is always positioned on the inside looking out, for example, through café windows, shop windows and car windows at Doob, whereas Doob is always located on the outside looking in, for example, through the window of the play house at Megan (Alexandra Kyle) and at the Hispanic woman through her kitchen window. In this way, therefore, *Eye for an Eye*, like the woman's film, employs the window to construct a distinction between public, masculine space and private, feminine space. The window, however, also acts as a framing device so that the woman standing at a window (in the case of the Hispanic woman) or looking out of one is constructed as much as 'to-be-looked-at' as looking. Furthermore, the scene in which Karen watches Doob watching the Hispanic woman, would seem to merely reproduce the relations of looking established in the post-credit sequence and succinctly summarized by John Berger: 'Men look at women. Women watch themselves being looked at.'[30] Indeed, at the end of this scene Doob returns Karen's gaze so that she too becomes the object of his look. Again, then, any implications of an active female gaze suggested by close-ups of Karen's eyes (here reflected in the rear-view mirror of her car) are undermined. Similarly, when Karen triumphantly tells Dolly (Beverly D'Angelo) about watching Doob she pointedly removes her glasses. As Doane has argued: 'Glasses worn by a woman in the cinema do not generally signify a deficiency in seeing but an active looking.'[31] Karen's admission of her appropriation of the gaze is, in other words, potentially so threatening and dangerous that it must be accompanied by a simultaneous rejection of the power to see, symbolized by the removal of her glasses. Finally, Dolly's response to Karen's admission is to suggest that Karen is mad: 'Jesus Christ, Karen, what are you doing. This is insane.'

Like the female gothic melodrama or paranoid woman's film, therefore, *Eye for an Eye* is characterized both by the heroine's investigation of a man and by a tendency to question or undermine her perceptions. This is particularly apparent in an early scene before Doob has been identified as the rapist and murderer. Karen, Mack and Megan visit a museum where Megan keeps running on ahead of them. As she becomes increasingly frantic about Megan's safety, Karen imagines that every man she encounters is the rapist and murderer. The apparent feminist point to this scene that all men are potential rapists is, however, undermined in the exchange that follows where Karen tells Mack to stop treating her like 'some neurotic', to which Mack retorts, 'Well don't act like one.' Furthermore, the evidence that Karen collects during her investigation of Doob is, on two occasions, systematically undermined by the detective in charge of the case.

Karen's job as director of public affairs at the Media Museum also suggests a concern with issues of spectatorship. However, while televisions are very frequently on in the background of scenes, people are rarely shown watching them. Consequently, although we briefly see Megan watching a cartoon and Doob watching a pop video, it is Karen who is privileged as a spectator. Doane proposes that:

> The pressure of the demand in the 'woman's film' for the depiction of female subjectivity is so strong, and often so contradictory, that it is not at all surprising that sections such as the projection scenes in *Caught* and *Rebecca* should dwell on the problems of female spectatorship.[32]

In *Eye for an Eye* we twice see Karen watching a video tape of Doob's arrest on the news. By means of the rewind, slow-play and freeze-frame functions she attempts to control Doob, to fix him as the object of her gaze. Her subsequent investigation of him is predicated not only on dissatisfaction with the narrative resolution of this 'story' (the dismissal of the case against Doob), but represents an attempt to recreate the conditions of this spectatorship. In other words, the pleasure of Karen's investigation of Doob, like that of the cinema spectator, is predicated on her presence not being acknowledged. As she says to Dolly after the first time she follows Doob: 'And he never even knew I was there.' In this respect, the windows through which Karen watches Doob can be seen as corresponding to the cinema screen, while she, usually immobile, can be seen as corresponding to the spectator in the auditorium. This fantasy of inviolability is, however, broken when Doob returns Karen's gaze. While Karen subsequently returns to watching the video tape, this functions to mark a new phase in the narrative – an apparent shift from investigation to punishment (Karen's plans for revenge). In this way, then, the film's narrative trajectory would appear to reverse the traditional gendered relations of looking in the cinema. In other words, Karen appears to have become the subject rather than the object of the voyeuristic gaze described by Laura Mulvey. Mulvey argues that voyeurism functions to guard against the castration anxiety brought about by the representation of the female through

> re-enactment of the original trauma (investigating the woman, demystifying her mystery), counterbalanced by the devaluation, punishment or saving of the guilty object ... pleasure lies in ascertaining guilt (immediately associated with castration), asserting control, and subjecting the guilty person through punishment or forgiveness.[33]

This avenue is, according to Mulvey, 'typified by the concerns of the *film noir*'.[34]

Certainly, this section of the film is marked by a shift from the issues and iconography of the gothic melodrama to the visual style and themes of film noir (although as several critics have argued the two are inextricably linked).[35] Particularly noteworthy in this respect are scenes of the city at night and of an urban landscape comprised of car parks and back-street garages. For example, in contrast to the forbidding Gothic façade of the building where the support group meetings are held, the garage where Karen plots her revenge with the help of Sidney (Philip Baker Hall) and Martin (Keith David) is dark and seedy, lit on the outside by a flickering neon sign, while the back office features the traditional noir venetian blinds.[36] The emphasis on the long, black shadows cast by the characters' bodies and on the sound of footsteps ringing out in the empty streets when Karen believes she is being followed one night, is also characteristic of the noir style. Moreover, the camera movement here, in which the camera tracks backwards before Karen as she quickens her pace, is remarkably similar to that described by Place and Peterson as one of the few moving shots found in film noir.[37] This incident also proves to be another example of Karen's paranoia (the man turns out to be friend not foe) and is reminiscent of gothic melodrama. It also serves to remind us that not all men are potential rapists. Most importantly, however, it functions to construct Karen, if not as a femme fatale, then at least as a 'fatal femme' – she lies in wait for her 'pursuer' and then violently attacks him.

What I want to suggest, therefore, is that the shift from the codes of gothic melodrama to those of film noir is accompanied by a concomitant shift in the subject of investigation. In other words, where gothic melodrama is frequently concerned with investigating and establishing the guilt of a man (here Doob), film noir is often concerned with investigating and establishing the guilt of a woman. This section of the film thus actually functions to establish Karen's guilt, variously constructing her as neglectful mother, as violent woman and as sexually aggressive – all significant attributes of the femme fatale. Here, then, it is Karen who is watched by the other characters. We see Angel (Charlayne Woodard) watching Karen approach Sidney at a support group meeting and we see Mack watching Karen distractedly pushing Megan's swing in the garden (it is perhaps significant here that Karen is positioned outside the home, while Mack is positioned inside looking out through the window). Retrospectively, we discover that Karen has been the object of both these characters' investigations (throughout this section of the film, several jarring high-angle shots work to suggest that the characters are being watched by some unknown presence). Angel, it transpires, is an FBI officer working undercover to investigate vigilante activity, while Mack, having found Karen's gun club membership card, has been making enquiries that reveal her duplicity. This doubling of the investigative structure 'with stories within stories, so that the investigation of one enigma frames another', according to Elizabeth Cowie, is characteristic of the film noir and explains its narrative complexity.[38] Indeed, the opening of the scene in which Mack confronts Karen about her membership of the gun club is straight out of film noir with Mack playing the role of Philip Marlowe. Karen arrives home to a darkened house, as she steps through the door, however, a lamp is switched on to reveal Mack sitting in an armchair waiting to cross-examine her. Throughout this section of the film, camera shots and visual motifs are also used to suggest imprisonment and construct Karen as guilty. For example, as she commits herself to killing Doob, we see her face framed in close-up between the head and shoulders of the two men standing in the foreground, echoing a similar shot of Doob at the preliminary hearing. Or, there is the tracking shot from in front of some railings as Karen leaves Angel's house having been warned of the consequences of exacting her revenge on Doob.

Karen is also shown to be guilty of neglecting her maternal responsibilities. In fact, there is a case to be made for arguing that the rape itself is constructed as a consequence of this neglect. In other words, Karen is unable to protect Julie (Olivia Burnette) because she is not at home but stuck in a traffic jam returning from work, a point underlined in this sequence by cutting between these two spaces and by showing Karen to be in possession of the full trappings of the career woman: smart hairstyle, business suit and mobile phone.[39] More specifically, the cross-cutting between this image of the career woman and the spectacular consumption of Megan's party preparations functions to suggest that, since the family is clearly wealthy, there is no economic imperative or justification for Karen's career. 'I won't leave you Julie', Karen says as she hears her daughter being attacked at the other end of the phone, but the point is surely that she already has. Indeed, Julie's response to the news that Karen is going to be late – 'What else is new?' – functions to assure us that Karen's failure to be there to protect Julie is not simply an unusual and unintentional coincidence of fate. Later in the film, moreover, responsibility for preventing unsolicited sexual advances is placed squarely with the woman and particularly the mother – as Karen and Angel work-out at the gym, the instructor can be heard intoning in the background, 'Knees together, ankles together. Remember what your mother told you'. Similarly, in *In My Daughter's Name*, the rape is implicitly set up not only as a result of Laura's abdication of maternal responsibilities – leaving her daughter to put the chicken in the oven and mind her younger sister while she is at work, making her buy the napkins – but as a form of wish-fulfilment on Laura's part. In a scene early in the film, Laura asks her husband if they can get rid of the car, which is continually breaking down and is 'so damned annoying'. 'So are the kids', her husband replies, 'we don't get rid of them.' 'Don't tempt me', Laura retorts. Indeed, the implication is that Carly only accepts a lift from her rapist for fear, as she later says, that her mother will, metaphorically at least, kill her if she fails to return promptly with the napkins.

Although after Carly's rape and murder, Laura attempts to compensate for her dereliction of duty by becoming increasingly overprotective of her remaining daughter, Lissa (Ellen Blain), she continues to neglect her maternal responsibilities, such as shopping for food. In *Eye for an Eye*, Karen is shown to be similarly neglectful but, unlike in *In My Daughter's Name*, this neglect also extends to her remaining daughter, Megan. In both films, moreover, the women's investigation and harassment of the men who raped and murdered their daughters is shown to radically compromise the safety of their surviving children suggesting, as Doane does, that 'a certain violence ... is coincident with the attribution of the gaze to the female'.[40] In *In My Daughter's Name*, for example, Peter Lipton takes out a restraining order on Laura, then comes to her home and implicitly threatens Lissa: 'Lissa, she's pretty. I like her.' Likewise, in *Eye for an Eye*, while Karen is at the gym with Angel, Doob visits Megan at school and afterwards warns Karen, 'Why don't you just stay out of my neighbourhood and I'll stay out of yours.' In recreating the conditions of the original rape – Megan, like Julie, is playing house, this time in the school's playhouse; Karen is absent; Doob tells Karen, 'I don't really like kiddy pussy, but I'm willing to make an exception' – this sequence not only suggests that Karen was similarly responsible for the earlier attack, but in many ways returns us to the beginning of the film. Indeed, the sequence of shots directly following Karen's confrontation with Doob – Karen putting Megan to bed and shutting and locking the window, followed by a long, static shot of the house – echo those which open the film, while the next scene, showing Karen enlisting Sidney's help in planning her revenge, would appear to answer in the affirmative the question this opening sequence posed: 'Do you kill for your child?'. Similarly, in *In My Daughter's Name*, the scene following the one in which Peter Lipton threatens Lissa shows Laura following him to a shopping centre where she shoots and kills him.

Although the decision to kill the man who has killed one daughter and is threatening the other would seem the ultimate act of maternal love and, therefore, morally justified, the ensuing narratives of both films work to undermine such a reading. In *Eye for an Eye*, for example, the series of short sequences that follow Karen's decision to kill Doob function to juxtapose Karen's increasing proficiency in using a gun and defending herself with her growing incompetence as a mother (signalled through her neglectful and distanced behaviour towards Megan). Particularly indicative of Karen's withdrawal from her role in the home is her failure to notice when Megan shows her a picture of a house she has drawn. Indeed, this crucial failure to see contrasts ironically with the unwavering, investigative gaze Karen directs at Doob. Also worth noting here is how, after Karen attacks the man she believes is pursuing her, her initial concern about the violence she has inflicted turns quickly to pleasure. This scene, moreover, cuts directly into one showing Karen and Mack having sex. While the editing here works to make a rather crude and already overworked connection between sex and violence, it also functions to position Karen within a lineage of representations of women who are not only violent but sexually active and aggressive; representations most commonly found in film noir and contemporary neo-noirs. The scene opens with Mack in the traditional, active masculine position on top of Karen. However, Karen then turns over so that she is on top of him and pins him down by the arms. Such a display of active and aggressive female sexuality is, nevertheless, immediately undermined as Mack pushes Karen off him, holds her at arms length and then returns her to her previous position beneath him.

This section of the film concludes with another visual echo of the film's opening sequence – a long tracking shot of the exterior of the house. Yet, whereas at the beginning of the film we hear Megan calling for her mother, here she is calling for Mack. The scene thus functions to mark the extent to which Karen has strayed from her maternal role but also, as she goes and comforts Megan, to reposition her in that role (just as Mack had repositioned her in her 'correct' sexual role in the previous scene). The tracking shot of the house also suggests that someone is again watching and it is in the following scenes that we learn that Karen has been the object of investigation. Consequently, Karen decides against killing Doob, a decision she arrives at during Dolly's birthday party. That the next scene depicts the rape and murder of the Hispanic woman is not merely ironic. Rather the juxtaposition of these two scenes also acts as another reminder of the beginning of the film, where, shortly before being raped and murdered, Julie is shown preparing Megan's birthday party. Indeed, lest we fail to make this connection, we have recently been reminded, via a conversation between Megan and Karen, that Julie's death occurred on Megan's birthday.

Tania Modleski, among others, has argued that such 'excessive repetition characterizes many film melodramas'.[41] Related to this, and also a point made by several critics of melodrama, is their tendency towards forming a circular pattern. As Christine Gledhill notes, 'many cinematic melodramas start out from a flashback so that their end literally lies in their beginning'.[42] While *Eye for an Eye* does not start out from a flashback, throughout the course of the narrative there are constant evocations of the film's beginning (themselves a form of flashback). As the film progresses, moreover, these become more frequent and insistent such that when Karen goes to see Detective Denillo (Joe Mantegna) after the rape and murder of the Hispanic woman, their conversation is actually punctuated by several brief flashbacks to earlier points in the film (Doob

attacking Julie and the Hispanic woman; Doob watching and deliv-
ering groceries to the latter). Indeed, this scene is actually a repetition of an earlier one in which Karen visited Denillo after Julie's
death to enquire how the case against Doob was progressing. However, whereas in the earlier scene Karen listened meekly as Denillo
outlined the various evidence he had collected against Doob, here it
is she who details her investigation of Doob (one which Denillo systematically undermines, causing her to retort, 'Fuck you'). In this
respect, these repetitions serve to mark Karen's transformation from
passive, life-preserving mother to active, aggressive woman. Yet,
these repetitions are not only signifiers of narrative progression.
Rather, they can also signify circularity and can thus function to
reverse narrative transformations.

Clearly, the rape-revenge structure is itself based on repetition,
something that the phrase 'an eye for an eye' explicitly points up.
However, as we have seen, the passage from rape to revenge, from
victim to aggressor, usually also necessitates some kind of transformation of the female protagonist. Of course, in the maternal rape-
revenge film, this narrative trajectory is complicated by the fact that
victim and avenger are not one and the same, so that the transformations that occur are not from victim to aggressor but from
mother to aggressor. This substitution of morally justified mothers
for female victim-avengers would seem the obvious way not only to
insert a New Right ideology of family values into the rape-revenge
cycle, but also to militate against or divert its potentially subversive
feminist politics. Yet, these narratives constantly work to construct
the mother not as morally justified but as guilty. Thus, in *In My
Daughter's Name*, rather than acting from some maternal moral
high ground, Laura acts out of a sense of her failure as a mother.
The film, therefore, is unable to legitimate her movement from the
feminine private realm (of motherhood) to the masculine public
realm (of revenge and violence) on the basis of moral righteousness
(as in the trauma drama). Laura, then, must not only be shown to be
punished for her actions, but the film's narrative trajectory must, in
fact, continuously work to reinscribe her in the realm of the private.
As her lawyer, Maureen Leeds (Lee Grant), emphasizes at the end
of the film: 'You're not a killer Laura, you're a *mother*.' Indeed,
despite Laura's attempts to insist that her actions were those of a
sane and rational woman, and despite the fact that she is found
guilty of voluntary manslaughter (rather than not guilty by reason

of insanity), her lawyer's defence strategies tend to function to undermine any sense of female agency. In addition, Laura's refusal to plead not guilty by reason of insanity ('I'm not going to lie to protect myself like he did') works to compound her guilt by implying that she desires punishment. Moreover, this guilt is often posited precisely as a consequence of narratives of transformation (for example, the movement of women from the home into the workplace brought about by feminism). *Eye for an Eye* makes this connection explicit by using the scenes depicting Karen's transformation to establish her guilt.

The maternal rape-revenge film, therefore, does not deploy the rape-revenge structure in order to articulate and negotiate the various transformations brought about by second-wave feminism. Rather, the narrative trajectories of these films is towards reversing these transformations and relocating women as mothers in the home. Indeed, even when the films construct apparently positive feminist representations of career women, such as the female defence lawyer in *In My Daughter's Name*, they simultaneously work to contain the feminist implications of these representations. For example, while the lawyer's career motivation can be traced to feminism – she too lost a daughter to male (domestic) violence – this motivation is ultimately channelled into a discourse of motherhood and particularly maternal guilt, with the lawyer having been oblivious to her daughter's plight. Thus the lawyer's motivation in taking on Laura's case can be read as arising not out of a feminist critique of male violence against women, but out of her need to assuage her own sense of guilt over her daughter's death. Such a reading is confirmed both by the specific form her defence takes and by her comment to Laura: 'I'm doing this for both of us'.

In My Daughter's Name, then, follows a similar narrative trajectory to the maternal melodrama in which, as Christian Viviani has observed, 'the partial or total rehabilitation of the mother is accomplished … through a cathartic trial scene'.[43] In *Eye for an Eye*, it is achieved by mapping the rape-revenge structure across both the generic discourses of melodrama and those of film noir. In other words, the codes of film noir are used to construct Karen as guilty, while the repetitive and circular narrative structure of melodrama, although initially used to chart her transformation, ultimately functions to reposition her in the space of the home from which she was absent at the beginning of the film. In this final section of the film,

then, Mack and Megan go off on holiday and Karen, having manu-
factured an excuse to temporarily stay behind, breaks into and ran-
sacks Doob's apartment, leaving her baseball hat behind as a
signifier of her presence. As Mack and Megan are shown driving
through the countryside, Doob is shown travelling towards his final
confrontation with Karen, while Karen is shown at home preparing
for this melodramatic resolution by putting on some classical music.
Having broken into the house by smashing a window (according to
Doane 'a potential point of violence in the paranoid woman's
films'), Doob climbs the stairs to the bathroom, where the shower is
running.[44] Pulling back the curtain to reveal not Karen but a towel,
he swings round to find her aiming a gun at him. The following
conversation ensues:

KAREN Sorry to disappoint you
DOOB What're you gonna do. Shoot me.
KAREN You broke into my house with the intent to do me bodily harm.
      The law says I have the right to protect myself.
DOOB You want me to say I'm sorry. It could've been anybody. I don't
      even remember what she looked like. It's nothin' personal.
KAREN She was seventeen years old. She was five foot two. She had
      brown eyes. Her name was Julie. She was my daughter.
DOOB She was a great fuck.

Doob then runs at Karen and knocks the gun from her hand to the
bottom of the stairs. A struggle follows during which Karen falls
down the stairs. As she lies on her back at the bottom, Doob walks
down the stairs towards her, repeating that it was nothing personal.
'It's very personal', Karen responds, as she grabs the gun and shoots
him four times. He falls and lands on top of her. She pushes him off
and the sequence ends with a close-up of Doob's face.

There are several issues I want to pick up on here. The first of
these is the way in which this sequence re-enacts the original rape.
Clearly, the very act of 'breaking and entering' the feminine space of
the home acts as a metaphor for rape. However, there is also the way
in which, at the end, Doob falls and lands face down on the pros-
trate Karen – a position with obvious sexual connotations. Finally,
the moment when Doob knocks the gun out of Karen's hand acts as
a visual echo of the moment during the original rape when Karen
falls over and her mobile phone skids away from her across the
pavement. The latter, in particular, functions to suggest that Karen

is now in the right place as opposed to the wrong place. Indeed, here it is the father/husband who is shown to be (justifiably) absent and impotent. Like Karen at the beginning, Mack is shown to be far from home unable to make contact because the phone is engaged.[45] In this respect, the end of *Eye for an Eye* would appear to be informed by the kind of melodramatic resolution identified by Griselda Pollock and summarized by Christine Gledhill:

> From Pollock's perspective the women's point-of-view movies and male oedipal dramas have one thing in common: the relocation of the woman as mother, a position that, while fathers may disappear, be rendered silent or impotent, dominates the conclusion of these films.[46]

The melodramatic nature of Karen's revenge is also ensured not only by having it occur in the home, but by specifically locating it on the staircase, which, as Gledhill points out, has 'become a standard feature of a cinematic rhetoric in the expression of melodramatic confrontation'.[47] While the film proffers a legal explanation for Karen's decision to exact her revenge on Doob in the feminine, private space of the home rather than the masculine, public space of the street, this need to act within the confines of the law can in turn be traced to Karen's role as a mother. As Angel says to Karen in the scene immediately preceding her decision not to go along with the planned public revenge: 'You've got to think about what kind of example you'll be setting Megan.' Moreover, this scene closes with a shot from outside of both women inside the home looking out of the window at children buying ice cream. At this point, it is worth noting that when Mack attacks Doob earlier in the film, he does so in the masculine, public space of the courtroom. A quick glance at other recent parental rape-revenge films reveals a similarly gendered use of space. In the paternal rape-revenge film, *A Time to Kill*, for example, the father's revenge on his daughter's rapists also takes place in the masculine, public space of the courthouse (equating his revenge, quite literally, with 'the law of the father'). In *In My Daughter's Name*, on the other hand, while Laura's revenge also takes place in a public space (the mall) it is one that is specifically designated as a feminine space for consumption. Furthermore, in the latter film, Laura is shown to be duly punished for her violent incursion into public space whereas, in the former film, the father is acquitted. The maternal rape-revenge film's emphasis on the private and individual nature of rape and revenge is finally perhaps nowhere more apparent than in Karen's retort to Doob, 'It's very personal.'

Despite second-wave feminism's claim that 'the personal *is* political', and despite pointedly referencing the O. J. Simpson trial and contemporary public debates about violence against women, *Eye for an Eye* makes no attempt to represent rape or revenge as feminist or even public issues.[48] In fact, as I hope to have shown, its project is rather to mobilize these issues in the service of articulating a private discourse of maternity. An analysis of the character of Angel proves especially illuminating in this respect. As a black, lesbian mother who is also an FBI officer, Angel's function within the narrative would appear to be to provide a positive, feminist representation of woman. Like the female lawyer in *In My Daughter's Name*, however, Angel's function is actually to investigate Karen, establish her guilt and to reposition her in relation to motherhood through continuously invoking a discourse of maternity. Angel is thus constructed as the moral guardian of the home and family; as, quite literally, the 'Angel in the House'. The function of these female characters can be seen as analogous to that of the doctor in the pre-1970 rape-revenge melodramas discussed in chapter 3, whose role similarly was to 'cure' the heroine of her rejection of the feminine career and to restore her to her proper role within the confines of the family. As such, these representations of women in positions of power and authority are not a cause for celebration, since their function, like that of the doctor, is simply to legitimate and authorize the discourses of maternity that these films articulate. Furthermore, while *Eye for an Eye* also places women in an investigative role, Angel's gaze is directed towards policing other women's behaviour, while Karen's is continually undermined or punished.

The final section of *Eye for an Eye* also returns us to the questions of specularity posed at the beginning of the film, particularly the question of 'who is looking?' suggested by the absence of an establishing shot to accompany the tracking point-of-view shot of the exterior of the house in the film's opening sequence. During the course of the film the combination of the codes of gothic melodrama and those of film noir has tended to complicate these issues by situating woman as both the subject and object of investigation (Doob watches women, Karen watches Doob, Mack and Angel watch Karen). The missing establishing shot is, however, provided in the film's final sequences, where a similar exterior shot of the house is followed by a tracking close-up of Doob's face accompanied by the sound of his footsteps on the soundtrack. The next shot is, moreover, of Karen closing the shower curtain. Given the way in which the shower has functioned within cinematic history as the locus for the erotic display of the female body (Alfred Hitchcock's 1960 *Psycho* being an obvious case in point), this series of shots would appear to function to re-establish and confirm traditional relations of looking: man as 'bearer of the look', woman as 'to-be-looked-at'. Nevertheless, unlike *Psycho*, *Eye for an Eye* denies us fetishistic shots of the woman's naked body by always positioning the camera on the wrong side of the shower curtain. Similarly, the staircase, according to Doane 'traditionally the locus of specularization of the woman', becomes a site not for erotic display but for violent confrontation.[49] Doane suggests that this despecularization of the woman is characteristic of the paranoid woman's film where the woman becomes the object of a de-eroticized medical gaze, so that 'in terms of spatial configuration and language the female figure is trapped within the medical discourse of these narratives'.[50] This argument would certainly seem to be applicable to the end of *In My Daughter's Name*, where the lawyer, like the doctor in the woman's film, traps Laura within a discourse of insanity. More significantly, in tracing the origins of this insanity to maternal guilt, the film's 'medical gaze' also functions to ensnare Laura within a discourse of maternity. What I want to suggest is that at the end of *Eye for an Eye*, while Karen is not the object of a specifically medical gaze, she is de-eroticized and that this functions similarly to trap her within a discourse of maternity.[51] In other words, in order to relocate Karen as mother she must simultaneously be desexualized, must be presented not as an erotic object.

Thus, perhaps the only form of physical transformation the maternal avenger can be seen to undergo is a process of what Feuer calls 'uglification'.[52] For Feuer this serves to democratize the trauma drama's 'charismatic individual'. Within the context of the rape-revenge cycle, however, this is clearly the opposite to what I have elsewhere identified as a process of eroticization. As I argued in chapter 1, as an articulation of one of the new public femininities described by Hilary Radner, the erotic female avenger functions not only to problematize the gendered binary implicit in the movement from rape (feminine) to revenge (masculine), but to destabilize the distinction between the masculine public sphere and the feminine private sphere.[53] Uglification, however, would appear to be virtually synonymous with masculinization (in so far as the binary ugliness/prettiness, like all binaries, is inherently gendered). Ugliness, nevertheless, also carries connotations of sexual unattractiveness and can thus also be understood in terms of the binary desexualized/sexualized, a binary with particular pertinence to the construction and representation of women as either madonnas or whores. While the madonna/whore distinction is somewhat archaic, its influence continues to be felt in contemporary attempts to distinguish between mothers and working girls or between private and public femininities. As the opposite of eroticization, the maternal rape-revenge film's process of uglification would appear to work to reverse the direction of the transformations found in the female rape-revenge film and, in particular, to re-establish the ideology of the separate spheres. In other words, uglification serves not to masculinize but to desexualize the maternal avenger, which in the context of my current arguments, places her firmly within the realm of the desexualized femininity of the mother. Contrary to the female rape-revenge film, therefore, the maternal rape-revenge film's process of uglification functions to steer its maternal avenger away from an exploration of the sexualized, public femininities articulated by the female avenger and towards the singular, desexualized, private femininity of the mother.

According to Radner, one of the key ways in which public femininities are constructed and reproduced is through consumer practices, such as the buying and wearing of clothes.[54] Interestingly, the opening sequences of *In My Daughter's Name* focus on shopping and particularly the buying of clothes. Clearly, within the context of my current arguments, this functions to set up an emphasis on public femininities from which the film can then depart. However, it also functions to set out the film's message in microcosm. In other words, Carly's failure to fulfil her private feminine role (putting the chicken in the oven) is shown to be the consequence of her pursuit of public femininities (buying a dress), in the same way that Laura's failure in her private role as a mother is shown to be a result of her public role as a working woman and organizer of social events. Furthermore, Laura's obsession with public appearances (having the right embossed napkins) crucially causes her to overlook her private role of policing her daughter's public appearance when she sends her out to get them. Indeed, the film links Laura's ill-defined concept of correct feminine/maternal behaviour with her ill-defined concept of correct feminine appearance. Thus, she will not let Carly wear the recently purchased long, flowery, distinctly girly dress to go out with her boyfriend, but she does allow her to go out alone at night to fetch the napkins in a short, black, distinctly sexy outfit. Laura's recognition of this mistake – signalled by the fact that it is the former outfit she chooses for Carly to be buried in – marks the end of the film's concern with public femininities as they are constructed through clothes and make-up and the beginning of the movement towards the more natural, private femininity of motherhood as it is articulated through uglification, or the shedding of clothes and make-up. At the beginning of the film, Laura's desire to be 'something else besides a mother' (to borrow a phrase from King Vidor's classic 1938 maternal melodrama, *Stella Dallas*) is shown not only through the fact that she has a job, but through the way in which she is represented as both sexualized (in an early scene showing she and her husband about to make love) and glamourized (at her husband's birthday party). By the end of the film, however, she is represented as dowdy, haggard and desexualized. Similarly, in *Eye for an Eye*, Karen relinquishes the smart suits, hairstyle and make-up that signify the public femininity of the career woman – lest we fail to register Karen's incursion into the public sphere, it is underlined in her title as director of *public* affairs – for the drab, asexual, private femininity of the mother.

This emphasis on the sanctity of motherhood is, however, not simply a feature of the maternal rape-revenge film. Rather, that it is a function of the cycle as a whole to construct the mother as sacrosanct is suggested by the infrequency with which mothers are featured as rape victims in these films (to my knowledge there are only two such examples: *Positive ID* and *The Rape of Dr Willis*). At this juncture, it is perhaps worth noting that also infrequent, to the point of non-existence, is the representation of black female victims or avengers. As far as I am aware, the only American rape-revenge films to include such representations are *Showgirls* and *A Time to Kill*.[55] This omission, I think, can be read alongside the construction of the white mother as sacrosanct and thus as exempt from rape, as a sign of the rape-revenge cycle's complicity with a racist discourse that constructs black women as already 'impure' and incapable of being raped.[56] The perceived 'impurity' of the black woman, moreover, also deprives her of the necessary moral justification for revenge.

Indeed, even *Showgirls* and *A Time to Kill* can be seen as complicit with such racist ideologies. In other words, despite the fact that both films feature black female victims, they simultaneously deny her the opportunity to exact her own revenge, preferring instead to allocate this task either to the victim's father (*A Time to Kill*) or to her white female friend (*Showgirls*). In so doing, these films can be seen as contributing to the construction of a hierarchy of vengeance in which black men and white women are considered to have a greater moral justification for avenging the rape of the black woman than the black woman herself. In these two films, then, black women are not only victimized, they are disempowered.

The marked absence of black female victims and avengers in the rape-revenge cycle, therefore, can be seen as stemming from a belief that black women are 'impure' and, thus, not only incapable of being raped, but morally excluded from exacting revenge. The infrequency with which white mothers feature as rape victims, on the other hand, can be seen as stemming from a desire to assure the purity of the white mother by exempting her from rape. It is perhaps for this reason that, in its final sequence, *Eye for an Eye* can only symbolically re-enact the original rape. Yet, while the film goes to some lengths not to represent Karen as an erotic object, the same visual treatment is, tellingly, not extended to Doob's victims (one a child, the other childless) whose bodies, both during and after their rape and murder, are the subject of brief but fetishistic close-ups. That we are denied similar shots of Doob's body suggests that the film operates firmly within the boundaries of the traditional relations of looking described by Laura Mulvey. In the film's closing scenes, then, Karen is once again the object of (masculine) investigation. Seated in a chair, her face is once more 'framed' in close-up by the police officers who stand before her barraging her with questions. Despite Denillo's interpretation of Doob's killing as 'a clear case of self-defence', Karen's guilt is not in question: 'I know what you've done here', he tells her, 'you haven't fooled me.' Finally, Mack's arrival, in echoing and reversing Karen's return home after the initial rape, suggests that, in terms of space, of inside and outside, traditional gender roles have also been re-established. In the film's penultimate shot, Mack and Karen sit together on the sofa and, as she bows her head in atonement, he takes her hand in a gesture of forgiveness.

That there have been no new articulations of the rape-revenge structure since *Eye for an Eye* and *A Time to Kill* would seem to suggest that the cycle has run its course. Certainly, from the evidence presented above, it would appear that the cycle has, at the very least, come full circle. In chapter 3, I examined the deployment of the rape-revenge structure over a range of genres, particularly melodrama, from the silent period to 1970. In so doing, I attempted to show how the structure functioned in relation to the discourses of gender and genre in the period prior to the rise of second-wave feminism. Here, I argued that the structure largely functioned to endorse and uphold the traditional conceptions of masculinity and femininity inscribed in melodrama. In particular, I showed how in these films rape tended to be cast as either resulting in, or resulting from, the heroine's rejection of the feminine career of heterosexual romance and family, and I demonstrated how, in both cases, the threat this represented was apparent in the way in which these narratives worked overtime to return the woman to her 'proper' place within the confines of the family and heterosexual relations.

The maternal rape-revenge film deploys the codes and conventions of melodrama to similar ideological effect. The occurrence of rape, for example, is similarly traced to the heroine's rejection of the feminine career, and specifically, given the emphasis on the maternal, to her abdication of her private maternal responsibilities within the home. Unlike the earlier films, however, the maternal rape-revenge film explicitly traces the heroine's rejection of a private feminine identity to her pursuit of the public femininity of the career woman. In this way, then, the maternal avenger's rejection of her feminine vocation, and the rape it is seen to engender, is traced specifically to the political and social changes brought about by feminism in the post-1970 period (such as the increase in working mothers). Indeed, that it is maternal guilt rather than maternal love that drives these women to commit acts of revenge suggests that the aim of these films is not simply to contain the feminist politics of the female rape-revenge cycle, but to effect a dual process of critique and co-option. In constructing the maternal avenger not as morally justified but as guilty of neglecting her maternal responsibilities, the films are able to lay the blame for rape on the transformations brought about by second-wave feminism, while simultaneously constructing an apparently feminist justification (rape prevention) for women's return to the home. Thus, while these films apparently make some concessions to feminist gains through the inclusion of independent career women such as Angel Kosinsky and Maureen Leeds, these gains are appropriated by and contained within a discourse of family values. The function of the independent career woman here, like that of the male protagonists of the earlier films, is to legitimate and authorize the maternal discourses these films articulate and to restore the heroine to her proper role within the family. Similarly, although the emphasis on male rather than female revenge found in the pre-1970 films would seem to have been reversed, the distinctions drawn between male and female revenge in these films remain. In other words, while male revenge on behalf of a woman continues to be depicted as a natural, inevitable and morally justified aspect of masculine identity, maternal revenge continues to be subject to the additional legitimating devices and/or punishment I identified in the films of the pre-1970 period.

In so far as the maternal rape-revenge film represents a return to the melodramatic discourses and ideology of these 'pre-feminist' films, its politics can be seen as resolutely those of a backlash against feminism as I defined it at the beginning of this chapter. Indeed, the persistently nostalgic vein that Christine Gledhill has identified in melodrama make it particularly suited to the articulation of a backlash politics, particularly since the melodramatic image of the past is that of 'the Edenic home and family, centring on the heroine as "angel in the house"'.[57] Yet, as Gledhill points out, because melodrama 'operates within the frameworks of the present social order', its address is not so much to 'how things ought to be than to how they should have been'.[58] That the backlash is driven by a similar desire to return to an impossible past allows me to temper the somewhat pessimistic tone of this chapter with a more optimistic conclusion. As Elizabeth Traube has argued:

> while right-wing antifeminism indeed became a powerful social force during the 1980s, it represents the residual ideology of a declining minority. Despite the political gains that the 'pro-family' movement has achieved, it remains a backlash movement, an attempt to repress newer, unequally distributed possibilities and to return to an idealized past. If studies from the 1990s are to be believed, the majority of women and men in America do not anticipate any such return.[59]

Notes

1. *Thelma and Louise* might also be included in this latter category since although its heroines evade the law, they do so only through death. Their evasion of the law can be read as equivalent to a form of symbolic containment.

2. Jane Feuer, *Seeing through the Eighties: Television and Reaganism* (London: BFI, 1995).

3. Ibid., p. 19.

4. Ibid., p. 19.

5. Ibid., p. 20.

6. Ibid., p. 36.

7. Ibid., p. 42n14 (my emphasis).

8. Ibid., p. 37.

9. Of the two films I intend to discuss here (*In My Daughter's Name* and *Eye for an Eye*), only one (*In My Daughter's Name*) is a TV movie. However, in terms of plot, structure and ideology the two films are remarkably similar and, in fact, *Eye for an Eye* conforms more closely to the structure of the made-for-TV trauma drama than *In My Daughter's Name*.

10. David Grimsted, 'Vigilante Chronicle: The Politics of Melodrama Brought to Life', in *Melodrama: Stage, Picture, Screen*, ed. by Jacky Bratton, Jim Cook and Christine Gledhill (London: BFI, 1994), pp. 199–213 (p. 199).

11. Ibid., p. 205.

12. Feuer, *Seeing through the Eighties*, p. 32.

13. Ibid., p. 30 and p. 31.

14. Ibid., p. 37 and p. 42n14.

15. Will Wright, *Six Guns and Society: A Structural Study of the Western* (Berkeley: University of California Press, 1975).

16. Feuer, *Seeing through the Eighties*, p. 25.

17. Ibid., p. 37 and p. 38.

18. The film's title, of course, functions to alert us to its reliance on such biblical allusions.

19. Christine Gledhill, 'The Melodramatic Field: An Investigation', in *Home Is Where The Heart Is: Studies in Melodrama and the Woman's Film*, ed. by Christine Gledhill (London: BFI, 1987), pp. 5–39 (p. 21).

20. Grimsted, 'Vigilante Chronicle', p. 200 (my emphasis).

21. J. C. J. Metford, *Dictionary of Christian Lore and Legend* (London: Thames and Hudson, 1983), p. 96.

22. Joan Comay, *Who's Who in the Old Testament together with the Apocrypha* (London: Weidenfeld and Nicolson, 1971), p. 126.

23. Grimsted, 'Vigilante Chronicle', p. 207.

24. The contrast drawn between the different neighbourhoods Karen and

Doob inhabit, and between Doob's job as a delivery man and the spectacular consumption of Megan's birthday preparations, also function to cement this class distinction. The visual excess apparent in the scenes depicting the preparation for Megan's party is, moreover, characteristic of the melodramatic style.

25 Thomas Elsaesser, 'Tales of Sound and Fury: Observations on the Family Melodrama', in *Film Theory and Criticism: Introductory Readings*, ed. by Gerald Mast, Marshall Cohen and Le Braudy, 4th edn (New York: Oxford University Press, 1992), pp. 512–35 (p. 515).

26 Feuer, *Seeing through the Eighties*, p. 31.

27 Ibid., p. 40.

28 See, for example, Simon Fanshawe, 'Long Running Marathon', *Sunday Times* (Section 10), 9 June 1996, pp. 12–13.

29 Mary Ann Doane, 'The "Woman's Film": Possession and Address', in *Re-Vision: Essays in Feminist Film Criticism*, ed. by Mary Ann Doane, Patricia Mellencamp and Linda Williams (Los Angeles: American Film Institute, 1984), pp. 67–82 (p. 72).

30 John Berger, *Ways of Seeing* (London: Penguin/BBC, 1972), p. 47.

31 Mary Ann Doane, 'Film and the Masquerade: Theorizing the Female Spectator', in *Issues in Feminist Film Criticism*, ed. by Patricia Erens (Bloomington: Indiana University Press, 1990), pp. 41–57 (p. 50).

32 Mary Ann Doane, '*Caught* and *Rebecca*: The Inscription of Femininity as Absence', in *Feminism and Film Theory*, ed. by Constance Penley (London: BFI, 1988), pp. 196–215 (p. 214).

33 Laura Mulvey, 'Visual Pleasure and Narrative Cinema', in *Feminism and Film Theory*, ed. by Constance Penley (London: BFI, 1988), pp. 57–68 (p. 64).

34 Ibid., p. 64.

35 Elizabeth Cowie outlines the various arguments for the connection between melodrama and film noir in '*Film Noir* and Women', in *Shades of Noir: A Reader*, ed. by Joan Copjec (London: Verso, 1993), pp. 121–65. *Mildred Pierce* (Michael Curtiz, 1945) represents a particularly interesting example of the combination of melodrama and film noir. For an analysis of this combination see: Pam Cook, 'Duplicity in *Mildred Pierce*', in *Women in Film Noir*, ed. by E. Ann Kaplan (London: BFI, 1978), pp. 68–82.

36 There is also an example of film noir lighting earlier in the film when Karen stumbles across the plot to kill the man who murdered the Gratz's son. Karen discovers Mr and Mrs Gratz (William Mesnich and Rand Reed) together with Sidney Hughes in a store room grouped under a harsh, low-slung ceiling light which casts unnatural shadows on their faces. As Paul Schrader notes, in film noir 'ceiling lights are hung low and floor lamps are seldom more than five feet high'. Paul Schrader,

'Notes on Film Noir', *Film Comment*, 8:1 (1972), 8–13 (p. 11).

37 J. A. Place and L. S. Peterson, 'Some Visual Motifs of Film Noir', in *Movies and Methods, Volume I: An Anthology*, ed. by Bill Nichols (Berkeley: University of California Press, 1976), pp. 325–38 (pp. 337–8).

38 Cowie, '*Film Noir* and Women', p. 126.

39 The use of cross-cutting during key sequences is characteristic of the melodramatic style. This technique can also be found in the sequence in which Doob visits Megan at school while Karen is at the gym and in the final sequence. The technique is also used in *In My Daughter's Name* where the rape is intercut with scenes of the father's birthday party.

40 Doane, 'The "Woman's Film"', p. 69.

41 Tania Modleski, 'Time and Desire in the Woman's Film', in *Film Theory and Criticism: Introductory Readings*, ed. by Gerald Mast, Marshall Cohen and Leo Braudy, 4th edn (New York: Oxford University Press, 1992), pp. 536–48 (p. 539).

42 Christine Gledhill, 'Melodrama', in *The Cinema Book*, ed. by Pam Cook (London: BFI, 1985), pp. 73–84 (p. 80). See also: Elsaesser, 'Tales of Sound and Fury', p. 525; Modleski, 'Time and Desire in the Woman's Film', p. 540.

43 Christian Viviani, 'Who Is Without Sin?: The Maternal Melodrama in American Film, 1930–1939', in *Home Is Where The Heart Is: Studies in Melodrama and the Woman's Film*, ed. by Christine Gledhill (London: BFI, 1987), pp. 83–99 (p. 86).

44 Doane, 'The "Woman's Film"', p. 72.

45 As I pointed out in chapter 3, muteness is a key motif of the 'woman's film'. In *Eye for an Eye*, this motif appears in the form of more generalized problems of communication: Julie has a stutter, the language difference prevents Karen from being able to articulate her concerns about Doob to the Hispanic woman, and both Karen at the beginning and Mack at the end are unable to contact home because the phone is engaged.

46 Gledhill, 'Melodrama', p. 78. Karen's first husband (and Julie's father) is rendered similarly absent and ineffectual. As Dolly says of him: 'Talk about deadbeat dads.'

47 Ibid., p. 81. Similarly, in *Johnny Belinda* (discussed in chapter 3), Belinda's killing of her rapist, Locky McCormick, is also represented via the motif of the staircase.

48 In an early scene depicting Karen at work, the camera ranges across a series of television screens variously showing a musical, a 'he-man' movie, and a black and white silent melodrama before briefly coming to rest on a screen relaying the O. J. Simpson trial. Despite the frequency with which televisions are shown broadcasting in the background of

scenes, this is the only instance where the subject matter of the broadcast is clearly and easily identifiable.

49 Doane, 'The "Woman's Film"', p. 72.

50 Ibid., p. 75.

51 At the beginning of the film, Karen is specifically constructed as both insane and neurotic.

52 Feuer, *Seeing through the Eighties*, p. 22.

53 Hilary Radner, 'Pretty Is as Pretty Does: Free Enterprise and the Marriage Plot', in *Film Theory Goes to the Movies*, ed. by Jim Collins, Hilary Radner and Ava Preacher Collins (London: Routledge, 1993), pp. 56–76 (p. 58).

54 Ibid., p. 58.

55 The female rape-revenge structure is not unique to US cinema but appears in the films of other countries and cultures, particularly in Indian cinema. For a discussion of such films see: Lalitha Gopalan, 'Avenging Women in Indian Cinema', *Screen*, 38:1 (Spring 1997), 42–59.

56 In many respects, this omission can also be read as an articulation of the racial bias implicit in feminist discourses of rape, which very rarely give any consideration to the rape of black women. One of the few exceptions is Susan Griffin's 'The Politics of Rape', in Susan Griffin, *Made From This Earth: Selections from her Writing, 1967–1982* (London: The Women's Press, 1982), pp. 39–58.

57 Gledhill, 'The Melodramatic Field', p. 21.

58 Ibid., p. 21.

59 Traube, *Dreaming Identities*, p. 165.

Conclusion

Textual and theoretical negotiations

Against the tendency of existing work in the area to categorize rape-revenge as a sub-genre of horror, I have argued that rape-revenge is better understood as a narrative structure which, on meeting the discourses of second-wave feminism in the 1970s, has produced a historically specific but generically diverse cycle of films. I have suggested, therefore, that the rape-revenge cycle might usefully be read as one of the key ways in which Hollywood has attempted to make sense of feminism and the changing shape of heterosexual femininity in the post-1970 period. Using a model of cultural analysis underpinned by the concept of hegemony, I have argued that it is in the various negotiations that take place between the feminist stories the rape-revenge structure attempts to tell and the feminine stories embedded in the genres over which it has been mapped that popular, common-sense understandings of feminism are produced. In the preceding chapters, then, I have analysed in some detail the various textual negotiations into which the rape-revenge structure has entered and, in so doing, I hope to have explicated some of the popular but ill-defined terms currently being used to define the contemporary feminist moment. In particular, against the wholesale rejection of feminism implied by terms such as 'post-feminism' and 'backlash', I have argued instead that feminism is currently undergoing a process of negotiation and transformation. While this project represents an attempt to understand this process of negotiation as it has been articulated through popular film, it also represents an attempt to enter into this process. In other words, my reading of the rape-revenge cycle has arisen not simply from an analysis of these textual negotiations, but from my own theoretical negotiations with feminism and feminist film theory. In what follows, then, I want to outline and summarize some of these processes of negotiation.

This project arose, in part at least, out of a sense of frustration at the limitations imposed on the study of the rape-revenge film by defining it as a sub-genre of horror. For me, rape-revenge was clearly not a genre, not only because it seemed to cut across genres, but because it lacked many of the elements used to define genres, such as a coherent iconography. Nor was it a movement since although, like rape-revenge, film movements tend to occur in specific historical periods and cut across genres, unlike rape-revenge, film movements are normally the product of a group of film-makers who share political and/or aesthetic beliefs and, as such, are unified by a common stylistic approach. Nor was it simply a narrative trope or motif. Rather, rape-revenge seemed to me to constitute a clear, though somewhat primitive, example of a narrative structure. While traditionally structural analyses of narrative have been more detailed and elaborate (Propp, for example, identified thirty-one narrative events and seven spheres of action in the Russian fairy-tale), rape-revenge was clearly understandable in these terms. In other words, rape-revenge can be seen as constituting a sequence of narrative events (rape, transformation, revenge) occurring in a particular order, combined with a specific set of character functions or spheres of action (victim, rapist, avenger). Understanding rape-revenge in this way has facilitated a close analysis not only of narrative events, character functions and the relationships between them, but of the extent to which variations in the structure might be historically determined. For example, I have shown how the rise of second-wave feminism in the 1970s, and the concomitant emergence of the figure of the independent woman, demanded a redefinition of character functions and, by extension, a transformation in the internal dynamics of the rape-revenge structure and the stories it told. In other words, while in the rape-revenge films of the pre-1970 period the victim was largely defined through her relation to men as daughter, wife or fiancée, so necessitating and legitimating the presence of a male avenger of her rape, in the films of post-1970 period the representation of the rape victim as an independent woman meant that she was increasingly able to become the credible avenger of her own rape. Consequently, if the rape-revenge films of the pre-1970 period largely told masculine stories in which women were, for the most part, passive victims, in the post-1970 period the rape-revenge film can be seen as increasingly telling feminine, and even feminist, stories.

As I have implied, however, changes at the level of the rape-revenge structure cannot be understood simply in terms of feminism. Rather, as the increase in legal and parental rape-revenge films in the late 1980s and 1990s suggests, changes in the structure can be seen as a product as much of the individual populism of the Reagan era and the family values agenda of the New Right as of feminism. Indeed, as I have argued throughout, the popular understandings of feminism that circulate around the figure of the female avenger are, in many respects, the result of a series of contemporary negotiations between the discourses of feminism and the discourses of the New Right. For example, while the shift from the male avengers of pre-1970 films such as *The Virgin Spring* and *Rancho Notorious* to the maternal avengers of *In My Daughter's Name* and *Eye for an Eye* can in some ways be seen as enabled by feminism, it can also be read as a response to a Reaganite discourse of family values and, therefore, as an articulation of the wider backlash against feminism these discourses have been understood as instigating. In this way, feminist gains are appropriated by and contained within the right-wing ideologies of the Reagan and Thatcher administrations. This process of appropriation need not, however, always be wholly reactionary. As I argued in my analysis of *The Last Seduction*, for example, while the film can be seen as merging feminist discourses around violence against women with a Reaganite yuppie ideology, this ideology simultaneously functions to legitimate feminist ambition and will to power. In *Eye for an Eye*, on the other hand, apparently feminist-inspired figures such as the black, lesbian FBI officer are, like the male protagonists of the pre-1970 rape-revenge melodramas discussed in chapter 3, employed to articulate a backlash discourse that demands women's return to the home and family.

Defining rape-revenge as a narrative structure has also enabled an exploration of what happens when the structure is mapped across the codes, conventions and narrative structures of specific genres. If the maternal avenger is, in part, the product of a series of negotiations between the discourses of feminism and the discourses of Reaganism, she is also a product of the negotiations that occur when the rape-revenge structure is mapped over the discourses of melodrama. Indeed, as I pointed out in the previous chapter, the persistently nostalgic vein Christine Gledhill has identified in melodrama makes it particularly suited to the articulation of a backlash politics.[1] This persistently nostalgic vein, however, also has something to do with the influence of post-modern aesthetics on the contemporary cultural landscape and, in particular, with the way in which genre texts from the past are increasingly being recycled in the present. Thus, the backlash politics the maternal rape-revenge film articulates must be understood, in part at least, as the product of the particular ways in which generic discourses from the past are circulating and functioning in the present. According to Jim Collins, this generic recycling manifests itself in two different ways: 'eclectic irony' and the 'new sincerity'. The maternal rape-revenge film clearly falls into the latter category since it deploys the codes and conventions of melodrama in order to facilitate and guarantee a 'move back in time' to an Edenic past centring on home and family where the 'unresolvable conflicts' of the present 'can be successfully resolved'.[2]

In contrast, the neo-noirs discussed in chapter 6 can be seen as examples of 'eclectic irony'. Here, various elements – the rape-revenge structure, the codes and conventions of film noir, the vampire narrative and the 1980s success story – are juxtaposed and given a self-conscious, ironic articulation. Unlike the maternal rape-revenge film, then, the neo-noir's recycling of these elements is not nostalgic. Rather, the neo-noir reconfigures these elements in a way that can be seen as an attempt to make sense of a contemporary moment in which the certainties of 1970's feminism are undergoing a process of negotiation and transformation. For example, while the figure of Catwoman in *Batman Returns* clearly owes something to the hyper-feminine, pre-feminist figures of the vamp and femme fatale, she also owes something to the female avenger who, as I have been arguing throughout, is a figure who has been enabled by second-wave feminism. However, in recycling these representations for the 1990s, Catwoman emerges neither as a wholly pre-feminist figure, nor as a wholly feminist figure. Rather, insofar as her combination of the 'feminine' vamp and the 'feminist' female avenger erodes the distinction between constructed feminine identities and authentic feminist identities on which 1970s feminism depended, she can be seen as a distinctly post-feminist figure.

To see the contemporary rape-revenge film as simply a decline from an original moment of political and aesthetic authenticity, as Clover does, is to attribute to the discourses of both genre and gender a unity and coherence they no longer possess. It also fails to recognize the way in which the recycling of genre texts not only militates against conventional accounts of generic development, but complicates conventional understandings of the way in which texts negotiate their cultural and social contexts. Instead, the meanings of feminism the rape-revenge structure produces must be understood as a product of the negotiations that occur within and between the various genres and discursive contexts across which it has been mapped. Since these are constantly shifting, so too are the meanings of feminism the structure generates. For this reason, I have argued that these meanings and, indeed, rape-revenge films themselves, are perhaps better understood not in terms of authentic moments but as narratives of transformation.

While understanding rape-revenge as a narrative structure helps to explain its generic diversity and facilitates an analysis of the various negotiations into which the structure enters, this term alone fails to explain the historical specificity of these narratives of transformation and the way in which they seemed to cohere following the rise of second-wave feminism in the 1970s. Of the available terms, 'cycle' seemed to me to best describe the ephemeral and transitional nature of rape-revenge, facilitating a discussion of its historical specificity and of the ideological significance of shifts and differences in the various deployments of the structure. In particular, the term 'cycle' not only seemed to describe the historical specificity and generic diversity of deployments of the rape-revenge structure in this period, it countered the evaluative narrative of decline from an authentic aesthetic and political moment apparent in approaches such as Clover's. In suggesting that, with the maternal avenger, the rape-revenge cycle may have run its course, then, I do not intend to reproduce this narrative of decline. Rather, I merely wish to suggest that the narrative possibilities the rape-revenge structure offers may have been exhausted. Instead, as feminism continues to evolve and new feminist stories emerge, I think the culture industries will devise new narratives to make sense of them. What I hope this book has provided are some theoretical tools and approaches with which to analyse those narratives when they appear. I want to finish, then, by shifting the focus from an analysis of the rape-revenge cycle's textual negotiation of feminism to a consideration of the various theoretical negotiations with feminism and feminist film theory that have underpinned this analysis. In particular, it is the question of the relationship between theory and politics, the academic and the public, that I want to address now; one that I think must be addressed by any intellectual work which claims to be informed by feminism.

Traditionally, feminist film theory has fallen into two broad categories: the theory of feminist films and film theory informed by feminism. The first has tended to concentrate on constructing and analysing a feminist canon of films, the second on producing feminist critiques of classical Hollywood cinema. Both assume, therefore, that feminism exists *a priori* film and both then proceed to evaluate films in terms of an authentic feminism, which is seen to exist outside the sphere of representation. The evolution of these two types of feminist film theory can largely be traced to the influence of Laura Mulvey's 'Visual pleasure and narrative cinema'.[3] Here Mulvey used an analysis of the patriarchal construction of femininity in classical Hollywood film to call for the development of a politically and aesthetically radical avant-garde that would challenge the basic assumptions of mainstream film. The distinction Mulvey's analysis drew between mainstream film (as the site where normative femininities are constructed and patriarchal ideology reproduced) and a feminist avant-garde cinema continues to inform the work of feminist film theorists today. This is particularly apparent in Carol Clover's work on the rape-revenge film, which, despite its radical revision of Mulvey's theories concerning spectatorship and the male gaze, continues to draw a subtle distinction between depoliticized, feminine mainstream film and politicized, feminist alternative film.

The distinctions drawn over twenty years ago in response to analyses of classical Hollywood cinema, however, are no longer applicable to a film industry that has not only seen massive changes in production, distribution and exhibition, but whose producers and consumers are now familiar with, at the very least, the most basic tenets of feminism. As I argued in chapter 1, the advent of new technologies such as television and video, and the subsequent growth in media literacy amongst consumers, has changed the historical development and function of genres, as well as the way in which they construct gender. As Annette Kuhn has recently argued, then, it is becoming 'decreasingly possible now to insist upon a qualitative break between dominant and alternative cinemas'.[4] Such changes clearly owe a good deal to the success of feminist film theory in putting political issues on the popular agenda. However, many films now also exhibit such a high degree of self-consciousness about the kinds of theoretical paradigms that have been used to analyse them that many of the central tenets of feminist film theory have become obsolete or at least in need of historicizing. This is particularly true of the kinds of psychoanalytic concepts that informed early feminist film theory, particularly Mulvey's work on the 'look'. Both *The Last Seduction* and *Batman Returns*, for example, contain such knowing references to castration anxiety, the phallic woman and fetishism that to attempt a serious psychoanalytically informed analysis would be to play straight into the films' hands.

For these reasons, I want to propose that the most appropriate and politically expedient form feminist film theory can take today is not one that attempts to separate feminist film from mainstream film, the political from the popular, but one that attempts to theorize the relationship between feminism and film, the political and the popular, the contextual and the textual. The influence on the development of feminist film theory of text-based structuralist analyses and ahistorical psychoanalytic theories has, however, left it ill-equipped to analyse such relationships. In attempting such an analysis, I have been forced to look beyond the theoretical parameters of feminist film theory to cultural studies, and particularly to a model of cultural analysis underpinned by the concept of hegemony. While it is generally recognized that films do not reflect, but rather construct, reality, the notion of hegemony allows us to go one stage further and argue that the reality that films construct is a product of a process of negotiation and struggle between competing and often contradictory versions of reality. Against feminist film theory's tendency to argue that films either tell dominant patriarchal stories (mainstream film) or oppositional feminist stories (alternative film or readings against the grain of mainstream film), the concept of hegemony allows us to see film as the site where dominant and oppositional meanings are negotiated and transformed. The benefits of such an approach for a politically informed feminist analysis are thus twofold. First, it enables us to account for and understand the process of change; a project that is surely crucial for any intellectual discipline with an investment in bringing about cultural, social and political change. Second, as Tony Bennett has observed:

> In suggesting that the political and ideological articulations of cultural practices are *movable* – that a practice which is articulated to bourgeois values today may be disconnected from those values and connected to socialist ones tomorrow – the theory of hegemony opens up the field of popular culture as one of enormous political possibilities.[5]

I want to explore some of those political possibilities here.

In the preceding chapters I have attempted to show how films, and indeed the business of analysing them, work to produce and construct various popular, public understandings of feminism. Given the cultural pessimism that pervades many recent accounts of popular film as simply an articulation of a right-wing backlash against feminism, I have been particularly concerned to analyse how popular film might attempt to negotiate the competing and sometimes contradictory demands of feminism and the New Right. In so doing, I hope to have shown how feminism was not simply rejected but negotiated, was both invoked and suppressed, legitimated and critiqued, appropriated and contained, popularized and depoliticized. I have argued, therefore, that this process of negotiation offers a challenge to accepted definitions of post-feminism as implying that feminism is somehow over or past. Rather, post-feminism is perhaps better understood as a process through which feminism is accommodated by dominant culture and various common-sense or public meanings of feminism produced. While many of these meanings are tailored to the perpetuation of a capitalist hegemony, they also retain some of their oppositional charge. Indeed, as Christine Gledhill has argued, 'the ambivalence of textual negotiation produces a wider address – more servicable to a capitalist industry – than a more purely feminist text, or counter-text could'.[6] This ambivalence, however, also opens up spaces for feminist negotiations and appropriations. As Gledhill goes on to suggest:

> The productivity of popular culture lies in its capacity to bring these different dimensions into contact and contest; their negotiations contribute to its pleasures. We need to attend to such pleasures if we are to appreciate what holds us back as well as what impels us forward, and if cultural struggle is to take place at the centre of cultural production as well as on the margins.[7]

For this reason, feminist film theory needs to continue to rethink and revise its perennial suspicion of popular culture, together with some of the received theoretical orthodoxies that fuel and reinforce this suspicion. This would free us to channel our energies into the more politically productive project of understanding how feminist orthodoxies are being constructed and circulated, received and negotiated, outside the academy, in the public domain. Indeed, such a project is surely crucial if we are to bridge the gap between theory and politics, the academic and the public, and intervene in this all-important process of meaning-making. Thus, as feminists, it is crucial that we not only understand, but enter into, this process, that our analyses of it are not only descriptive but productive. As Stuart Hall argues, we need a theoretical practice 'which always thinks about its intervention in a world in which it would make some difference, in which it would have an effect'.[8] For this reason, I want to conclude this discussion with an exploration of the implications of my research for feminist pedagogy, since it is through teaching that we make our first, and often only, interventions into the world outside the academy.

Twice during the last academic year I have been surprised to find my female students producing articulate feminist critiques of the Spice Girls. I was surprised for two reasons. First, these were first year students with little or no formal training in feminist theory, yet they spoke eloquently of how the Spice Girls reinforced feminine stereotypes, of how they were appropriating and exploiting feminism for financial gain and of how, at the very least, their brand of feminism was depoliticized and did little to address the very real problems facing women today (particularly inequality in the workplace and the home). Second, I was surprised because, despite their seemingly feminist-inspired critiques of the Spice Girls, none of my students would explicitly identify themselves as a feminist. Instead, they projected an identity that seemed remarkably similar to the stylized performance of femininity for which they had criticized the Spice Girls. There are, I think, a number of reasons for this apparent contradiction. The simplest of these is that feminist ideas have become so much part of young people's common sense that they no longer explicitly identify the ideas or themselves with feminism. The second reason is a pedagogical one. In other words, they produced what they thought was the correct feminist reading, despite the fact that it contradicted their own lived experience of femininity.[9] Of course, in terms of its application of certain theoretical paradigms it did represent one correct reading, and learning to apply such paradigms is clearly an important part of gaining an academic qualification. But feminism is surely about more than academic qualifications. With the decline of movement feminism and the institutionalization of academic feminism it is often easy to lose sight of the fact that feminism is essentially a movement for political and social change. We will lose sight of this aspect of feminism, however, if we continue to uncritically teach a feminism that contradicts the lived experience of our students, which fails to take account of the way in which, as Angela McRobbie points out,

> the old binary opposition which put femininity at one end of the polit-
> ical spectrum and feminism at the other is no longer an accurate way
> of conceptualizing young female experience ... It is no longer a ques-
> tion of those who know (the feminists, the academics) against those
> who do not, or who are the 'victims' of ideology.[10]

If we are to make feminism mean more to our students than a degree certificate, we need to find a model of feminist theory and pedagogy that acknowledges and attempts to negotiate the contra-dictions between their lived experience of femininity/feminism and academic feminism, and which allows them to make sense of their own, historically and culturally specific, relationship to feminism. This would mean acknowledging the changing political and institu-tional context in our feminist teaching and historicizing feminist theory. It would mean acknowledging the way in which the univer-sity is no longer the locus of radical politics and protest it was in the 1960s and 1970s, but an increasingly commercial, corporate ven-ture. It would mean recognizing, therefore, that the political context in which academic feminism was originally produced and under-stood no longer exists for our students and that, with the introduc-tion of loans and tuition fees, education is increasingly being viewed as a commodity, rated not for its cultural and social 'use value' but for its economic 'exchange value' in the jobs market. In acknowl-edging this changing context, it would mean trying to retain a sense of the existence and viability of feminist politics against those that would characterize this period as simply one of post-feminism or backlash. It would mean recognizing, in other words, that while ideas about post-feminism have clearly been formed in the wake of popular understandings of Reaganism and Thatcherism, they do not simply reflect those ideologies. Rather, as I argued in my analysis of *The Last Seduction*, these ideas arise out of a process of negotiation between the discourses of Reaganism and the discourses of femi-nism, articulated here through the film's combination of a Reagan-ite success story and a feminist revenge story. Consequently, as I have already suggested, while in some ways the film can be seen as blend-ing feminist discourses about violence against women with a Rea-ganite ideology, its specific articulation of this ideology can also be seen as enabling and justifying feminist desires to 'have it all'. In so doing, however, the film also negotiates and redefines the very notion of 'having it all'. In other words, while in traditional feminist discourse, 'having it all' more often than not meant giving things up (particularly heterosexual femininity as it is constructed through adornment and consumerism), the negotiations that occur between 1970s feminism and the 1980s culture of consumption in *The Last Seduction* suggest that it is now possible to 'have', for some women at least, both femininity *and* feminism. Indeed, as it has long been recognized in feminist subcultural analyses, feminine competencies and practices, especially those centred around consumption and dressing up, can in many ways be read as forms of resistance to fixed images of femininity. As I argued in my analysis of the figure of Catwoman, the challenge this represents to the notion of stable, discreet, unified identities suggests that the distinction between constructed feminine identities and authentic feminist identities on which early second-wave feminism depended is perhaps no longer tenable.

We also need to acknowledge, therefore, the way in which, with the decline of movement feminism and the increasing cost of higher education, popular culture has become one of the primary ways in which feminism is now lived and experienced by the majority of women. This would mean, then, not presenting popular culture as simply a debased feminine realm, but as a realm in which popular understandings of feminism are constructed and circulated, received and negotiated. Indeed, as I pointed out in my analyses of *The Last Seduction* and *Batman Returns*, many films are extremely knowing about both the feminine and the feminist stories they invoke and address their spectators as equally knowledgeable. In so doing, they allow their spectators to view the versions of feminism and femininity they construct with a degree of irony and critical detachment, and thus open up spaces for the appropriation and negotiation of these versions of feminism and femininity. As such, these texts provide a rich source of critical and political debate about the meanings of and relationship between femininity and feminism, a debate which, more importantly, frequently extends beyond or originates outside of the classroom. While the controversy surrounding *Thelma and Louise* discussed in chapter 4 is, of course, a case in point, the Spice Girls represent a perhaps more contemporary and more pervasive example. The much-maligned notion of 'Girl

Power', for example, can be seen as representing an attempt to negotiate a reconciliation between femininity and feminism. In a section
entitled 'I've got Girl Power because …' in their book *Girl Power!*,
each member of the group outline the specific negotiations this has
involved for them.[11] In suggesting that 'Girl Power'/feminism is neither exclusive nor unitary, the section opens up an important space
in which young women might begin to think about what feminism
means to them and in which, in addressing why they might have
'Girl Power', they can begin to gain a sense of their own power and
agency in the world.

As Lorraine Gamman and Margaret Marshment argue, then, as
feminists 'we cannot afford to dismiss the popular by always positioning ourselves outside it'.[12] Instead, they suggest we need to find
ways in which we can intervene in the mainstream to make feminist
meanings both a part of our common sense and 'a part of our pleasures'.[13] The way in which films such as *Thelma and Louise* and
Batman Returns articulate popular, common-sense versions of feminism can perhaps be seen as a testament to the success of this project. We still need, however, 'to convert commonsense into "good
sense"', while recognizing that we do not have a monopoly on
either.[14] In re-appropriating these common-sense meanings for the
purposes of teaching good sense, we would need, for example, to
remain alert to the symbiotic relationship between feminism and
popular culture I have been arguing for throughout. In other words,
we would need to recognize that good sense does not exist prior to,
but emerges out of our negotiations with, common sense. In particular, we would need to attend to the problems inherent in the versions of feminism constructed and circulated in popular culture,
while acknowledging our own complicity in the production and perpetuation of such understandings of feminism. For example, while
we might want to criticize the rape-revenge cycle for constructing a
version of feminism that is unequivocally white, heterosexual and
middle-class, we would also need to recognize the way in which this
is, in some ways, simply an articulation of a bias already implicit in
feminism.[15] I am only too aware that this study, in many ways,
merely serves to perpetuate that bias and the hegemony of white,
heterosexual, middle-class feminism. I do not, however, feel autho-
rized to speak from any other position than that constructed for me
by my race, class and sexual identity. What I have tried to do is to
problematize the historically specific identity 'feminist', particularly

its tendency to exclude the overtly erotic or feminine woman, while remaining alert to the fact that the liberated, sexualized, post-feminist identities the rape-revenge cycle constructs are not available to all women. As bell hooks argues in her discussion of Madonna, for example, 'the very image of sexual agency' such figures project 'has been the stick this society has used to justify its continued beating and assault on the black female body'.[16] It is not, however, that either of these interpretations is wrong but, as Ien Ang points out, that they represent 'two different points of view, constructed from two distinct speaking positions'.[17] It is for this reason that the much-maligned phrase 'I'm a feminist, but…' might usefully be appropriated by feminism since, as Ang argues, in problematizing and detotalizing feminist identity, it provides a position from which both black and white women can speak.[18]

I am also aware of the fact that as a single, childless woman for whom feminism has opened up opportunities beyond the traditional feminine career of the wife and mother, I may appear to have reproduced some of the old exclusions and biases associated with 1970s feminism. In particular, I am conscious of the fact that my less sympathetic reading of the maternal avenger may be seen as an articulation of traditional feminist animosity towards the identities of wife and mother. I hope it is clear from my analysis, however, that this vilification of the mother is a product of the text itself and not of my feminist reading of it. Indeed, as an older generation of feminists have grown up and themselves become mothers, many feminists have begun to rethink their traditional animosity towards motherhood.[19] It is for this reason, I think, that the backlash against feminism manifested itself so clearly in the representation of (working) mothers. In other words, it addressed itself to women who were already finding that the experience of motherhood was, in the words of Susan Douglas, challenging 'every feminist principle you've ever had'.[20] We need to be alert, therefore, to the fact that our female student body is not comprised simply of young, white, middle-class, childless women and that when they proclaim 'I'm not a feminist, but…' or 'I am a feminist, but…' there may be a different set of contradictions and exclusions in play than simply the opposition between feminism and lipstick.

Rather than decrying the appropriation of feminism by dominant consumerist culture or the pressure on universities to become more entrepreneurial, then, we need to reappropriate the power of feminism to 'sell' anything from pop music to vigilante politics, to 'sell' to our students not only the 'exchange value' of an academic qualification, but the cultural and social 'use value' of feminist politics. Speaking of the way in which feminist ideas have been co-opted to sell bras and tampons, Gamman and Marshment argue that:

> not even the whizz-kids at Saatchi and Saatchi have total control over polysemy: if the ad talks about 'liberation', in whatever context, liberation is still what it is talking about, not confinement, and if it can sell bras perhaps it can change lives. It can work both ways ... if the language of popular culture changes in our direction, then maybe we can re-appropriate it for our own purposes.[21]

As Yvonne Tasker has observed, however, the problem facing feminist appropriations of popular culture is that they 'can all too easily reduce into an attempt to establish a fit between these forms and a pre-existing agenda'.[22] Thus, we need to acknowledge that we cannot define or prescribe the 'good sense' or the 'use value' of feminist politics in advance, that there is no authentic feminism or feminist identity that exists independently of its insertion into cultural forms, practices and contexts. Rather, feminism, like femininity, is culturally and historically specific, is constantly being negotiated and transformed. For this reason, the popularity of phrases such as 'I'm not a feminist, but...' or 'I am a feminist, but...' are not causes for concern, but important indicators of the way in which ordinary women are entering into the struggle to negotiate and define the public, everyday meanings of feminism and femininity. Those of us who unequivocally define ourselves as feminists would do well to climb down from our academic ivory towers and join this struggle since, if we are to bridge the gap between the academic and the public, the theoretical and the political, we need, as Andrea Stuart has argued, 'to build bridges and create alliances, based not so much on fixed identities but on flexible *identifications*'.[23]

Notes

1 Christine Gledhill, 'The Melodramatic Field: An Investigation', in *Home is Where the Heart Is: Studies in Melodrama and the Woman's Film*, ed. by Christine Gledhill (London: BFI, 1987), pp. 5–39 (p. 21).

2 Jim Collins, 'Genericity in the Nineties: Eclectic Irony and the New Sincerity', in *Film Theory Goes to the Movies*, ed. by Jim Collins, Hilary

Radner and Ava Preacher Collins (London: Routledge, 1993), pp. 242–63 (p. 259).

3 Laura Mulvey, 'Visual Pleasure and Narrative Cinema', in *Feminism and Film Theory*, ed. by Constance Penley (London: BFI, 1988), pp. 57–68.

4 Annette Kuhn, *Women's Pictures: Feminism and Cinema*, 2nd edn (London: Verso, 1994), p. 220.

5 Tony Bennett, 'Introduction: Popular Culture and "the turn to Gramsci"', in *Popular Culture and Social Relations*, ed. by Tony Bennett, Colin Mercer and Janet Woollacott (Milton Keynes: Open University Press, 1986), pp. xi–xix (p. xvi).

6 Christine Gledhill, 'Pleasurable Negotiations', in *Female Spectators: Looking at Film and Television*, ed. by E. Deidre Pribram (London: Verso, 1988), pp. 64–89 (p. 87).

7 Ibid., p. 87.

8 Stuart Hall, 'Cultural Studies and Its Theoretical Legacies', in *Cultural Studies*, ed. by Lawrence Grossberg, Cary Nelson and Paula A. Treichler (London: Routledge, 1992), pp. 277–94 (p. 286).

9 Charlotte Brunsdon discusses the problems of feminist pedagogy at greater length in 'Pedagogies of the Feminine: Feminist Teaching and Women's Genres', *Screen*, 32:4 (Winter 1991), 364–81.

10 Angela McRobbie, *Postmodernism and Popular Culture* (London: Routledge, 1994), p. 158.

11 The Spice Girls, *Girl Power!* (London: Zone/Chameleon Books, 1997), pp. 6–7.

12 Lorraine Gamman and Margaret Marshment, 'Introduction', in *The Female Gaze: Women as Viewers of Popular Culture*, ed. by Lorraine Gamman and Margaret Marshment (London: The Women's Press, 1988), pp. 1–7 (p. 2).

13 Ibid., p. 2.

14 Ibid., p. 2.

15 The racial bias is, significantly, particularly evident in feminist discourses of rape which very rarely give any consideration to the rape of black women.

16 bell hooks, *Black Looks: Race and Representation* (London: Turnaround, 1992), p. 160.

17 Ien Ang, 'I'm a Feminist but... "Other" Women and Postnational Feminism', in *Transitions: New Australian Feminisms*, ed. by Barbara Caine and Rosemary Pringle (St. Leonards: Allen and Unwin, 1995), pp. 57–73 (p. 64).

18 Ibid., pp. 57–73.

19 See for example: Rosalind Coward, *Our Treacherous Hearts: Why Women Let Men Get Their Way* (London: Faber and Faber, 1992); Susan J. Douglas, *Where the Girls Are: Growing Up Female with the*

Mass Media (London: Penguin, 1995).

20 Douglas, *Where the Girls Are*, p. 278. The final chapter, from which this quote is taken, is significantly entitled 'I'm Not a Feminist, But…' and offers an interesting and informative account of feminism and the media in the 1990s.

21 Gamman and Marshment, 'Introduction', p. 4.

22 Yvonne Tasker, 'Having It All: Feminism and the Pleasures of the Popular', in *Off-Centre: Feminism and Cultural Studies*, ed. by Sarah Franklin, Celia Lury and Jackie Stacey (London: Harper Collins, 1991), pp. 85–96 (p. 95).

23 Andrea Stuart, 'Feminism: Dead or Alive?', in *Identity*, ed. by Jonathan Rutherford (London: Lawrence and Wishart, 1990), pp. 28–42 (p. 41).

Filmography of primary texts

The Accused
Country/Year: USA, 1988
Production company: Paramount Pictures
Director: Jonathan Kaplan
Producers: Stanley R. Jaffe and Sherry Lansing
Screenplay: Tom Topor
Leading players: Jodie Foster (*Sarah Tobias*), Kelly McGillis (*Katheryn Murphy*), Bernie Coulson (*Kenneth Joyce*), Ann Hearn (*Sally Frazer*), Steve Antin (*Bob Joiner*).

Anatomy of a Murder
Country/Year: USA, 1959
Production company: Carlyle
Director: Otto Preminger
Producer: Otto Preminger
Screenplay: Wendell Mayes, from the novel by Robert Traver
Leading players: James Stewart (*Paul Biegler*), Lee Remick (*Laura Manion*), Ben Gazzara (*Lt Frederick Manion*), Arthur O'Connell (*Parnell McCarthy*), Eve Arden (*Maida*), Kathryn Grant (*Mary Pilant*).

Batman Returns
Country/Year: USA, 1992
Production company: Warner Bros
Director: Tim Burton
Producers: Denise Di Novi and Tim Burton
Screenplay: Daniel Waters
Leading players: Michael Keaton (*Batman/Bruce Wayne*), Danny DeVito (*The Penguin/Oswald Cobblepot*), Michelle Pfeiffer (*Catwoman/Selina Kyle*), Christopher Walken (*Max Shreck*), Michael Gough (*Alfred*), Michael Murphy (*Mayor*), Cristi Conaway (*Ice Princess*), Andrew Bryniarski (*Chip*), Pat Hingle (*Commissioner Gordon*).

The Birth of a Nation
Country/Year: USA, 1915
Production company: Epoch Producing Corporation
Director: D. W. Griffith
Producer: D. W. Griffith
Screenplay: D. W. Griffith, Thomas Dixon and Frank Woods, from the novel *The Clansman* by Rev Thomas Dixon Jr.
Leading players: Henry B. Walthall (*Col Ben Cameron*), Mae Marsh (*Flora Cameron*), Miriam Cooper (*Margaret Cameron*), Josephine Crowell (*Mrs Cameron*), Spottiswoode Aitken (*Dr Cameron*), André Beranger (*Wade Cameron*), Lillian Gish (*Elsie Stoneman*).

Blackmail
Country/Year: GB, 1929
Production company: British International Pictures
Director: Alfred Hitchcock
Producer: John Maxwell
Screenplay: Benn W. Levy, Charles Bennett, Alfred Hitchcock and Garnett Weston, from the play by Charles Bennett
Leading players: Anny Ondra (*Alice White*), Sara Allgood (*Mrs White*), John Longden (*Frank Webber*), Charles Paton (*Mr White*), Donald Calthorp (*Tracy*), Cyril Ritchard (*Crewe*).

Broken Blossoms
Country/Year: USA, 1919
Production company: D. W. Griffith Inc.
Director: D. W. Griffith
Producer: D. W. Griffith
Screenplay: D. W. Griffith, based on the story 'The Chink and the Child' by Thomas Burke
Leading players: Lillian Gish (*Lucy Burrows*), Richard Barthelmess (*Cheng Haun, The Yellow Man*), Donald Crisp (*Battling Burrows*), Arthur Howard (*Burrows' Manager*), Edward Peil (*Evil Eye*), George Beranger (*The Spying One*).

Eye for an Eye
Country/Year: USA, 1995
Production company: Paramount Pictures
Director: John Schlesinger
Producer: Michael I. Levy
Screenplay: Amanda Silver and Rick Jaffa, based on the novel by Erika Holzer
Leading players: Sally Field (*Karen McCann*), Ed Harris (*Mack McCann*),

Olivia Burnette (*Julie McCann*), Alexandra Kyle (*Megan McCann*), Kiefer Sutherland (*Robert Doob*), Joe Mantegna (*Detective Sergeant Denillo*), Beverly D'Angelo (*Dolly Green*), Darrell Larson (*Peter Green*), Charlayne Woodard (*Angel Kosinsky*), Philip Baker Hall (*Sidney Hughes*), Keith David (*Martin*).

Handgun (a.k.a. *Deep in the Heart*)
Country/Year: USA, 1982
Production company: Kestrel Films
Director: Tony Garnett
Producer: Tony Garnett
Screenplay: Tony Garnett
Leading players: Karen Young (*Kathleen Sullivan*), Clayton Day (*Larry Keeler*), Suzie Humphreys (*Nancy*), Helena Humann (*Miss Davis*), Ben Jones (*Chuck*).

Hannie Caulder
Country/Year: GB, 1971
Production company: Tigon British Film Productions Ltd
Director: Burt Kennedy
Producer: Patrick Curtis
Screenplay: Z. X. Jones
Leading players: Raquel Welch (*Hannie Caulder*), Robert Culp (*Thomas Price*), Christopher Lee (*Bailey*), Jack Elam (*Frank*), Strother Martin (*Rufus*), Ernest Borgnine (*Emmett*), Diana Dors (*Madame*).

In My Daughter's Name
Country/Year: USA, 1992
Production company: Cates/Doty Productions
Director: Jud Taylor
Producer: Dennis E. Doty
Screenplay: Mimi Rothman Schapiro and Bill Wells, from a story by Sharon Michaels and Phyllis Vernick
Leading players: Donna Mills (*Laura Elias*), John Getz (*Michael Elias*), Ari Meyer (*Carly Elias*), Ellen Blain (*Lissa Elias*), John Rubinstein (*Ben Worrall*), Lee Grant (*Maureen Leeds*), Adam Storke (*Peter Lipton*), Penelope Branning (*Blair Lipton*), Ron Frazier (*Missildine*).

Johnny Belinda
Country/Year: USA, 1948
Production company: Warner Bros
Director: Jean Negulesco
Producer: Jerry Wald

Screenplay: Irmgard VonCube and Allen Vincent, from the play by Elmer Harris
Leading players: Jane Wyman (*Belinda McDonald*), Lew Ayres (*Dr Robert Richardson*), Charles Bickford (*Black McDonald*), Agnes Moorehead (*Aggie McDonald*), Stephen McNally (*Locky McCormick*), Jan Sterling (*Stella McGuire*).

The Last Seduction
Country/Year: USA, 1993
Production company: ITC Entertainment Ltd
Director: John Dahl
Producer: Jonathan Shestack
Screenplay: Steve Barancik
Leading players: Linda Fiorentino (*Bridget Gregory*), Peter Berg (*Mike Swale*), Bill Pullman (*Clay Gregory*), J. T. Walsh (*Frank Griffith*), Bill Nunn (*Harlan*), Herb Mitchell (*Bob Trotter*), Brien Varady (*Chris*), Dean Norris (*Shep*), Donna Wilson (*Stacy*).

Outrage
Country/Year: USA, 1950
Production company: Filmmakers
Director: Ida Lupino
Producer: Collier Young
Screenplay: Ida Lupino, Collier Young and Marvin Wald
Leading players: Mala Powers (*Ann Walton*), Tod Andrews (*Doc Ferguson*), Robert Clarke (*Jim Owens*), Raymond Bond (*Mr Walton*), Lillian Hamilton (*Mrs Walton*).

The Quick and the Dead
Country/Year: USA, 1995
Production company: TriStar Pictures
Director: Sam Raimi
Producers: Joshua Donen, Allen Shapiro and Patrick Markey
Screenplay: Simon Moore
Leading players: Sharon Stone (*Ellen*), Gene Hackman (*John Herod*), Russell Crowe (*Cort*), Leonardo DiCaprio (*Kid*), Tobin Bell (*Dog Kelly*), Roberts Blossom (*Doc Wallace*), Kevin Conway (*Eugene Dred*), Keith David (*Sergeant Cantrell*), Lance Henriksen (*Ace Hanlon*), Pat Hingle (*Horace, the bartender*).

Rancho Notorious
Country/Year: USA, 1952
Production company: Fidelity Pictures-RKO Radio

Director: Fritz Lang
Producer: Howard Welsch
Screenplay: Daniel Taradash, from a story by Sylvia Richards
Leading players: Marlene Dietrich (*Altar Keane*), Arthur Kennedy (*Vern Haskell*), Mel Ferrer (*Frenchy Fairmont*), Gloria Henry (*Beth*).

Sleeping with the Enemy
Country/Year: USA, 1991
Production company: Twentieth-Century Fox
Director: Joseph Ruben
Producer: Leonard Goldberg
Screenplay: Ronald Bass, based on the novel by Nancy Price
Leading players: Julia Roberts (*Laura/Sara*), Patrick Bergin (*Martin*), Kevin Anderson (*Ben*), Elizabeth Lawrence (*Chloë*), Kyle Secor (*Fleishman*).

Thelma and Louise
Country/Year: USA, 1991
Production company: Pathé Entertainment Inc, A Percy Main Production
Director: Ridley Scott
Producers: Ridley Scott and Mimi Polk
Screenplay: Callie Khouri
Leading players: Susan Sarandon (*Louise Sawyer*), Geena Davis (*Thelma Dickinson*), Harvey Keitel (*Hal Slocombe*), Michael Madsen (*Jimmy*), Christopher McDonald (*Darryl*), Stephen Tobolowsky (*Max*), Brad Pitt (*J. D.*), Timothy Carhart (*Harlan*).

Unforgiven
Country/Year: USA, 1992
Production company: Warner Bros.
Director: Clint Eastwood
Producer: Clint Eastwood
Screenplay: David Webb Peoples
Leading players: Clint Eastwood (*William Munny*), Gene Hackman ('*Little Bill' Daggett*), Morgan Freeman (*Ned Logan*), Richard Harris (*English Bob*), Jaimz Woolvett ('*Schofield Kid'*), Saul Rubinek (*W. W. Beauchamp*), Frances Fisher (*Strawberry Alice*), Anna Thompson (*Delilah Fitzgerald*), David Mucci (*Quick Mike*), Rob Campbell (*Davey Bunting*), Anthony James (*Skinny Dubois*).

The Virgin Spring
Country/Year: Sweden, 1959
Production company: Svensk Filmindustri
Director: Ingmar Bergman

Producers: Ingmar Bergman and Allan Ekelund
Screenplay: Ulla Isaksson
Leading players: Max von Sydow (*Herr Töre*), Brigitta Pettersson (*Karin Töre*), Birgitta Valberg (*Mareta Töre*), Gunnel Lindblom (*Ingeri*), Axel Duberg (*Thin Herdsman*), Tor Isedal (*Mute Herdsman*), Ove Porath (*Boy*).

The Wind
Country/Year: USA, 1928
Production company: Metro-Goldwyn-Mayer Picture Corp.
Director: Victor Seastrom
Producer: No producer credited
Screenplay: Frances Marion, from the novel by Dorothy Scarborough
Leading players: Lillian Gish (*Letty*), Lars Hanson (*Lige*), Montagu Love (*Roddy Wirt*), Dorothy Cummings (*Cora*), Edward Earle (*Beverly*), William Orlamond (*Sourdough*).

Filmography of secondary texts

Films

Bad Girls (Jonathan Kaplan, USA, 1994)
The Ballad of Little Jo (Maggie Greenwald, USA, 1993)
Basic Instinct (Paul Verhoeven, USA, 1992)
Batman (Leslie Martinson, USA, 1966)
Batman (Tim Burton, USA, 1989)
The Beguiled (Donald Siegel, USA, 1970)
The Birds (Alfred Hitchcock, USA, 1963)
Blue Steel (Kathryn Bigelow, USA, 1990)
Body Heat (Lawrence Kasdan, USA, 1981)
Body of Evidence (Uli Edel, USA, 1992)
Bram Stoker's Dracula (Francis Ford Coppola, USA, 1992)
The Bravados (Henry King, USA, 1958)
Buffy the Vampire Slayer (Fran Rubel Kuzui, USA, 1992)
Carrie (Brian De Palma, USA, 1976)
Chinatown (Roman Polanski, USA, 1974)
Dances with Wolves (Kevin Costner, USA, 1990)
Deliverance (John Boorman, USA, 1972)
Dirty Weekend (Michael Winner, GB, 1992)
Doña Barbara (Fernando de Fuentes, Mexico, 1942)
Double Indemnity (Billy Wilder, USA, 1944)
Extremities (Robert M. Young, USA, 1986)
Fatal Attraction (Adrian Lyne, USA, 1987)
Final Analysis (Phil Joanou, USA, 1992)
A Fistful of Dollars (Sergio Leone, Italy/West Germany/Spain, 1964)
Frenzy (Alfred Hitchcock, GB, 1972)
The Greatest Question (D. W. Griffith, USA, 1919)
Halloween (John Carpenter, USA, 1978)
The Handmaid's Tale (Volker Schlöndorff, USA/Germany, 1990)
The Hand that Rocks the Cradle (Curtis Hanson, USA, 1992)
Hunter's Blood (Robert C. Hughes, USA, 1986)

Innocent Blood (John Landis, USA, 1992)
I Spit on Your Grave (a.k.a *Day of the Woman*, Meir Zarchi, USA, 1977)
Kill Me Again (John Dahl, USA, 1989)
Kiss Me Deadly (Robert Aldrich, USA, 1955)
Last House on the Left (Wes Craven, USA, 1972)
Last Train from Gun Hill (John Sturges, USA, 1959)
Lipstick (Lamont Johnson, USA, 1976)
The Man from Laramie (Anthony Mann, USA, 1955)
Marnie (Alfred Hitchcock, USA, 1964)
Mortal Thoughts (Alan Rudolph, USA, 1991)
Ms. 45 (a.k.a *Angel of Vengeance*, Abel Ferrara, USA, 1981)
My Darling Clementine (John Ford, USA, 1946)
Nevada Smith (Henry Hathaway, USA, 1966)
Nosferatu: Eine Symphonie des Grauens (F. W. Murnau, Germany, 1922)
Now Voyager (Irving Rapper, USA, 1942)
One-Eyed Jacks (Marlon Brando, USA, 1961)
Pale Rider (Clint Eastwood, USA, 1985)
Play Misty for Me (Clint Eastwood, USA, 1971)
Positive I.D. (Andy Anderson, USA, 1987)
Pretty Woman (Garry Marshall, USA, 1990)
Prom Night (Paul Lynch, USA, 1980)
Psycho (Alfred Hitchcock, USA, 1960)
The Rape of Dr Willis (Lou Antonio, USA, 1992)
Red Rock West (John Dahl, USA, 1993)
Settle the Score (Edwin Sherin, USA, 1989)
Sexual Intent (Kurt MacCarley, USA, 1992)
Shame (Steve Jodrell, Australia, 1988)
She Said No (John Patterson, USA, 1990)
Showgirls (Paul Verhoeven, USA, 1995)
Sliver (Philip Noyce, USA, 1993)
Stagecoach (John Ford, USA, 1939)
Stella Dallas (King Vidor, USA, 1938)
Sudden Impact (Clint Eastwood, USA, 1983)
Terror Train (Roger Spottiswoode, Canada, 1979)
The Texas Chainsaw Massacre (Tobe Hopper, USA, 1974)
A Time to Kill (Joel Schumacher, USA, 1996)
Under Capricorn (Alfred Hitchcock, GB, 1949)
The Velvet Vampire (Stephanie Rothman, USA, 1971)
Without Her Consent (Sander Stern, USA, 1990)
Working Girl (Mike Nichols, USA, 1988)

Television programmes

'Dracula', *The South Bank Show*, (LWT, UK), transmitted in January 1993

Bibliography

Acker, Ally, *Reel Women: Pioneers of the Cinema 1896 to the Present* (London: B. T. Batsford, 1991)

Agnew, Thelma, '*The Accused*: Review', *Spare Rib*, 199 (March 1989), 36

Allen, Jeanne Thomas, 'The Representation of Violence to Women: Hitchcock's *Frenzy*', *Film Quarterly*, 38:3 (Spring 1985), 30–9

Allen, Sandra, Lee Sanders and Jan Willis, eds, *Conditions of Illusion* (Leeds: Feminist Books, 1974)

Andrews, Nigel, 'Bearing the Rape Victim's Cross', *Financial Times*, 16 February 1989, p. 31

Ang, Ien, *Watching Dallas: Soap Opera and the Melodramatic Imagination* (London: Methuen, 1985)

Ang, Ien, 'Melodramatic Identifications: Television Fiction and Women's Fantasy', in *Television and Women's Culture: The Politics of the Popular*, ed. by Mary Ellen Brown (London: Sage, 1990), pp. 75–88

Ang, Ien, 'I'm a Feminist but... "Other" Women and Postnational Feminism', in *Transitions: New Australian Feminisms*, ed. by Barbara Caine and Rosemary Pringle (St Leonards: Allen and Unwin, 1995), pp. 57–73

Ang, Ien, *Living Room Wars: Rethinking Media Audiences for a Postmodern World* (London: Routledge, 1996)

Bader, Eleanor J., '*Thelma and Louise*: Review', *Spare Rib*, July 1991, 19–20

Baehr, Helen, and Gillian Dyer, eds, *Boxed In: Women and Television* (London: Pandora, 1987)

Barker, Martin, ed., *The Video Nasties: Freedom and Censorship in the Media* (London: Pluto Press, 1984)

Barrett, Michele, and Anne Phillips, 'Introduction', in *Destabilizing Theory: Contemporary Feminist Debates*, ed. by Michele Barrett and Anne Phillips (Cambridge: Polity Press, 1992), pp. 1–9

Barrett, Michele, and Anne Phillips, eds, *Destabilizing Theory: Contemporary Feminist Debates* (Cambridge: Polity Press, 1992)

Bennett, Tony, 'Introduction: Popular Culture and "the turn to Gramsci"', in *Popular Culture and Social Relations*, ed. by Tony Bennett, Colin

Mercer and Janet Woollacott (Milton Keynes: Open University Press, 1986), pp. xi–xix

Bennett, Tony, ed., *Popular Fiction: Technology, Ideology, Production, Reading* (London: Routledge, 1990)

Bennett, Tony, Colin Mercer and Janet Woollacott, eds, *Popular Culture and Social Relations* (Milton Keynes: Open University Press, 1986)

Berger, John, *Ways of Seeing* (London: Penguin/BBC, 1972)

Best, Steven, and Douglas Kellner, *Postmodern Theory: Critical Interrogations* (Basingstoke: Macmillan, 1991)

Birch, Helen, ed., *Moving Targets: Women, Murder and Representation* (London: Virago, 1993)

Bonner, Hilary, 'Asking For It?: The Provocative Question Raised by Jodie Foster's New Movie', *Daily Mirror*, 10 February 1989, p. 13

Bottigheimer, Ruth B., *Grimms' Bad Girls and Bold Boys: The Moral and Social Vision of the Tales* (New Haven: Yale University Press, 1987)

Bratton, Jacky, Jim Cook and Christine Gledhill, eds, *Melodrama: Stage, Picture, Screen* (London: BFI, 1994)

Bremner, Charles, 'Giving as Bad as they Get', *Times* (Saturday Review), 20 June 1991, p. 6

Brown, Geoff, 'Bosom Buddies Take to the Road', *Times*, 11 July 1991

Brown, Jeffrey A., 'Gender and the Action Heroine: Hardbodies and the *Point of No Return*', *Cinema Journal*, 35:3 (Spring 1996), 52–71

Brown, Mary Ellen, ed., *Television and Women's Culture: The Politics of the Popular* (London: Sage, 1990)

Brown, Mick, 'Revenge of the Abused "Accessories"', *Daily Telegraph*, 5 July 1991, p. 15

Brownmiller, Susan, *Against Our Will: Men, Women and Rape*, 2nd edn (Harmondsworth: Penguin, 1976)

Brunsdon, Charlotte, 'A Subject for the Seventies', *Screen*, 23:3–4 (1982), 20–9

Brunsdon, Charlotte, 'Men's Genres for Women', in *Boxed In: Women and Television*, ed. by Helen Baehr and Gillian Dyer (London: Pandora, 1987), pp. 184–202

Brunsdon, Charlotte, 'Pedagogies of the Feminine: Feminist Teaching and Women's Genres', *Screen*, 32:4 (1991), 364–81

Brunsdon, Charlotte, *Screen Tastes: Soap Opera to Satellite Dishes* (London: Routledge, 1997)

Bruzzi, Stella, *Undressing Cinema: Clothing and Identity in the Movies* (London: Routledge, 1997)

Burchill, Julie, 'To Have and Have Not', *Guardian* (Weekend), 14 March 1998, p. 7

Burgin, Victor, James Donald and Cora Kaplan, eds, *Formations of Fantasy* (London: Methuen, 1986)

Buscombe, Edward, 'Cowboys', *Sight and Sound*, 6:8 (August 1996), 32–5

Buscombe, Edward, ed., *The BFI Companion to the Western* (London: Museum of the Moving Image, 1991)

Butler, Judith, *Gender Trouble: Feminism and the Subversion of Identity* (London: Routledge, 1990)

Butler, Judith, and Joan W. Scott, eds, *Feminists Theorize the Political* (London: Routledge, 1992)

Byars, Jackie, *All That Hollywood Allows: Re-reading Gender in 1950s Melodrama* (London: Routledge, 1991)

Caine, Barbara, and Rosemary Pringle, eds, *Transitions: New Australian Feminisms* (St. Leonards: Allen and Unwin, 1995)

Calman, Stephanie, 'Shocking Truth of How Men Turn Beast', *Sunday Express*, 19 February 1989, p. 18

Campbell, Beatrix, '*The Accused* On Release', *Marxism Today*, March 1989, pp. 42–3

Campbell, Jeremy, 'Revenge of the Feminists', *Evening Standard*, 5 June 1991, p. 19

Carr, Helen, ed., *From My Guy to Sci-Fi: Genre and Women's Writing in the Postmodern World* (London: Pandora, 1989)

Clarke, David B., ed., *The Cinematic City* (London: Routledge, 1997)

Clover, Carol, *Men, Women and Chainsaws: Gender in the Modern Horror Film* (London: BFI, 1992)

Clover, Carol, 'High and Low: The Transformation of the Rape-Revenge Movie', in *Women and Film: A Sight and Sound Reader*, ed. by Pam Cook and Philip Dodd (London: Scarlet Press, 1993), pp. 76–85

Cohan, Steven, and Ina Rae Hark, eds, *Screening the Male: Exploring Masculinities in Hollywood Cinema* (London: Routledge, 1993)

Collins, Jim, 'Genericity in the Nineties: Eclectic Irony and the New Sincerity', in *Film Theory Goes to the Movies*, ed. by Jim Collins, Hilary Radner and Ava Preacher Collins (London: Routledge, 1993), pp. 242–63

Collins, Jim, Hilary Radner and Ava Preacher Collins, eds, *Film Theory Goes to the Movies* (London: Routledge, 1993)

Comay, Joan, *Who's Who in the Old Testament together with the Apocrypha* (London: Weidenfeld and Nicolson, 1971)

Cook, Pam, 'Duplicity in *Mildred Pierce*', in *Women in Film Noir*, ed. by E. Ann Kaplan (London: BFI, 1978), pp. 68–82

Cook, Pam, 'Authorship and Cinema', in *The Cinema Book*, ed. by Pam Cook (London: BFI, 1985), pp. 114–206

Cook, Pam, 'Women', in *The BFI Companion to the Western*, ed. by Edward Buscombe (London: Museum of the Moving Image, 1991), pp. 240–3

Cook, Pam, 'Outrage', in *Queen of the 'B's: Ida Lupino Behind the Camera*, ed. by Annette Kuhn (Trowbridge: Flicks Books, 1995), pp. 57–72

Cook, Pam, *Fashioning the Nation: Costume and Identity in British Cinema* (London: BFI, 1996)

Cook, Pam, ed., *The Cinema Book* (London: BFI, 1985)

Cook, Pam, and Philip Dodd, eds, *Women and Film: A Sight and Sound Reader* (London: Scarlet Press, 1993)

Copjec, Joan, *Read My Desire: Lacan against the Historicists* (London: M.I.T. Press, 1994)

Copjec, Joan, ed., *Shades of Noir: A Reader* (London: Verso, 1993)

Coppock, Vicki, Deena Haydon and Ingrid Richter, *The Illusions of 'Post-Feminism': New Women, Old Myths* (London: Taylor & Francis, 1995)

Cottam, Hilary, 'Blessed Margaret', *Guardian* (The Week), 17 January 1998, p. 4

Coward, Rosalind, *Our Treacherous Hearts: Why Women Let Men Get Their Way* (London: Faber and Faber, 1992)

Cowie, Elizabeth, '*Film Noir* and Women', in *Shades of Noir: A Reader*, ed. by Joan Copjec (London: Verso, 1993), pp. 121–65

Creed, Barbara, 'From Here to Modernity: Feminism and Postmodernism', *Screen*, 28:2 (Spring 1987), 47–67

Creed, Barbara, *The Monstrous-Feminine: Film, Feminism, Psychoanalysis* (London: Routledge, 1993)

Crofts, Stephen, 'Identification, Gender and Genre in Film: The Case of *Shame*', *The Moving Image*, 2 (1993), 3–88

Curran, James, David Morley and Valerie Walkerdine, eds, *Cultural Studies and Communications* (London: Arnold, 1996)

D'Acci, Julie, 'The Case of *Cagney and Lacey*', in *Boxed In: Women and Television*, ed. by Helen Baehr and Gillian Dyer (London: Pandora, 1987), pp. 203–25

Dargis, Manohla, 'Guns N' Poses', *Village Voice*, 16 July 1991, p. 22

Dargis, Manohla, '*Thelma and Louise* and the Tradition of the Male Road Movie', in *Women and Film: A Sight and Sound Reader*, ed. by Pam Cook and Philip Dodd (London: Scarlet Press, 1993), pp. 86–92

Davenport, Hugo, 'Taking to the Refuge of the Road', *Daily Telegraph*, 11 July 1991, p. 14

Davis, Kathy, 'Remaking the She-Devil: A Critical Look at Feminist Approaches to Beauty', *Hypatia*, 6:2 (Summer 1991), 21–43

'Daws', '*Thelma and Louise*: Review', *Variety*, 13 May 1991

De Lauretis, Teresa, *Technologies of Gender: Essays on Theory, Film, and Fiction* (Basingstoke: Macmillan, 1987)

De Lauretis, Teresa, 'Guerrilla in the Midst: Women's Cinema in the 80s', *Screen*, 31:1 (Spring 1990), 6–25

Denzin, Norman K., *Images of Postmodern Society: Social Theory and Contemporary Cinema* (London: Sage, 1991)

Doane, Mary Ann, 'The "Woman's Film": Possession and Address', in

Re-Vision: Essays in Feminist Film Criticism, ed. by Mary Ann Doane, Patricia Mellencamp and Linda Williams (Los Angeles: American Film Institute, 1984), pp. 67–82

Doane, Mary Ann, '*Caught* and *Rebecca*: The Inscription of Femininity as Absence', in *Feminism and Film Theory*, ed. by Constance Penley (London: BFI, 1988), pp. 196–215

Doane, Mary Ann, 'Film and the Masquerade: Theorizing the Female Spectator', in *Issues in Feminist Film Criticism*, ed. by Patricia Erens (Bloomington: Indiana University Press, 1990), pp. 41–57

Doane, Mary Ann, *Femmes Fatales: Feminism, Film Theory, Psychoanalysis* (London: Routledge, 1991)

Doane, Mary Ann, Patricia Mellencamp and Linda Williams, eds, *Re-Vision: Essays in Feminist Film Criticism* (Los Angeles: American Film Institute, 1984)

Docherty, Thomas, ed., *Postmodernism: A Reader* (Hemel Hempstead: Harvester Wheatsheaf, 1993)

Douglas, Susan J., *Where the Girls Are: Growing Up Female with the Mass Media* (London: Penguin, 1995)

Dumaresq, Delia, 'Rape: Sexuality in the Law', *m/f*, 5:6 (1981), 41–59

Dworkin, Andrea, *Letters From A War Zone: Writings 1976–1987* (London: Secker & Warburg, 1988)

Dyer, Richard, 'Resistance through Charisma: Rita Hayworth and *Gilda*', in *Women in Film Noir*, ed. by E. Ann Kaplan (London: BFI, 1978), pp. 91–9

Dyer, Richard, *Stars* (London: BFI, 1979)

Dyer, Richard, *Heavenly Bodies: Film Stars and Society* (Basingstoke: Macmillan, 1987)

Dyer, Richard, 'Children of the Night: Vampirism as Homosexuality, Homosexuality as Vampirism', in *Sweet Dreams: Sexuality, Gender and Popular Fiction*, ed. by Susannah Radstone (London: Lawrence and Wishart, 1988), pp. 47–72

Dyer, Richard, 'Dracula and Desire', *Sight and Sound*, 3:1 (January 1993), 8–12

Dyer, Richard, 'A White Star', *Sight and Sound*, 3:8 (August 1993), 22–4

Dyer, Richard, *White* (London: Routledge, 1997)

Easthope, Anthony, 'Notes on Genre', *Screen Education*, 32:33 (Autumn 1979–Winter 1980), 39–44

Ebert, Roger, 'Why Movie Audiences Aren't Safe Anymore', *American Film*, 6:5 (March 1981), 54–6

Ebert, Roger, '*The Accused*: Review', *Chicago Sun-Times*, 14 October 1988

Ehrenstein, David, 'One From the Art', *Film Comment*, 29:1 (January–February 1993), 27–30

Ellsworth, Elizabeth, 'Illicit Pleasures: Feminist Spectators and *Personal Best*', in *Becoming Feminine: The Politics of Popular Culture*, ed. by Leslie

G. Roman, Linda K. Christian-Smith and Elizabeth Ellsworth (London: Falmer Press, 1988), pp. 102–19

Elsaesser, Thomas, 'Tales of Sound and Fury: Observations on the Family Melodrama', in *Film Theory and Criticism: Introductory Readings*, ed. by Gerald Mast, Marshall Cohen and Leo Braudy, 4th edn (New York: Oxford University Press, 1992), pp. 512–35

Erens, Patricia, ed., *Issues in Feminist Film Criticism* (Bloomington: Indiana University Press, 1990)

Evans, Mary, ed., *The Woman Question: Readings on the Subordination of Women* (London: Fontana, 1982)

Eyüboglu, Selim, 'The Authorial Text and Postmodernism: Hitchcock's *Blackmail*', *Screen*, 32:1 (Spring 1991), 58–78

Faludi, Susan, *Backlash: The Undeclared War Against Women* (London: Vintage, 1992)

Fanshawe, Simon, 'Long Running Marathon', *Sunday Times* (Section 10), 9 June 1996, pp. 12–13

Feminist Anthology Collective, eds, *No Turning Back: Writings from the Women's Liberation Movement 1975–1980* (London: The Women's Press, 1981)

Feuer, Jane, *Seeing through the Eighties: Television and Reaganism* (London: BFI, 1995)

Feuer, Jane, 'Feminism on Lifetime: Yuppie TV for the Nineties', *Camera Obscura*, 33–4 (1994–95), 133–45

Fischer, Lucy, *Cinematernity: Film, Motherhood, Genre* (Princeton: Princeton University Press, 1996)

Flitterman-Lewis, Sandy, 'The Blossom and the Bole: Narrative and Visual Spectacle in Early Film Melodrama', *Cinema Journal*, 33:3 (Spring 1994), 3–15

Francke, Lizzie, 'Interview with Callie Khouri', *Guardian*, 9 July 1991, p. 17

Franklin, Sarah, Celia Lury and Jackie Stacey, eds, *Off-Centre: Feminism and Cultural Studies* (London: Harper Collins, 1991)

Frayling, Christopher, *Spaghetti Westerns: Cowboys and Europeans from Karl May to Sergio Leone* (London: Routledge and Kegan Paul, 1981)

Frayling, Christopher, '*Unforgiven*: Review', *Sight and Sound*, 2:6 (October 1992), 58

Frayling, Christopher, '*Dracula*', in *The BFI Companion to Horror*, ed. by Kim Newman (London: BFI, 1996), pp. 98–9

Frayling, Christopher, 'Vampirism (Before *Dracula*)', in *The BFI Companion to Horror*, ed. by Kim Newman (London: BFI, 1996), pp. 320–1

French, Marilyn, *The War Against Women* (London: Penguin, 1993)

French, Philip, 'Beware of Brutal Brunettes', *Guardian* (Review), 7 August 1994, p. 10

French, Sean, 'A Flirt with Danger', *Observer*, 19 February 1989, p. 42

Friedan, Betty, *The Feminine Mystique* (Harmondsworth: Penguin, 1965)

Gaines, Jane, 'Introduction: Fabricating the Female Body', in *Fabrications: Costume and the Female Body*, ed. by Jane Gaines and Charlotte Herzog (London: Routledge, 1990), pp. 1–27

Gaines, Jane, and Charlotte Herzog, eds, *Fabrications: Costume and the Female Body* (London: Routledge, 1990)

Gamman, Lorraine, and Margaret Marshment, 'Introduction', in *The Female Gaze: Women as Viewers of Popular Culture*, ed. by Lorraine Gamman and Margaret Marshment (London: The Women's Press, 1988), pp. 1–7

Gamman, Lorraine, and Margaret Marshment, eds, *The Female Gaze: Women as Viewers of Popular Culture* (London: The Women's Press, 1988)

Garber, Majorie, *Vested Interests: Cross-Dressing and Cultural Anxiety* (London: Routledge, 1992)

Gelder, Ken, *Reading the Vampire* (London: Routledge, 1993)

Gerrard, Nicci, 'The New Feminsim: Hello, boys...', *Observer* (Review), 27 April 1997, p. 5

Gledhill, Christine, '*Klute* 1: A Contemporary Film Noir and Feminist Criticism', in *Women in Film Noir*, ed. by E. Ann Kaplan (London: BFI, 1978), pp. 6–21

Gledhill, Christine, '*Klute* 2: Feminism and *Klute*', in *Women in Film Noir*, ed. by E. Ann Kaplan (London: BFI, 1978), pp. 112–28

Gledhill, Christine, 'Developments in Feminist Film Criticism', in *Re-Vision: Essays in Feminist Film Criticism*, ed. by Mary Ann Doane, Patricia Mellencamp and Linda Williams (Los Angeles: American Film Institute, 1984), pp. 18–45

Gledhill, Christine, 'Genre', in *The Cinema Book*, ed. by Pam Cook (London: BFI, 1985), pp. 58–64

Gledhill, Christine, 'Melodrama', in *The Cinema Book*, ed. by Pam Cook (London: BFI, 1985), pp. 73–84

Gledhill, Christine, 'The Western', in *The Cinema Book*, ed. by Pam Cook (London: BFI, 1985), pp. 64–72

Gledhill, Christine, 'The Melodramatic Field: An Investigation', in *Home Is Where The Heart Is: Studies in Melodrama and the Woman's Film*, ed. by Christine Gledhill (London: BFI, 1987), pp. 5–39

Gledhill, Christine, 'Pleasurable Negotiations', in *Female Spectators: Looking at Film and Television*, ed. by E. Deidre Pribram (London: Verso, 1988), pp. 64–89

Gledhill, Christine, 'Women Reading Men', in *Me Jane: Masculinity, Movies and Women*, ed. by Pat Kirkham and Janet Thumin (London: Lawrence and Wishart, 1995), pp. 73–93

Gledhill, Christine, ed., *Home Is Where the Heart Is: Studies in Melodrama and the Woman's Film* (London: BFI, 1987)

Glover, David, and Cora Kaplan, 'Guns in the House of Culture?: Crime Fiction and the Politics of the Popular', in *Cultural Studies*, ed. by Lawrence Grossberg, Cary Nelson and Paula A. Treichler (London: Routledge, 1992), pp. 213–26

Gopalan, Lalitha, 'Avenging Women in Indian Cinema', *Screen*, 38:1 (Spring 1997), 42–59

Grant, Barry Keith, ed., *Planks of Reason: Essays on the Horror Film* (London: The Scarecrow Press, 1984)

Grant, Linda, 'I'm Sexy. So Promote Me', *Guardian* (G2), 23 June 1998, p. 6

Greer, Germaine, *The Female Eunuch* (London: Paladin, 1971)

Griffin, Susan, *Made From This Earth: Selections from her Writing, 1967–1982* (London: The Women's Press, 1982)

Griggers, Cathy, '*Thelma and Louise* and the Cultural Generation of the New Butch-Femme', in *Film Theory Goes to the Movies*, ed. by Jim Collins, Hilary Radner and Ava Preacher Collins (London: Routledge, 1993), pp. 129–41

Grimsted, David, 'Vigilante Chronicle: The Politics of Melodrama Brought to Life', in *Melodrama: Stage, Picture, Screen*, ed. by Jacky Bratton, Jim Cook and Christine Gledhill (London: BFI, 1994), pp. 199–213

Gross, Larry, 'Film Áprès Nóir', *Film Comment*, 12:4 (1976), 44–9

Grossberg, Lawrence, Cary Nelson and Paula A. Treichler, eds, *Cultural Studies* (London: Routledge, 1992)

Gunew, Sneja, ed., *A Reader in Feminist Knowledge* (London: Routledge, 1991)

Haag, Pamela, '"Putting Your Body on the Line": The Question of Violence, Victims, and the Legacies of Second-Wave Feminism', *Differences: A Journal of Feminist Cultural Studies*, 8:2 (Summer 1996), 23–67

Hall, Stuart, *The Hard Road to Renewal: Thatcherism and the Crisis of the Left* (London: Verso, 1988)

Hall, Stuart, 'Cultural Studies and Its Theoretical Legacies', in *Cultural Studies*, ed. by Lawrence Grossberg, Cary Nelson and Paula A. Treichler (London: Routledge, 1992), pp. 277–94

Hallam, Julia, '*Working Girl*: A Woman's Film for the Eighties', in *Gendering the Reader*, ed. by Sara Mills (Hemel Hempstead: Harvester, 1994), pp. 173–98

Haraway, Donna, 'A Manifesto for Cyborgs: Science, Technology, and Socialist Feminism in the 1980s', in *Feminism/Postmodernism*, ed. by Linda J. Nicholson (London: Routledge, 1990), pp. 190–233

Hart, Lynda, *Fatal Women: Lesbian Sexuality and the Mark of Aggression* (London: Routledge, 1994)

Harvey, Sylvia, 'Woman's Place: The Absent Family of Film Noir', in *Women in Film Noir*, ed. by E. Ann Kaplan (London: BFI, 1978), pp. 22–34

Haskell, Molly, *From Reverence to Rape: The Treatment of Women in the Movies* (London: New English Library, 1975)

Heal, Sue, '*The Accused*: Review', *Today*, 17 February 1989, p. 26

Hebdige, Dick, *Subculture: The Meaning of Style* (London: Routledge, 1991)

Higgins, Lynn A., and Brenda R. Silver, eds, *Rape and Representation* (New York: Columbia University Press, 1991)

Hitchcock, Alfred, 'Direction', in *Focus on Hitchcock*, ed. by Albert J. LaValley (New Jersey: Prentice-Hall, 1972), pp. 32–9

Holloway, Wendy, '"I Just Wanted to Kill a Woman" Why?: The Ripper and Male Sexuality', *Feminist Review*, 9 (October 1981), 33–40

Holmlund, Christine, 'A Decade of Deadly Dolls: Hollywood and the Woman Killer', in *Moving Targets: Women, Murder and Representation*, ed. by Helen Birch (London: Virago, 1993), pp. 127–51

hooks, bell, *Black Looks: Race and Representation* (London: Turnaround, 1992)

Hutcheon, Linda, *The Politics of Postmodernism* (London: Routledge, 1989)

Hutchinson, Tom, 'How One Girl's Ordeal Put Humanity on Trial', *Mail on Sunday*, 19 February 1989, p. 36

Jameson, Fredric, 'Postmodernism, or The Cultural Logic of Late Capitalism', in *Postmodernism: A Reader*, ed. by Thomas Docherty (Hemel Hempstead: Harvester Wheatsheaf, 1993), pp. 62–92

Jefferson, Ann, and David Robey, eds, *Modern Literary Theory: A Comparative Introduction*, 2nd edn (London: B. T. Batsford, 1986)

Jeffords, Susan, 'The Big Switch: Hollywood Masculinity in the Nineties', in *Film Theory Goes to the Movies*, ed. by Jim Collins, Hilary Radner and Ava Preacher Collins (London: Routledge, 1993), pp. 196–208

Jeffords, Susan, *Hard Bodies: Hollywood Masculinity in the Reagan Era* (New Brunswick: Rutgers University Press, 1994)

Jeffreys, Sheila, *Anticlimax: A Feminist Perspective on the Sexual Revolution* (London: The Women's Press, 1990)

Jermyn, Deborah, 'Rereading the Bitches from Hell: A Feminist Appropriation of the Female Psychopath', *Screen*, 37:3 (Autumn 1996), 251–67

Johnston, Claire, '*Double Indemnity*', in *Women in Film Noir*, ed. by E. Ann Kaplan (London: BFI, 1978), pp. 100–11

Johnstone, Iain, '*The Accused*: Review', *Sunday Times*, 4 December 1988, p. 10

Johnstone, Iain, 'Doing Justice to the Victim', *Sunday Times*, 19 February 1989, p. 7

Johnstone, Iain, 'Buddy Can You Spare a Dame?', *Sunday Times*, 14 July 1991

Kaplan, E. Ann, *Women and Film: Both Sides of the Camera* (London: Methuen, 1983)

Kaplan, E. Ann, *Motherhood and Representation: The Mother in Popular Culture and Melodrama* (London: Routledge, 1992)

Kaplan, E. Ann, ed., *Women in Film Noir* (London: BFI, 1978)

Kempley, Rita, '*The Accused*: Review', *Washington Post*, 14 October 1988

Kirkham, Pat, and Janet Thumin, eds, *Me Jane: Masculinity, Movies and Women* (London: Lawrence and Wishart, 1995)

Knee, Adam, 'The Dialectic of Female Power and Male Hysteria in *Play Misty for Me*', in *Screening the Male: Exploring Masculinities in Hollywood Cinema*, ed. by Steven Cohan and Ina Rae Hark (London: Routledge, 1993), pp. 87–102

Knight, P. G., 'Naming the Problem: Feminism and the Figuration of Conspiracy', *Cultural Studies*, 11:1 (1997), 40–63

Krutnik, Frank, *In a Lonely Street: Film Noir, Genre, Masculinity* (London: Routledge, 1991)

Kuhn, Annette, 'Sexual Disguise and Cinema', in *Popular Fiction: Technology, Ideology, Production, Reading*, ed. by Tony Bennett (London: Routledge, 1990)

Kuhn, Annette, *The Women's Companion to International Film* (London: Virago, 1990)

Kuhn, Annette, *Women's Pictures: Feminism and Cinema*, 2nd edn (London: Verso, 1994)

Kuhn, Annette, ed., *Queen of the 'B's: Ida Lupino Behind the Camera* (Trowbridge: Flicks Books, 1995)

Lacan, Jacques, *Ecrits: A Selection*, trans. by Alan Sheridan (London: Tavistock, 1977)

LaValley, Albert J., ed., *Focus on Hitchcock* (New Jersey: Prentice-Hall, 1972)

Lawson, Nigella, 'Furore Triggered by Women on the Loose', *Sunday Times*, 7 July 1991

Lederer, Laura, ed., *Take Back The Night: Women on Pornography* (New York: William Morrow, 1980)

Leeds Revolutionary Feminist Group, 'Political Lesbianism: The Case Against Heterosexuality', in *The Woman Question: Readings on the Subordination of Women*, ed. by Mary Evans (London: Fontana, 1982), pp. 63–72

Lehman, Peter, '"Don't Blame this on a Girl": Female Rape-revenge Films', in *Screening the Male: Exploring Masculinities in Hollywood Cinema*, ed. by Steven Cohan and Ina Rae Hark (London: Routledge, 1993), pp. 103–17

Lentz, Kirsten Marthe, 'The Popular Pleasures of Female Revenge (or Rage Bursting in a Blaze of Gunfire)', *Cultural Studies*, 7:3 (October 1993), 374–405

Lesage, Julia, 'Artful Racism, Artful Rape: Griffith's *Broken Blossoms*', in *Jump Cut: Hollywood, Politics and Counter Cinema*, ed. by Peter Steven (Toronto: Between the Lines, 1985), pp. 247–68

Levitin, Jacqueline, 'The Western: Any Good Roles for Feminists?', *Film Reader*, 5 (1982), 95–108

Light, Alison, 'Putting on the Style: Feminist Criticism in the 1990s', in *From My Guy to Sci-Fi: Genre and Women's Writing in the Postmodern World*, ed. by Helen Carr (London: Pandora, 1989), pp. 24–35

Lippe, Richard, '*Anatomy of a Murder*', in *International Dictionary of Films and Filmmakers*, ed. by Nicholas Thomas, 2nd edn, 5 vols (Chicago: St James Press, 1990), Volume I, 38–40

Malcolm, Derek, 'The Lust Picture Show', *Guardian*, 16 February 1989, p. 21

Marcus, Sharon, 'Fighting Bodies, Fighting Words: A Theory and Politics of Rape Prevention', in *Feminists Theorize the Political*, ed. by Judith Butler and Joan W. Scott (London: Routledge, 1992), pp. 385–403

Margolis, Harriet E., '*Blue Steel*: Progressive Feminism in the '90s?', *Postscript*, 13:1 (1993), 67–76

Marriott, John, 'The Film That Puts Men in the Dock', *Daily Mail*, 17 February 1989, p. 30

Mars-Jones, Adam, 'Unmoving Violation', *Independent*, 16 February 1989, p. 15

Mars-Jones, Adam, 'Getting Away from It All', *Independent*, 12 July 1991, p. 18

Marwick, Arthur, *British Society Since 1945*, 2nd edn (London: Penguin, 1990)

Mast, Gerald, Marshall Cohen and Leo Braudy, eds, *Film Theory and Criticism: Introductory Readings*, 4th edn (New York: Oxford University Press, 1992)

Mather, Victoria, 'Guilty Witnesses to a Violent Crime', *Daily Telegraph*, 16 February 1989, p. 18

Mathews, Tom Dewe, *Censored* (London: Chatto and Windus, 1994)

McArthur, Colin, 'Chinese Boxes and Russian Dolls: Tracking the Elusive Cinematic City', in *The Cinematic City*, ed. by David B. Clarke (London: Routledge, 1997), pp. 19–45

McGlen, Nancy E., and Karen O'Connor, *Women's Rights: The Struggle for Equality in the Nineteenth and Twentieth Centuries* (New York: Praeger, 1983)

McRobbie, Angela, 'New Times in Cultural Studies', *New Formations*, 13 (Spring 1991), 1–17

McRobbie, Angela, *Postmodernism and Popular Culture* (London: Routledge, 1994)

McRobbie, Angela, '*More!*: New Sexualities in Girls' and Women's Magazines', in *Cultural Studies and Communications*, ed. by James Curran, David Morley and Valerie Walkerdine (London: Arnold, 1996), pp. 172–94

Metford, J. C. J., *Dictionary of Christian Lore and Legend* (London: Thames and Hudson, 1983)

Millett, Kate, *Sexual Politics* (London: Virago, 1977)

Mills, Sara, ed., *Gendering the Reader* (Hemel Hempstead: Harvester, 1994)

Milne, Tom, ed., *Time Out Film Guide*, 3rd edn (London: Penguin, 1993)

Modern Humanities Research Association, *MHRA Style Book: Notes for Authors, Editors, and Writers of Theses*, 4th edn (London: Modern Humanities Research Association, 1991)

Modleski, Tania, 'Time and Desire in the Woman's Film', in *Film Theory and Criticism: Introductory Readings*, ed. by Gerald Mast, Marshall Cohen and Leo Braudy, 4th edn (New York: Oxford University Press, 1992), pp. 536–48

Modleski, Tania, *The Women Who Knew Too Much: Hitchcock and Feminist Theory* (New York: Methuen, 1988)

Modleski, Tania, *Feminism Without Women: Culture and Criticism in a 'Postfeminist' Age* (London: Routledge, 1991)

Moi, Toril, 'Feminist Literary Criticism', in *Modern Literary Theory: A Comparative Introduction*, ed. by Ann Jefferson and David Robey, 2nd edn (London: B. T. Batsford, 1986), pp. 204–21

Moore, Suzanne, 'Asking for It?', *New Statesman and Society*, 17 February 1989, 16–17

Moore, Suzanne, 'A Sliver Off the Old Block', *Guardian* (G2), 10 September 1993, p. 11

Moretti, Franco, *Signs Taken For Wonders: Essays in the Sociology of Literary Forms*, trans. by Susan Fischer, David Forgacs and David Miller, rev. edn (London: Verso, 1988)

Morgan, Robin, 'Theory and Practice: Pornography and Rape', in *Take Back The Night: Women on Pornography*, ed. by Laura Lederer (New York: William Morrow, 1980), pp. 134–40

Morgan, Robin, ed., *Sisterhood is Powerful: An Anthology of Writings from the Women's Liberation Movement* (New York: Random House, 1970)

Mulvey, Laura, 'Visual Pleasure and Narrative Cinema', in *Feminism and Film Theory*, ed. by Constance Penley (London: BFI, 1988), pp. 57–68

Murphy, Kathleen, 'Only Angels Have Wings', *Film Comment*, 27:4 (1991), 26–9

Neale, Stephen, *Genre* (London: BFI, 1980)

Neale, Steve, 'Questions of Genre', *Screen*, 31:1 (Spring 1990), 45–66

Neale, Steve, 'The Big Romance or Something Wild?: Romantic Comedy Today', *Screen*, 33:3 (Autumn 1992), 284–99

Neale, Steve, and Frank Krutnik, *Popular Film and Television Comedy* (London: Routledge, 1990)

Newman, Kim, ed., *The BFI Companion to Horror* (London: BFI, 1996)

Nichols, Bill, ed., *Movies and Methods, Volume I: An Anthology* (Berkeley: University of California Press, 1976)

Nichols, Bill, ed., *Movies and Methods, Volume II: An Anthology* (Berkeley: University of California Press, 1985)

Nicholson, Linda J., ed., *Feminism/Postmodernism* (London: Routledge, 1990)

Oakley, Ann, and Juliet Mitchell, eds, *Who's Afraid of Feminism?: Seeing through the Backlash* (London: Penguin, 1997)

Paglia, Camille, *Vamps and Tramps: New Essays* (London: Viking, 1995)

Paramount Pictures Corporation, 'Production Information for *The Accused*' (1988)

Pearson, Roberta E., and William Uricchio, eds, *The Many Lives of the Batman: Critical Approaches to a Superhero and his Media* (London: BFI, 1991)

Peary, Danny, *Cult Movies 2* (London: Vermillon, 1983)

Pendreigh, Brian, 'Focus on an American Nightmare', *Scotsman*, 2 February 1989, p. 11

Penley, Constance, ed., *Feminism and Film Theory* (London: BFI, 1988)

Pidduck, Julianne, 'The 1990s Hollywood Fatal Femme: (Dis)Figuring Feminism, Family, Irony, Violence', *Cineaction*, 38 (1995), 65–72

Place, Janey, 'Women in Film Noir', in *Women in Film Noir*, ed. by E. Ann Kaplan (London: BFI, 1978), pp. 35–67

Place, J. A., and L. S. Peterson, 'Some Visual Motifs of Film Noir', in *Movies and Methods Volume I: An Anthology*, ed. by Bill Nichols (Berkeley: University of California Press, 1976), pp. 325–38

Plaza, Monique, 'Our Costs and Their Benefits', *m/f*, 4 (1980), 28–39

Powell, Anna, 'Blood on the Borders: *Near Dark* and *Blue Steel*', *Screen*, 35:2 (1994), 136–56

Prawer, S. S., *Caligari's Children: The Film as Tale of Terror* (Oxford: Oxford University Press, 1980)

Pribram, E. Deidre, ed., *Female Spectators: Looking at Film and Television* (London: Verso, 1988)

Probyn, Elspeth, 'New Traditionalism and Post-Feminism: TV Does the Home', *Screen*, 31:2 (Summer 1990), 147–59

Radner, Hilary, '"This Time's For Me": Making Up and Feminine Practice', *Cultural Studies*, 3:3 (1989), 301–21

Radner, Hilary, 'Pretty Is as Pretty Does: Free Enterprise and the Marriage Plot', in *Film Theory Goes to the Movies*, ed. by Jim Collins, Hilary

Radner and Ava Preacher Collins (London: Routledge, 1993), pp. 56–76

Radner, Hilary, *Shopping Around: Feminine Culture and the Pursuit of Pleasure* (London: Routledge, 1995)

Radstone, Susannah, ed., *Sweet Dreams: Sexuality, Gender and Popular Fiction* (London: Lawrence & Wishart, 1988)

Riley, Denise, *'Am I That Name?': Feminism and the Category of 'Women' in History* (Basingstoke: Macmillan, 1988)

Riviere, Joan, 'Womanliness as a Masquerade', in *Formations of Fantasy*, ed. by Victor Burgin, James Donald and Cora Kaplan (London: Methuen, 1986)

Roberts, Yvonne, *Mad About Women: Can There Ever Be Fair Play Between The Sexes?* (London: Virago, 1992)

Rogin, Michael Paul, *Ronald Reagan, the Movie and Other Episodes in Political Demonology* (Berkeley: University of California Press, 1987)

Roiphe, Katie, *The Morning After* (London: Hamish Hamilton, 1993)

Roman, Leslie G., Linda K. Christian-Smith and Elizabeth Ellsworth, eds, *Becoming Feminine: The Politics of Popular Culture* (London: Falmer Press, 1988)

Romney, Jonathan, 'Vital Video: Sleazy Does It', *Guardian* (G2), 2 December 1994, p. 17

Ross, Andrew, 'Ballots, Bullets, or Batmen: Can Cultural Studies Do the Right Thing?', *Screen*, 21:1 (Spring 1990), 26–44

Rowland, Robyn, and Renate D. Klein, 'Radical Feminism: Critique and Construct', in *A Reader in Feminist Knowledge*, ed. by Sneja Gunew (London: Routledge, 1991), pp. 271–303

Russell, Sharon, 'The Witch in Film: Myth and Reality', in *Planks of Reason: Essays on the Horror Film*, ed. by Barry Keith Grant (London: Scarecrow Press, 1984), pp. 113–25

Rutherford, Jonathan, ed., *Identity* (London: Lawrence and Wishart, 1990)

Ryan, Michael, and Douglas Kellner, *Camera Politica: The Politics and Ideology of Contemporary Hollywood Film* (Bloomington: Indiana University Press, 1990)

Sadie, Stanley, ed., *The New Grove Dictionary of Music and Musicians*, 20 vols (London: Macmillan, 1980), Volume II

Schatz, Thomas, 'The New Hollywood', in *Film Theory Goes to the Movies*, ed. by Jim Collins, Hilary Radner and Ava Preacher Collins (London: Routledge, 1993), pp. 8–36

Schickel, Richard, *D. W. Griffith and the Birth of Film* (London: Pavilion, 1984)

Schlesinger, Philip, R. Emerson Dobash, Russell P. Dobash and C. Kay Weaver, *Women Viewing Violence* (London: BFI, 1992)

Schrader, Paul, 'Notes on Film Noir', *Film Comment*, 8:1 (1972), 8–13

Schwichtenberg, Cathy, ed., *The Madonna Connection: Representational*

Politics, Subcultural Identities, and Cultural Theory (Boulder: Westview Press, 1993)

Searles, Patricia, and Ronald J. Berger, eds, *Rape and Society: Readings on the Problem of Sexual Assault* (Oxford: Westview Press, 1995)

Sharman, Leslie Felperin, 'Bad Girls: Review', *Sight and Sound*, 4:7 (July 1994), 37–8

Sharpe, Sue, *Just Like a Girl: How Girls Learn to be Women From the Seventies to the Nineties* (London: Penguin, 1994)

Showalter, Elaine, *Sexual Anarchy: Gender and Culture at the Fin-de-Siècle* (London: Virago, 1992)

Simpson, Mark, *Male Impersonators: Men Performing Masculinity* (London: Cassell, 1994)

Sinfield, Alan, *Literature, Politics and Culture in Postwar Britain* (Oxford: Basil Blackwell, 1989)

Skal, David J., *Hollywood Gothic: The Tangled Web of 'Dracula' from Novel to Stage to Screen* (London: André Deutsch, 1990)

Smith, Joan, 'Road Testing', *Guardian*, 9 July 1991, p. 17

Smith, Paul, *Clint Eastwood: A Cultural Production* (Minneapolis: University of Minnesota Press, 1993)

The Spice Girls, *Girl Power!* (London: Zone/Chameleon Books, 1997)

Starr, Marco, 'J. Hills is Alive: A Defence of *I Spit on Your Grave*', in *The Video Nasties: Freedom and Censorship in the Media*, ed. by Martin Barker (London: Pluto Press, 1984), pp. 48–55

Steven, Peter, ed., *Jump Cut: Hollywood, Politics and Counter Cinema* (Toronto: Between the Lines, 1985)

Stoker, Bram, *Dracula*, ed. by Maurice Hindle (London: Penguin, 1993)

Stuart, Andrea, 'Feminism: Dead or Alive?', in *Identity*, ed. by Jonathan Rutherford (London: Lawrence and Wishart, 1990), pp. 28–42

Tasker, Yvonne, 'Having It All: Feminism and the Pleasures of the Popular', in *Off-Centre: Feminism and Cultural Studies*, ed. by Sarah Franklin, Celia Lury and Jackie Stacey (London: Harper Collins, 1991), pp. 85–96

Tasker, Yvonne, *Spectacular Bodies: Gender, Genre and the Action Cinema* (London: Routledge, 1993)

Tasker, Yvonne, 'Approaches to the New Hollywood', in *Cultural Studies and Communications*, ed. by James Curran, David Morley and Valerie Walkerdine (London: Arnold, 1996), pp. 213–28

Thomas, Nicholas, ed., *International Dictionary of Films and Filmmakers*, 2nd edn, 5 vols (Chicago: St. James Press, 1990), Volume I

Thompson, Ben, 'The Quick and the Dead: Review', *Sight and Sound*, 5:9 (September 1995), 58–9

Thumin, Janet, '"Maybe He's Tough But He Sure Ain't No Carpenter": Masculinity and In/Competence in *Unforgiven*', in *Me Jane: Masculinity,*

Movies and Women, ed. by Pat Kirkham and Janet Thumin (London: Lawrence and Wishart, 1995), pp. 234–48

Tomaselli, Sylvana, and Roy Porter, eds, *Rape: A Historical and Social Enquiry* (Oxford: Basil Blackwell, 1986)

Traube, Elizabeth G., *Dreaming Identities: Class, Gender, and Generation in 1980s Hollywood Movies* (Oxford: Westview Press, 1992)

Uricchio, William, and Roberta E. Pearson, '"I'm Not Fooled By That Cheap Disguise"', in *The Many Lives of the Batman: Critical Approaches to a Superhero and his Media*, ed. by Roberta E. Pearson and William Uricchio (London: BFI, 1991), pp. 182–213

Usher, Shaun, 'Men Get the Bullet from Tough Girls', *Daily Mail*, 12 July 1991, p. 30

Viviani, Christian, 'Who Is Without Sin?: The Maternal Melodrama in American Film, 1930–1939', in *Home Is Where The Heart Is: Studies in Melodrama and the Woman's Film*, ed. by Christine Gledhill (London: BFI, 1987), pp. 83–99

Wade, Dorothy, 'Why this Violence is Justified', *Sunday Times*, 12 February 1989, p. 5

Walker, Alexander, 'A Letter from Thelma's Hide-Out', *Evening Standard*, 11 July 1991, p. 26

Walter, Natasha, *The New Feminism* (London: Little Brown, 1998)

Walters, Margaret, 'Silent Witness', *Listener*, CXXI: 3101 (16 February 1989), 32

Walters, Margaret, 'American Gothic: Feminism, Melodrama and the Backlash', in *Who's Afraid of Feminism?: Seeing through the Backlash*, ed. by Ann Oakley and Juliet Mitchell (London: Penguin, 1997), pp. 56–76

Wandor, Micheline, ed., *The Body Politic: Women's Liberation in Britain* (London: Stage 1, 1972)

Weiss, Andrea, *Vampires and Violets: Lesbians in the Cinema* (London: Jonathan Cape, 1992)

Whelehan, Imelda, *Modern Feminist Thought: From the Second Wave to 'Post-Feminism'* (Edinburgh: Edinburgh University Press, 1995)

White, Mimi, 'Representing Romance: Reading/Writing/Fantasy and the "Liberated" Heroine of Recent Hollywood Films', *Cinema Journal*, 28:3 (1989), 41–56

Wicke, Jennifer, 'Celebrity Material: Materialist Feminism and the Culture of Celebrity', *South Atlantic Quarterly*, 93:4 (Fall 1994), 751–78

Williams, Linda, 'When the Woman Looks', in *Re-Vision: Essays in Feminist Film Criticism*, ed. by Mary Ann Doane, Patricia Mellencamp and Linda Williams (Los Angeles: American Film Institute, 1984), pp. 83–99

Williams, Linda, '"Something Else Besides a Mother": *Stella Dallas* and the Maternal Melodrama', in *Home Is Where the Heart Is: Studies in*

Melodrama and the Woman's Film, ed. by Christine Gledhill (London: BFI, 1987), pp. 299–325

Williams, Linda, 'Feminist Film Theory: *Mildred Pierce* and the Second World War', in *Female Spectators: Looking at Film and Television*, ed. by E. Deidre Pribram (London: Verso, 1988)

Williams, Linda Ruth, 'Sisters Under the Skin: Video and Blockbuster Erotic Thrillers', in *Women and Film: A Sight and Sound Reader*, ed. by Pam Cook and Philip Dodd (London: Scarlet Press, 1993), pp. 105–14.

Williams, Raymond, *Marxism and Literature* (Oxford: Oxford University Press, 1977)

Williamson, Judith, *Deadline at Dawn: Film Criticism 1980–1990* (London: Marion Boyars, 1993)

Willis, Sharon, 'Hardware and Hardbodies, What Do Women Want?: A Reading of *Thelma and Louise*', in *Film Theory Goes to the Movies*, ed. by Jim Collins, Hilary Radner and Ava Preacher Collins (London: Routledge, 1993), pp. 120–28

Willows, Terry, 'This is My Revenge Against the Animals Who Raped Me', *Today*, 21 October 1988, p. 29

Wilson, Elizabeth, 'Tell It Like It Is: Women and Confessional Writing', in *Sweet Dreams: Sexuality, Gender and Popular Fiction*, ed. by Susannah Radstone (London: Lawrence & Wishart, 1988), pp. 21–45

Winship, Janice, '"A Girl Needs to Get Street-wise": Magazines for the 1980s', *Feminist Review*, 21 (1985), 25–46

Winship, Janice, *Inside Women's Magazines* (London: Pandora, 1987)

Wolf, Naomi, *The Beauty Myth: How Images of Beauty Are Used Against Women* (London: Vintage, 1991)

Wolf, Naomi, *Fire with Fire: The New Female Power and How It Will Change the 21st Century* (London: Chatto and Windus, 1993)

Wollen, Peter, 'Delirious Projections', *Sight and Sound*, 2:4 (August 1992), 24–7

Wood, Robert E., 'Somebody Has To Die: *Basic Instinct* as White Noir', *Postscript*, 12:3 (1993), 44–51

Wood, Robin, *Ingmar Bergman* (London: Studio Vista, 1969)

Wood, Robin, 'Neglected Nightmares', *Film Comment*, 16:2 (1980), 24–32

Wood, Robin, 'An Introduction to the American Horror Film', in *Movies and Methods, Volume II: An Anthology*, ed. by Bill Nichols (Berkeley: University of California, 1985), pp. 195–220

Wood, Robin, *Hollywood from Vietnam to Reagan* (New York: Columbia University Press, 1986)

Wright, Will, *Six Guns and Society: A Structural Study of the Western* (Berkeley: University of California Press, 1975)

Wyatt, Justin, *High Concept: Movies and Marketing in Hollywood* (Austin: University of Texas Press, 1994)

Zimmerman, Bonnie, 'Daughters of Darkness: The Lesbian Vampire on Film', in *Planks of Reason: Essays on the Horror Film*, ed. by Barry Keith Grant (London: Scarecrow Press, 1984), pp. 153–63

Index

Note: 'n' after a page reference indicates a note number on that page.